Pilgrimage Yesterday and Today
Why? Where? How?

J. G. DAVIES

Pilgrimage
Yesterday and Today
Why? Where? How?

SCM PRESS LTD

British Library Cataloguing in Publication Data

Davies, J. G.
Pilgrimage yesterday and today: why?
where? how?
1. Christian pilgrimage
I. Title
248.4'6

ISBN 0-334-02254-1

First published 1988
by SCM Press Ltd
26–30 Tottenham Road London N1 4BZ

Typeset at The Spartan Press Ltd
Lymington, Hants
and printed in Great Britain by
The Camelot Press Ltd
Southampton

Contents

Preface		vii
List of Plates		ix
List of Figures		xi
Acknowledgments		xiii

1	Christian Pilgrimage in the Later Middle Ages	1
	The Universality of Pilgrimages	1
	Motives	2
	Destinations	7
	Exilic Pilgrimages	13
	Penitential Pilgrimages and the Quest for Indulgences	14
	Judicial Pilgrimages	16
	Crusades	17
	Pilgrimage Literature:	
	(a) Itineraries	19
	(b) Pilgrim-diaries	20
	(c) *Libri indulgentiarum*	21
	(d) Maps	22
	(e) Aids to devotion and their use	26
	(f) Guide books	33
	(g) Travel accounts	37
	Preparation for Pilgrimage	42
	The Journey	46
	The Mini-Pilgrimage or Devotions at the Holy Places	55
	The Return Home	77

2	Criticisms of Pilgrimage and the Protestant Condemnation	80
	Pre-Reformation Criticism:	
	(a) From within the ranks of the faithful	80
	(b) Wyclif and the Lollards	89

The Barbed Wit of Erasmus of Rotterdam   93
Martin Luther and the Reformation Condemnation of
     Pilgrimages   96
Aspects of the Catholic Response   108

3 The Death and Resurrection of Protestant Pilgrimages 115
   The Aftermath of the Reformation   115
   The Continuity of Roman Catholic and Eastern
        Orthodox Pilgrimages:
        (a) Roman Catholic Pilgrims   130
        (b) Eastern Orthodox Pilgrims   136
   The Attraction of the Holy Land to Protestants in the
        Nineteenth Century   140
   The Contribution of Thomas Cook   147
   The Re-emergence of Local Pilgrimages within Protestantism 152
   The Resurrection of Pilgrimages to the Holy Land among
        Protestants in the Twentieth Century   160

4 The Meaning of Pilgrimage Today   168
   Hints from the Past   168
   Pilgrimage as a Spiritual Exercise   184
   Pilgrimage as an Imitation of Christ and his Saints   189
   Pilgrimage, Identity and Unity   202
   Pilgrimage and the Bible   206

5 Devotions for Today's Pilgrims   214
   At the Point of Departure   215
   A Service for the Commissioning of Pilgrims   216
   Form of Prayer for the Outward Journey   220
   The Use of the Bible   221
   Meditation   227
   Prayers, Hymns and Psalms   228
   Stations of the Cross, Processions, Re-enactment
        and Movement-Prayers   231
   Pilgrimage and the Gospel Sacraments   234
   The Return Home   238
   Form of Prayer to be Used on the Return Journey   239

References   241
Bibliography   252
Index   265

Preface

'All pilgrimages should be stopped.' These are the words of Martin Luther, but they could equally well have come from the lips of any one of the Protestant Reformers of the sixteenth century. Without exception they condemned a devotional practice that had had a continuous history from at least the second century AD. Why did they do this?

To answer this question that history has to be examined to find out what were the pilgrims' motives, how they understood what they were doing and how they conducted themselves throughout the exercise. This basic survey, which occupies the first chapter of the present study, covers in the main the late Middle Ages but with sufficient reference back to the patristic period to show continuity. It culminates with the dawn of the Reformation and so provides the necessary background to understand the criticisms of the Protestants which are presented in detail in chapter 2.

The effects of this wholesale condemnation are described in the next chapter where the continuing visits to such centres as Rome and Jerusalem by a few Protestants are chronicled and their attitude to what they were doing is described. But then notice has to be taken of a profound change. In the nineteenth century the Holy Land began once again to exercise a powerful attraction even upon the heirs of the Reformation who began to travel there in steadily increasing numbers. Indeed in the opening decades of the present century there took place what can only be described as the resurrection of pilgrimages, both locally and overseas, amongst those who counted Luther or Calvin or Cranmer as their spiritual forebears. What were the factors that resulted in this *volte-face*? The remainder of chapter 3 is devoted to answering this question.

The re-emergence of Protestant pilgrimages was not accompanied by any examination in depth of the criticisms previously levelled against them. Little attempt was made to develop a theological interpretation or justification of the renewed practice. Chapter 4 attempts to supply this gap, drawing on hints from the past, considering it as a spiritual exercise, as a way of imitating Christ and his saints, and relating it to the biblical writings as the foundation documents of the Christian faith. This is all the more necessary if a pilgrimage is to be distinguished from a tour – if the former is something more than the latter, what constitutes that 'something more'? In the final chapter the devotional aspects of modern pilgrimages are reviewed with suggestions about forms of services, the use of the Bible, meditation, prayers and hymns.

Pilgrimage is a complex subject because it is the point of intersection of many themes: devotional, liturgical, historical, theological, social and anthropological. Because of this variety, this study should be of general interest as well as appealing to those with specialist concerns. It is however today's pilgrims that are principally in view in the hope that it may assist them to make an enriching experience even more profound.

A final word is needed to explain the format of the notes and references. This is twofold: biblical references are printed in the body of the text to allow ease of identification. The sources of quotations and cross references are printed after the final chapter, where they can be safely ignored by those who do not wish to check them or follow the topics further, except for a few which do add a little to the text and are therefore designated by an asterisk.

Birmingham   J. G. Davies

List of Plates

I   Pilgrims on the façade of Saint-Jouin-de Marnes   12

II   Mediaeval pilgrim found buried in Worcester Cathedral   45

III   Cockleshells decorating a capital of Saint-Hilaire, Melle   76

IV   Jesus as a pilgrim on the Way to Emmaus (San Domingo de Silos near Burgos, 1085–1100)   88

V   A modern Greek ex-voto   139

VI   A Thomas Cook tent in the Holy Land, 1880   150

VII   Archbishop Geoffrey Fisher at the Jordan   163

VIII   In the steps of St Paul. Modern pilgrims in the theatre at Ephesus (Acts 19.23–41)   196

IX   One of the lions guarding the entrance to the harbour at Miletus (Acts 20.15)   198

X   Pilgrims before the tribunal of Gallio at Corinth (Acts 18.12)   200

XI   The Pilgrim Way from Neapolis: the Via Egnatia (Acts 16.11f.)   212

XII   The renewal of baptismal vows at Philippi (Acts 16.13–15)   236

List of Figures

1 Crusaders (from the French edition of von Breydenbach, *Journey to the Holy Land*, Paris 1522) 18

2 Map of Rhodes 1534 (from B. Bordone, *Isolario*, N. Zoppino, Venice) 24

3 Plan of Mount Sinai (from Giacomo de Verona, *Liber peregrinationis*, 1355) 24

4 Panoramic view of Jerusalem (from the Latin edition of von Breydenbach, Mainz 1486) 25

5 Title page of the second edition of *Information for Pilgrims unto the Holy Land*, Wynkyn de Worde, 1515 34

6 Pilgrims' galley off Rhodes (from the Latin edition of von Breydenbach) 35

7 Plan of a pilgrimage church, Santiago de Compostela 37

8 Alphabets: Coptic and Ethiopic (from the Latin edition of von Breydenbach); Armenian (from the Spanish edition of Zaragoza, 1498) 40

9 A pilgrim with scrip, staff and tokens (on a tomb stone in Llandyfodwg church, Glamorgan) 44

10 Venice (from the Latin edition of von Breydenbach) 53

11 Pilgrims burrowing into limb holes in a thirteenth-century shrine. Measuring wicks for 'trindles' are in the foreground 61

12 Canterbury pilgrims' tokens 78

13 Chaucer's Wife of Bath (from *The Canterbury Tales*, William Caxton 1484) 83

14   Rome (from the Spanish edition of von Breydenbach)   116

15   The Holy Sepulchre (from G. Sandys, *Relation of a Journey Begun An: Dom: 1610*, 3rd edn Allet 1632)   125

16   The tattooed cross (from J. Sanderson, *Travels 1584–1602*, f. 127a)   128

17   Holy Year. The Jubilee Medal of Clement VIII. One side depicts the beginning of the celebration and the other the walling up of the Holy Door at the end   130

Acknowledgments

I am happy to record my gratitude to Canon Lorys M. Davies for first arousing my interest in the subject of this book by inviting me to be liturgical consultant for the Birmingham Diocesan Pilgrimage to Canterbury. It was however my wife Mary who suggested that I might use the material I had collected as the basis for a full length study and I am naturally grateful to her. My thanks are also due to my daughter Sally whose gift of *Maps of the Bible Lands* by K. Nebenzahl drew my attention to an aspect of pilgrimage literature that I would otherwise have neglected. Information about the 'limb holes' in the church of St Wite, Whitchurch Canonicorum, was volunteered by Dr Ruth Padel.

Canon Arthur Payton, the founder of Inter-Church Travel Ltd, kindly supplied me with information about the establishment of the firm which has done so much to promote pilgrimage in the twentieth century. Canon Ronald Brownrigg further filled out the picture for me, drawing on his rich experience of organizing pilgrimages for over forty years. Douglas Cady, Director and General Manager of Inter-Church Travel, has enabled me to enjoy practical experience of pilgrimages by inviting me to be a leader on numerous occasions. It was Nicholas Day, at the time Senior Product Assistant of the same firm, who told me of the riches of Thomas Cook's archives and arranged for me to have access to them. The archivist, E. Swinglehurst, was most kind in helping me find my way through the mass of material and in supplying Plate VI. Dr B. S. Benedikz, Sub-Librarian of Special Collections in the University of Birmingham, has given me continual assistance in tracing rare books. I gladly acknowledge the help of the Dean and Chapter of Worcester Cathedral together with P. A. Barker, in obtaining Plate II; that of Anthony Bryer, Professor of Byzantine Studies in the University of Birmingham for Plate V and of Canon William Purcell for Plate VII.

It is finally my pleasure to record my appreciation of the help of Miss Margaret Lydamore, Associate Editor of SCM Press, for once again preparing a manuscript of mine for the printer with her customary care and attention to detail.

November 1987 J. G. Davies

I

Christian Pilgrimage in the Later
Middle Ages

The principal character in one of the stories of Boccacio's *Decameron* is a certain Father Cipolla.[1] His name immediately indicates that the tale is to be taken humorously because it is the Italian for 'onion'. Father Onion, then, has recently been on a pilgrimage to Jerusalem and he announces that he is about to display for veneration some of the precious relics he has brought back with him. Amongst the items he has obtained from the patriarch is 'a little bottle containing some of the noise of the bells of Solomon's temple', but the *pièce de résistance* is 'one of the feathers of the Archangel Gabriel which he dropped in the bedroom of the Virgin Mary when he came to make the announcement to her in Nazareth'. The quest for such relics – authentic or not – was intense prior to the Reformation, but the practice of pilgrimage was not in itself, nor has it remained, distinctive of Christianity.

The Universality of Pilgrimages

Jews go to Jerusalem and so also Christians. Hindus visit the Ganges; Muslims make their way to Mecca, Buddhists to Sarnath near Benares and members of the Tenri-Kyo sect of Shintoism to Tenri Shi in Japan. When they do so, each and every one is performing an act of practical piety; they are embodying in a journey what is related to the experimental, ritualistic and social dimensions of religion. They are engaged in a search for meaning and for spiritual advancement and their pilgrimage dramatizes their quest for the divine. Indeed a pilgrimage centre is universally regarded as a place of intersection between everyday life and the life of God. It is a geographical location that is worthy of reverence because it has been the scene of a manifestation of divine power or has an association with a holy person.

Here is a fund of ideas that is common to almost every world religion. There is a parallelism too not only between the most important aspects but in insignificant details. So mediaeval Christians regarded pilgrimage as a penitential activity which could reach its climax with the remission of their sins, and Muslims, when entering the gates of Mecca, pray that they too may receive forgiveness. Of less importance is the common use of shells as symbols of a completed task such as the cockles at Compostela and the conches at Rameshwaran. Yet that which fundamentally distinguishes a Christian pilgrimage from any other is its Christo-centric character. He who is believed to be the beginning and the end, the door and the way, summons his disciples to take up their crosses and follow him, as he himself walked the *via crucis* and thereby voluntarily submitted himself to the will of his heavenly Father. Even when the destination is the tomb of a saint, the Christo-centric nature of the devotion is not lost because all the saints are only of importance as so many examples of different ways to imitate their Master. Yet the extent of this distinction can only be made fully apparent by an examination in depth of Christian pilgrimages throughout the ages, of the devotional practices associated with them and of their meaning. But exactly why should anyone go on a pilgrimage at all?

Motives

The Middle Ages, as noted already above in the case of Father Cipolla, were marked by a great eagerness to obtain relics. There is, for instance, the case of Fulk de Neuilly, d. 1202, who was a famous preacher with a reputation for outstanding sanctity. The crowds who flocked to hear him would try to tear off pieces of his clothing. On one occasion he frustrated their efforts by announcing that there was little point as his garments had not been blessed, but that he was about to pronounce a benediction on the clothing of a bystander. No sooner had he made the sign of the cross over him than the unfortunate man had every stitch stripped from him, leaving him stark naked![2]

This passion for relics in part arose from their commercial potential which Cipolla fully appreciated, but here is an example drawn from history rather than from the creative imagination of

Boccacio. Guibert de Nogent, *c.* 1100, has preserved an account of the money-raising travels of the monks of Laon. They went about bearing a reliquary which was said to contain parts of the robe of the Virgin Mary. They even crossed into England where some remarkable cures were apparently effected. Guibert concludes: 'Out of the many things the queenly Virgin did in England, it should be enough to have culled these instances.'[3] In these words there is an important clue to the mediaeval understanding of relics; they are to be sought after and cherished because they are identical with the saint or saints whose remains they are – it was not simply the relics of the queenly Virgin but herself who accomplished these marvels in England. Hence to the men and women of the period the relics of a saint were the saint himself. This belief was constant and had been clearly expressed by John Chrysostom (d. 407) when he spoke of the remains of the martyr Babylas as 'a living, acting good patron and protector'.[4] It can be further illustrated by one of the spiritual anecdotes that make up *The Dialogue of Miracles*, compiled for the edification of novices, by Caesarius of Heisterbach (*c.* 1180–1240). The story relates to a time of civil war in Thuringia when, for fear of desecration, the bodies of two virgin saints were transferred to a secret location, the whereabouts of which were then forgotten.

> Being indignant at this treatment, twice they shook their resting place so violently that the shock could be heard by all. Twice also they appeared in dreams to the sacristan saying that they wished to leave the place where they were held in contempt.[5]

Move now to the dawn of the Reformation and to the account of his pilgrimage by Arnold von Harff (1496–99): he records his visit to one of the great pilgrimage churches in Toulouse, St Sernin, and says that there are twenty-five saints there 'in person' viz. six apostles, four bishops, seven martyrs, two confessors, two abbots and four unspecified.[6]

Not that the folk who noted the presence of such athletes of the faith were totally credulous and unaware of the possibility of forgeries, like those perpetrated by or on Father Cipolla. Even the devout, like Felix Fabri who paid two separate visits to the Holy Land in the late fifteenth century, could be highly critical as when he was told that there were preserved on St Michael's Mount the weapons with which the archangel had driven Lucifer and his followers from heaven. Michael, retorted Felix, 'had no need of a corporeal shield and sword, and these things have been untruthfully invented by the avarice of monks. They are childish fictions.'[7] Others, such as von Harff, were occasionally sceptical as when, on the road to Santiago, he reached San Domingo de la Calzada, reported that the saint is there 'in person' and then observed that his body and grave had already been shown to him at Bologna; he comments: 'I leave God to decide these disputes among priests who never allow that they are wrong.'[8]

But these self-same priests were not lost for an answer. Caesarius, who has already been quoted as an authority on these matters, declared to a novice who was worried about inauthentic relics:

> In my judgment ignorance in such matters excuses the fault and piety always wins grace. It is certain that this seems to be true, since sometimes the Lord works miracles through false relics to the honour of the saints to whom they are ascribed, and for those who do honour them in good faith.[9]

Yet, long before, Augustine had castigated the 'base commercialization' of 'the many hypocrites in the garb of monks, who go through the provinces, sent by no authority, never stationary, stable or settled. Some sell the relics of martyrs or so-called martyrs'.[10]

However, many priests did try to establish the genuineness of their treasures. Among such attempts was that undertaken by St Meinwerc of Paderborn (d. 1036). He used trial by fire to assure himself of the identity of the body of the martyr Felix.[11] There were in fact special liturgical texts devised for such ceremonies and these appropriately included a reference to the preservation of the three holy children in the fiery furnace described in the book of Daniel, and a petition that similarly the relics might be safeguarded as long as they were genuine, otherwise they should be consumed in the flames.[12] The rationale is clear: since the relics are the saint in person, if they are not spurious he will protect himself. This same manner of thinking underlies what has been called *furta sacra*, i.e. holy thefts which the mediaeval divines were quite prepared to condone. Their argument ran like this: since relics embody a personal holy presence, the desire to possess them is unobjectionable. If possession can only be obtained by theft, there is nothing wrong in this because the persons, whose relics they are, will simply abort the theft should they not wish to remove their place of residence.[13] If they did not, this was proof positive that they were ready to be at home elsewhere – the word 'home' is used advisedly since Caesarius could apply it to Rome as the 'home' of Peter and Paul.[14] This did not mean that custodians of relics left their protection entirely to the saints. They took the utmost care to guard them and threats of the divine punishment to descend upon thieves are frequent in the hagiographical literature.

There was in fact a certain familiarity on the part of mediaeval Christians *vis à vis* the saints; indeed on occasion if they failed to grant requests even their statues could be taken and whipped, as at Quency.[15] Moreover it was not simply the earthly remains of a holy person that constituted their continuing presence but the extension of that presence by means of contact-relics i.e. of objects that had been rubbed against or otherwise brought into touch with the original remains. But why were so many people prepared to go to great trouble to travel as pilgrims to the shrines where the relics were preserved? The answer turns upon knowing who the saints were and what functions they were believed to perform.

The shrine of a saint was a potentially active source of spiritual energy. Although dead in the flesh, the saint was there, a formidable and powerful being who, if approached properly, could bring help to the suppliant. The supreme witnesses to Christ had been those who had died during the persecutions; they were regarded as having shared in the suffering of their Master, and consequently some of the mediaeval miniatures depicting their lives drew on the iconography of Christ's arrest and judgment. So outstanding was their act of witness that the very word *martus* (witness) was eventually confined to them. With the end of the persecutions, a new concept of sanctity emerged; asceticism was assimilated to martyrdom and holiness was ascribed to those who spread the gospel among the heathen, governed the church with piety or became monks and nuns. So the roll of saints was increased and to all of them could be applied the dictum of Jerome (d. 420): 'We honour the servants that their honour may be reflected upon their Lord who himself says, "He that receives you receives me"' (Matt. 10.40)[16] This honour (*dulia*) – at least as far as the theologians were concerned – was less than worship (*latria*), although in popular devotion the one could easily merge into the other. Not surprisingly, the saints came to be regarded as having an intercessory function, so Paulinus of Nola (d. 431), in his fourteenth poem to St Felix, says: 'receive these prayers of your followers and recommend them to God.'[17] Prudentius (d.c. 410) was prepared to go even further. In one of his hymns he declared that a martyr 'listens to every entreaty and grants all prayers he finds deserving of God's grace . . . Blessings, believe me, he will obtain for all who invoke him.'[18] Consequently the motives for going on a pilgrimage included the search for a variety of blessings. Foremost among these must be noted the quest for health. Saints were regarded as doctors, more capable than soi-disants professionals and often less costly. So, to give one example, St Clare of France was believed to cure eye infections, a belief that owed something to a false etymology i.e. she was able to help, because, named Clare, she could restore clear (*claire*) vision.[19] To this can be added assistance when crops failed or when storms threatened. Then, among the slightly bizarre, there were pilgrimages by young maidens seeking marriage, certain saints, such as St John and St Anne in Brittany, being experts in these matters. To some French shrines even still-born infants were conveyed in the hope that they might be resuscitated for baptism.[20]

Some pilgrims were motivated by a special devotion to a particular saint and would therefore choose to journey to that saint's shrine. Such was the Italian notary, Nicolas di Martoni, whose desire to honour St Catherine led him to include Sinai in his itinerary to the Holy Land in 1394–5.[21]

Pilgrimages to ask saints for specific favours were frequent; for instance in 1487 Henry VII went to Walsingham to pray that he might be preserved from the wiles of his enemies.[22] Often such a journey could be in fulfilment of a vow, as a kind of thanksgiving for benefits received or hoped for. So Pero Tafur of Cordoba was horror stricken at the prospect of an early death when caught in a storm as he sailed towards Genoa and he made a vow that if he survived he would go on a pilgrimage.[23] Erasmus tells of Ogygius going to Compostela because his mother-in-law had vowed that if her daughter bore a live male child he, Ogygius, would go and salute St James and express gratitude.[24] The thanks, then, did not always have to be conveyed in person: one might also pay the expenses of a substitute – such a replacement would then have as his motive monetary gain. Compare the will of Roger of Wansford in which he directed his executors to send someone on a pilgrimage to implement 'a solemn vow which I made when gravely threatened and almost suffocated by the waves of the sea between Ireland and Norway'.

In sum, although without mention of vows, John Chrysostom at an early date provided a compendium of pilgrimage objectives when he wrote as follows in his panegyric on Ignatius of Antioch:

I beseech you all that if any is in despondency, if in disease, if in insult, if in any other circumstances of his life, if in the depth of sin, let him come hither with faith, and he will lay aside all those things, and will return with much joy, having procured a lighter conscience from the sight alone.[25]

Destinations

If such be some of the motives with which pilgrims set out, where did they go? Some destinations have already been mentioned: Laon, Toulouse, Walsingham and Compostela. Of these the last, Compostela was included in what were known as the major pilgrimages together with Canterbury (where Thomas à Becket was honoured), Cologne (which was associated with the Three Wise Men), Constantinople (which possessed many relics) but above all Rome. The growing importance in this respect of the old imperial capital is evident from the poems of Prudentius whose *Peristephanon*, published in 405, celebrates a host of martyrs and from the *Ecclesiastical History* of Bede (completed 731) where it is stated that going to Rome is 'reckoned to be of great moment.'[26] Indeed the bishops of Rome actively encouraged such pilgrimages. In the fourth century Damasus had opened up the catacombs, restored the tombs of the martyrs and placed therein beautifully lettered inscriptions, engraved by Furius Filocalus; he thus changed the character of these subterranean burial places so that they became more pilgrimage shrines than cemeteries.[27] Gregory the Great, too, (540–604) had lent his considerable authority to the practice.[28] For him his most precious relic was the chains of St Peter and it was his custom to send filings to his friends enclosed in crosses; so in 603 he sent such a gift to Eulogius who had weak vision, recommending him to apply it regularly to his eyes.[29] And not only Peter's chains but Paul's also attracted devotion and we find Chrysostom speaking of his desire to go and enter Paul's cell, 'consecrated by this prisoner' and behold his fetters.[30]

The draw of the two apostles was very powerful as evidenced by Aravatus, a sixth-century bishop of Tongres. Deeply disturbed at the advance of the Huns and concerned about the efficacy of his prayer that they would not be allowed to penetrate deep into Gaul, he decided to go to Rome, 'that he might be strengthened by the miraculous power of the apostles, and thereby better deserve to obtain that for which he made humble supplication to God'.[31] But it was Peter above all that exercised the greatest pull for to visit Rome was not only to venerate his relics but to honour his living embodiment: Peter lives on in the pope. This identification explains a passage in von Harff's account. He describes a metal statue of the apostle seated, with his right foot extended:

and I was told that whoever kissed the foot with devotion and repentance of his sins obtains daily as many pardons and indulgences as if he had kissed the foot of the pope himself.[32]

Many pilgrims also went to Rome with the specific intention of settling there permanently in the belief that on the day of resurrection their proximity to the key bearer would be of benefit: 'I will give you the keys of the kingdom of heaven' (Matt. 16.19).[33]

Yet Rome had other treasures to display. In the church of S. Maria Maggiore there was a painting of the Virgin Mary said to have been done by St Luke himself. Even better than this was the Vernicle, the veil or kerchief of Veronica with which, according to tradition, she had wiped Jesus' face on the way to Calvary and which had preserved his image upon it. Each pilgrim, in the words of Petrarch, could then look upon the very 'likeness of his Lord',[34] while Dante speaks of the many who 'go to see the blessed portrait left us by Jesus Christ as a copy of his most beautiful face'.[35] When Boniface VIII declared the year 1300 to be a Jubilee and so provided an additional incentive to those who would come as pilgrims, some 200,000 are said to have responded to his initiative and set the seal on an age-long devotion.

Rome, however, had one all-important rival – one to which attention would have been called previously if the presentation were intended to be strictly chronological rather than thematic – and that rival was the Holy Land. Indeed it is possible to discern an historical sequence of pilgrimages differentiated by their destinations. In the first place was Palestine, to be followed by visits to the tombs of the martyrs, with Rome exercising the most attraction. Other saints came next, with James of Compostela much favoured. Fourthly there were the confessors, such as Martin of Tours. Fifthly there were locations famed for supernatural apparitions, such as Monte Sant'Angelo in the Gargano Peninsula where the archangel was believed to have revealed himself in 490. Finally there were pilgrimages in honour of the Virgin. It is perhaps not excessive to suggest that there developed a certain pilgrimage-itis, which is perhaps best exemplified by the visits to Job's dunghill, strongly advocated by John Chrysostom who, in the course of a sermon delivered on Tuesday 9 March 388, declared it to be more venerable than the seat of any earthly monarch.

> For from seeing a royal throne no advantage results to the spectator, but only a temporary pleasure which has no profit; but from the sight of Job's dunghill one may derive every kind of benefit, yea, much divine wisdom and consolation, in order to patience . . . Therefore to

this day many undertake a long pilgrimage, even across the sea, hastening from the extremities of the earth, as far as Arabia, that they may kiss the ground of such a victor.[36]

Yet Jerusalem had pride of place and was not only the goal *par excellence* chronologically but also the one that most Christians desired to attain because there was the tomb of the first victor and martyr, Jesus himself. The title of first martyr is often given to Stephen, but the account of his death in Acts, with his forgiveness of his persecutors, is obviously modelled on that of Jesus and his words – 'Father forgive them for they know not what they do.' In this way emphasis is placed on the extent to which the death of a follower of Jesus may be linked to that of his Master. Yet the tomb of Jesus did differ from those of his saints in that it was empty, and moreover was for a long time inaccessible. Hadrian, according to Jerome, had deliberately built a temple to Venus on the site.[37] So the first recorded pilgrim, Melito of Sardis (*c.* 170) was motivated less by a desire to worship than by a wish to see the locations 'where these things were preached and done',[38] i.e. his concern was partly historical. Indeed for many the visit was a means of confirming the gospel accounts.[39]* So Leo (440–61), in his letter to Juvenal of Jerusalem, extolled the value of living in the city and so by implication of visiting it.

A person there is taught to understand the power of the gospel, not only by the written words but by the witness of the places themselves, and what elsewhere may not be disbelieved cannot there remain unseen. Why is the understanding in difficulty when the eyes are its instructors? And why are things read or heard doubtful where all the mysteries of man's salvation obtrude themselves upon the sight and touch?[40]

This motive for going to Palestine readily merges with another succinctly expressed by Jerome:

One understands holy scripture better when one has seen with one's own eyes Judaea and contemplated the ruins of its ancient cities.[41]

A thousand years later Felix Fabri, the preaching friar from Ulm, was to formulate the same idea:

Even unlearned laymen return theologians from the holy places . . . and men of small learning will return learned to no small degree.[42]

Closely associated with this motive of letting the Bible come alive before their eyes was the ardent desire of Christians, according to

Origen (d. c. 254), to go 'in search of the traces of Jesus and his disciples and prophets'.[43] To similar effect was the view of Paulinus of Nola in his forty-ninth epistle.

> No other sentiment draws men to Jerusalem but the desire to see and touch the places where Christ was physically present, and to be able to say from their very own experience: 'We have gone into his tabernacle, and have adored in the places where his feet stood' (Ps. 131.7).

It is not difficult to imagine the fervour of those who knelt in the Church of the Holy Sepulchre, believing they were praying for the forgiveness of their sins on the very spot where Christ had given his life as a ransom for many, or who climbed the Mount of Olives, entered the Church of the Ascension and saw what were considered to be the footprints of Jesus marked in the very rock. So a Russian abbot named Daniel, who came to the Holy Land in 1106–7, spoke of visiting the places 'which Christ our God pressed with his feet'.[44] Almost identical words were put in the mouth of Henry IV in Shakespeare's play – the king speaks of

> those holy fields
> Over whose acres walk'd those blessed feet
> Which fourteen hundred years ago were nail'd
> For our advantage on the bitter cross.[45]

No wonder that one pilgrim remarked to Felix Fabri: 'Nowhere have I received the grace of God in so large a measure as I did at the places where our redemption was wrought.'[46] Indeed von Harff records that he set out 'for the comfort and well being of my soul'.[47] The pilgrimage then became an act of thanksgiving 'undertaken with a view to the praise of God'.[48] Others stressed the sense of unity they experienced as they mingled with pilgrims from so many diverse lands. Indeed it would have seemed to have been Constantine's original intention to promote such unity when he launched what has been termed his Holy Land plan in the third decade of the fourth century.[49] He did much to promote Jerusalem, and Bethlehem too, as foci of devotion by the imposing buildings he had erected. According to his keen supporter Eusebius of Caesarea (d. c. 340) the emperor had actually been inspired by Christ to make the place of his resurrection 'a centre of attraction and venerable to all'.[50] Further the belief that the Second Coming would take place at Jerusalem was yet another incentive (like proximity to Peter at Rome) to draw the crowds, either to live out the remainder of their lives there in anticipation or to stay for a short time according to the maxim: you never know your luck.

This concept is enshrined in stone on the Romanesque façade of Saint-Jouin-de-Marnes where those standing before Christ at the Last Judgment wear the garb of pilgrims (Pl. I).

Cyril of Jerusalem (d. 386) was building on the foundation laid by Constantine when he devised a series of services, particularly for Holy Week, closely linked with the topography of the city where he presided as bishop. He was well aware of the evidential and didactic value of the sacred sites; thus, speaking in the Martyrium, he told candidates for baptism: 'Christ was truly crucified for our sins. Even supposing you were disposed to contest this, your surroundings rise up before you to refute you, this sacred Golgotha where we now come together because of him who was crucified here.'[51] On another occasion he affirmed that there are many true testimonies to Christ: 'the palm tree of the valley, which provided branches to the children of those days who hailed him. Gethsemane bears witness still, to the imagination all but haunted by the form of Judas. This Golgotha, sacred above all such places, bears witness by its very look. The most holy sepulchre bears witness and the stone lies there to this day.'[52] It was to see these very places and to participate in the celebrations that were arranged at each one that pilgrims began to arrive in droves.

One such pilgrim, who arrived in Jerusalem about the time of Cyril's death, was the Spanish nun Egeria. In the report she prepared for her sisters at home, she never ceased to marvel how the hymns, antiphons, readings and prayers were all 'suitable to the place and the day'. Yet if it was the pull of the Bible that induced folk to make Palestine their destination, the events recorded in it were by no means confined within its borders; consequently a natural extension or prelude to a Holy Land visit included the route of the Israelites through the wilderness with Mount Sinai as a station of great importance. The indefatigable Egeria was one of the first recorded to have made this circuit and her vivid description shows the extent to which she understood her pilgrimage to be a quest for the biblical past.

We were shown everything that the Books of Moses tell us took place in the valley beneath holy Sinai, the Mount of God. I know it has been rather a long business to write down these places one after another, and it makes far too much to remember, but it may help you, loving sisters, the better to picture what happened in these places when you read the holy Books of Moses . . . All the way I kept asking to see the different places mentioned in the Bible, and they were all pointed out to me by the holy men, the clergy and the monks with us. Some of the places were to the right and others to the left of our route, some a long way off

Plate I Pilgrims on the façade of Saint-Jouin-de-Marnes

and others close by. So, as far as I can see, loving sisters, you must take it that the Children of Israel zigzagged their way to the Red Sea, first right, then back left again, now forwards and now back.[53]

There was clearly an interplay between the destinations and the motives for going to Mount Sinai and to the Holy Land: here were the scenes of God's decisive acts in history; this was the place where redemption was achieved. These are not the same reasons that impelled people to visit the shrines of the saints, yet there was inevitably some overlap. In fact any pilgrimage, no matter what the destination, could be undertaken because of a vow; any one could involve a search for assistance culminating in requests for intercession and all were related to the concept of Christian discipleship in terms of imitation. So Chrysostom, stressing the value of places associated with the apostles, had no doubt that 'only seeing these places where they sat or where they were imprisoned, mere lifeless spots, we often transport our minds thither and imagine their virtues, and are excited by it, and become more zealous'.[54] According to Fabri, men and women go to Jerusalem 'to follow the holy footsteps of his shameful passion, even as Peter bids us do in the second chapter of his first epistle' (I Peter 2.21).[55] They were conscious in so doing that they were following the example of Abraham when he left Ur of the Chaldees at the divine command and they deemed their own pilgrimage to be a true *imitatio Christi* for Christ himself had been regarded as a pilgrim on the road to Emmaus on the first Easter Day.

When Archbishop Siegfried of Mainz set out for Palestine in the autumn of 1064, he informed the pope that his purpose was to venerate the tomb of Christ, to be edified by worshipping in the places where the Lord's feet had stood and to do penance for past sins.[56] It is this last intention that points to the need to consider certain types of pilgrimage other than those so far passed in rapid view. These are, in chronological order, exilic pilgrimages; pentitential ones, including the quest for indulgences; judicial pilgrimages and finally the Crusades – this last being, as is now generally recognized, a particular form of pilgrimage.

Exilic Pilgrimages

Hitherto the word 'pilgrimage' has been employed in the sense of a journey with devotional and other motives to a particular destination, be it the Holy Land, Rome or one of the many shrines of the saints. However there was a second meaning current from the early Middle

Ages which derived from the idea, based upon several scriptural verses such as Heb. 11.13 and I Peter 2.11, that Christians are 'exiles' in this world. Alienation is stressed together with the view that here below is not one's true homeland – indeed the believer is a foreigner. To go on a pilgrimage and so to quit one's native country could then be envisaged as an acted parable of a refusal to settle down. But the departure from the land of one's birth was not with a view to following a planned itinerary with a predetermined destination. The intention was to embark upon an unorganized wandering since God might lead you where he wished. In this way the affirmation in the Epistle to the Hebrews that we have here no lasting city (13.14) was dramatized.

It was the Irish monks of the sixth and seventh centuries who in particular embraced this mode of life as an ascetic exercise; they denied themselves the joy experienced by pilgrims *ad loca sancta* upon returning home. In a sense they were fulfilling Matt. 10.37f.: 'He who loves father and mother more than me is not worthy of me; and he who loves son or daughter more than me is not worthy of me; and he who does not take up his cross and follow me is not worthy of me.' So attachments to family, neighbourhood and country were disrupted on an exilic pilgrimage; that they are strangers in this world was effectively translated into reality; they were pilgrims *ex patria*. This exilic condition was daily recalled in that the pilgrims were wont to sleep with head on a stone as did Jacob when, similarly on a journey, he saw the angels ascending and descending. (Gen. 28.11f.)[57]

Penitential Pilgrimages and the Quest for Indulgences

The exilic type of pilgrimage was eventually to cease because of the insistence, especially in the Benedictine rule, of stability as the mark of a monk, and the *gyrovagus*, as such a wanderer was called, passed out of fashion, to be replaced in Ireland by the anchorite whose isolated cell became the scene of his continued exile.[58] However the ascetic aspect of the exilic pilgrimage was not lost to the extent that any and every pilgrimage to a holy place could be interpreted in penitential categories and this appealed more to lay men and women as a form of spiritual discipline than the entering into a commitment to a lifetime in a monastery.

Of course because of the extreme hardship of travel throughout this period, every pilgrimage was in a sense a penitential event. But a penitential pilgrimage properly so-called designates a recognized element within the church's disciplinary system. It constituted either a work of expiation as a part of the ecclesiastical process whereby a sinner obtained the remission of his sins or an authentic variety of sacramental penance, i.e. a penitential pilgrimage was not a voluntary effort on the part of the individual but an exercise imposed by the parish priest or sometimes by the bishop.

By the thirteenth century, having begun like the exilic type in Ireland, the penitential pilgrimage became fully institutionalized and was recognized as one of three legitimate forms of penance:

(*i*) Solemn public penance, imposed by a bishop alone

(*ii*) Public penance *non solemnis* – this is the penitential kind

(*iii*) Private penance[59]

The pentitential pilgrimage, it is worth noting, made a contribution to the pre-eminence of Rome as a destination, because in some cases where a bishop was undecided about the precise penance to order he would direct the person concerned to go to the pope and abide by his verdict.

From the same root, i.e. the penitential system, there sprang the granting of indulgences. The quest for these eventually became a primary motive for going on a pilgrimage as William Brewyn appreciated when he noted in his guide book (*c.* 1470) that many set out 'with the devout intention of acquiring indulgences'.[60] Certainly from 1300 onwards no traveller penned an account without listing the indulgences available, but their origin goes back long before and to understand them some further idea of the development of the penitential system is necessary.

If a person commits a sin and then confesses it, he or she becomes liable to the appropriate penalty before remission can be bestowed. This order – sin, confession, penalty, absolution – was followed up to the sixth and seventh centuries during the period of public penance, and forgiveness accordingly was not granted until the penalty imposed by the bishop had been carried out. From the seventh to the eleventh centuries the practice of private penance became the norm, and the previous sequence was then changed -- the penalty was executed *after* the absolution. These penalties were graded and their duration specified in days, weeks and years. However a confessor could reduce these periods by demanding the performance of good works, which included pilgrimage, and these were held to have equivalent values as regards the length of time.

In the eleventh and twelfth centuries a further step was taken in that these reductions in time were institutionalized by being incorporated into the official penitential system and there was a tendency to emphasize good works rather than ascetic exercises. It is to these reductions that the term 'indulgences' refers. However there was one further stage in their evolution in that they were finally dissociated from the penance imposed in the confessional. They were no longer linked to specific sins committed and confessed. Indulgences then constituted a gracious remission of the sentence to which all human beings are subject in that they fall short of the glory of God (Rom. 3.23). They could be sought and obtained by all, even by those who would not previously have resorted to the confessional. However, they continued to be reckoned in days, weeks and years, exactly as they had been when they were the equivalent of penalties of precise duration. This explains why many pilgrims speak of indulgences of forty days, seven weeks and seven years, which constitute partial indulgences, and of plenary ones which liberate totally.[61]

Indulgences received a great impetus and became even more closely bound up with pilgrimages because of two events. First, there was the launching of the Crusading movement by Urban II in 1095; he declared that anyone who took up the cross would receive full remission of enjoined penance.[62] Second was the introduction of the Jubilee Year by Boniface VIII in a bull of 22 February 1300 which granted indulgences for all who came to Rome during the twelve month period – this was also extended to the Holy Land and successive popes recognized other centres, e.g. Eugenius IV in 1445 approved of Mont-Saint-Michel.[63]

The practice of indulgences was founded upon the belief that the merits of Jesus and his saints form an inexhaustible treasury on which the pope who has the power of the keys may draw. So Eugenius III, who with Bernard of Clairvaux promoted the second Crusade in 1147, claimed that as Christ's vicar he could absolve from divine as well as ecclesiastical punishment.[64] No wonder that the popularity of pilgrimages increased and that certificates, specifying the indulgences acquired and authenticated with special seals, were eagerly sought.

Judicial Pilgrimages

It is not difficult to appreciate how a penitential pilgrimage could become less an act of expiation and more one of punishment, although the dividing line between the two is not very precise. It was perfectly reasonable for one found guilty of murder or parricide to be required to leave the country and go on a pilgrimage. In effect the sentence of Cain was served upon them: 'You shall be a fugitive and a wanderer on the earth' (Gen. 4.12). Hence in the eighth century it was decreed that the condemned should have no fixed abode but must be continually on the move, often for as many as seven years but sometimes for more. However by the ninth century the practice had arisen of despatching the culprits to a named place, usually Rome, where they were to obtain signed certificates to prove they had accomplished their appointed tasks. The journey was then interpreted as a true act of penitence that could lead to absolution for the fault committed.

The Inquisition, established by Gregory IX in 1231, adopted this procedure as a penalty for heretics in the south of France. Embodied in canon law, it was but a short step for it to pass into the civil and criminal codes and become a punishment inflicted by magistrates and judges upon those who had been found guilty of creating a public scandal or of breaching the peace. These judicial pilgrimages, as they came to be known, were often little more than scarcely disguised periods of forced exile although they are obviously not to be confused with the exilic type pursued as an ascetic exercise.[65]

Crusades

To travel to the Holy Land as a Crusader was, in marked contrast to being a judicial pilgrim, a voluntary undertaking, but it was certainly regarded as a form of pilgrimage. Indeed Urban II when launching the first one at Claremont in 1095 referred to it as 'this holy pilgrimage'. He further asserted that it was a means of fulfilling the apostle's exhortation in Romans 12.1 to present themselves as living sacrifices, holy, acceptable to God.

The Crusaders were at first known as *peregrini*, but towards the end of the twelfth century they began to be designated as *cruce signati*. This signing with the cross referred originally to the affixing of one on their clothing at Claremont, but there was no formal ceremony. A special service was soon drawn up and all Crusaders participated in it before leaving for the Middle East.[66] (Fig. 1)

The Crusades have not always had a good press: the idea of a holy war has not commended itself to Christians; the motives of some warriors were questionable, in particular their greed for land and riches; the sack of Constantinople in 1204 was outrageous – yet the religious motives of the majority should not be underestimated. Robert II of Flanders, for example, on the first Crusade, began each day with devotions and eagerly venerated any relic he could obtain;

Fig. 1 Crusaders (from the French edition of von Breydenbach, *Journey to the Holy Land*, Paris 1522)

the Turks eventually nicknamed him 'the Arm of St George' because he had secured that sacred object when passing through Romania.[67] Moreover, Urban had encouraged this immense adventure as destined to achieve several objects, each of high moral value: first, to defend Constantinople and by so doing to heal the schism between East and West; second, to be a repentant act of faith that would culminate in the moral reformation and total renewal of Christendom; third, it was to be a mass pilgrimage of believers united in the expectation of the imminent return of Christ.[68] Very much to the fore was the penitential aspect, as can be illustrated by the way the confessor of St Louis of France applied to him the words of Ephesians 5.4, i.e. 'He gave himself up for us, a fragrant offering and a sacrifice to God.'[69] It would be churlish to question the genuineness of the first Crusaders' feelings when in 1099 they reached Jerusalem and approached the Holy Sepulchre 'creeping on their knees and elbows, watering the pavement with their tears'.[70]

Pilgrimage Literature

Whereas the first pilgrims were departing on a virtually uncharted and unknown journey, those who followed in their footsteps were able to gain assistance from a variety of books which the pioneers themselves had produced. During the period under survey, however, which largely predates the invention of printing, such works were limited both in extent and in circulation; moreover, being in manuscript form, they were too costly for many and would have been of use only to the literate. Most were too bulky for easy conveyance, although one guide book of 1471, which has survived with its original binding of sheep leather on press-boards and brass fastenings, measures only 125/99 mm.[71]

This pilgrimage literature may be divided into seven categories, although they are by no means discrete and tend to merge into one another. Under the first head may be grouped itineraries, under the second pilgrim diaries and under the third lists of indulgences. Fourthly there are maps and plans, and next aids to devotion. The sixth type consists of guide books, which may be seen as a development of the first category and often include the third, with travel accounts in the seventh and final place.

(a) Itineraries

Amongst the military equipment discovered during the excavations at Dura-Europos on the Euphrates was the shield of a soldier who had perished there when the city was attacked shortly after AD 256. This soldier had served previously by the Black Sea and he had carefully noted on his shield distances and stopping places on his march from there to Syria.[72] In effect therefore he had kept a log and had transcribed it on one of his most precious possessions. Such an itinerary is little more than a list of stations en route and a record of the mileage between them. This particular example was individual, but there existed more public ones copied and circulating freely. Such were the two Antonine itineraries that contain lists of ways by land and sea throughout the Roman empire. First produced in the early third century, these have survived in an edition of a hundred years later.[73]

An identical format, but specifically related to travel as a Christian, is the document produced by the Bordeaux pilgrim to Jerusalem in the year 333.[74] Some 557 years later a similar type of document, this time with Rome as the goal, was written by Sigeric, Archbishop of

Canterbury, when he went there to receive the pallium from John XV. He recorded the several halts and in addition named the churches in the city that he visited over a two-day period.[75]

Similar information had been included previously in the *Itinerarium Salisburgense* which is found in a manuscript of the tenth century, but it reproduces an original of the early seventh and probably includes material from the fifth and even the fourth centuries. It describes routes to be followed in the holy city, and it provides information about the points of the compass, the position of the main shrines to the left or right of the road, the nature of each holy place, whether above or below ground, whether a sepulchral chamber or a church.[76] The Malmesbury *Notitia Portarum*, *c.* 675, which William of Malmesbury was later to copy into his history, specifies churches and graves outside the walls of Rome,[77] while the *Itinerarium Einsiedlense*, of which the first version dates back to the latter part of the eighth century, also provides a series of eleven walks around Rome in every possible direction and is virtually a street guide.[78] Belonging to the same genre is Brother Bernard of Ascoli's itinerary to Jerusalem (1112–20) which is similarly terse but not lacking in detail, so, for example, the Probatic Pool is recorded as being a quarter of a mile from the Temple and there are thirty steps down to the tomb of the Virgin Mary.[79] The thirteenth-century *Peregrinationes Terrae Sanctae* simply lists the stations and is no more nor less than a log.[80]

The necessity for travellers whatever their destination to possess one of these itineraries and their continuing utility is further indicated by the survival of one exclusively for commercial travel from Avignon to Rome, *c.* 1350,[81] and of another of use to pilgrims inscribed on the end-leaf of a fifteenth-century manuscript under the heading: 'The weye vnto Rome and so too Venyse and Jerusalem'.[82] No wonder that itineraries were incorporated into devotional manuals and eventually formed a standard section in complete guide books.

(b) Pilgrim-diaries

These rather stark road-books soon developed into pilgrim-diaries simply by the addition of details about the places visited together with personal comments. If we take what the Bordeaux pilgrim had to say in his itinerary about Bethlehem and set it side by side with the notice provided by the Piacenza pilgrim, *c.* 570, this elaboration will be evident.

Four miles from Jerusalem, on the right of the highway to Bethlehem, is the tomb in which was laid Jacob's wife Rachel. Two miles further on, on the left, is Bethlehem, where the Lord Jesus was born, and where a basilica has been built by command of Constantine.[83]

On the way to Bethlehem, at the third milestone from Jerusalem, lies the body of Rachel, on the edge of the area called Ramah. There I saw standing water which came from a rock, of which you can take as much as you like up to seven pints. Every one has his fill, and the water does not become less or more. It is indescribably sweet to drink, and people say that St Mary became thirsty on the flight to Egypt and that when she stopped here this water immediately flowed. Nowadays there is also a church building there. From there it is three miles to Bethlehem, which is a most renowned place. There are many servants of God there; there is the cave where the Lord was born, and, inside it, there is the manger decorated with gold and silver, at which lights are burning day and night. As you go in, the mouth of the cave is very narrow.[84]

From a later period one has only to contrast Sigeric's bald list (990) with that of the Anglo-Saxon merchant Saewulf (1102–3) who filled out his itinerary with many personal observations[85] or with the diary of Nikolas, abbot of the Benedictine monastery at Munkathvera in Iceland. The abbot set out for the Holy Land in 1154 and duly recorded routes, stopping places, and the time taken to travel between them, but at every turn he enriched this itinerary with details concerning the places he named; he reported on churches, landscape, dialects, climate and even the fair ladies of Siena. He included religious anecdotes and echoed German legends with such Wagnerian characters as Fafnir.[86]

(c) Libri indulgentiarum

Two hundred years on from abbot Nikolas, in the course of the fourteenth century, the quest for indulgences was in full cry and this promoted another genre of pilgrim literature, viz. books of indulgences which listed places and the corresponding benefits to be gained if they were visited. In effect, therefore, since the information had to be related to specific locations, these were a form of guide book but with a new emphasis on the remission of penalties for sin. Sometimes the facts were presented in rhyming form the easier to commit to memory. Such is the Vernon manuscript (1370) which includes a section entitled *The Stacyons of Rome*. This particular document is a commendation of the superior benefits of a visit to the papal city in contrast with Santiago or Jerusalem and it contains the affirmation that if a pilgrim attends mass in St Paul's every Sunday for a whole year

> You shall have as much pardon
> As you to St James went and come.[87]

Later the author argues that there is no need to go to St Catherine's on Mount Sinai; instead one should journey to Rome 'for pardon here is without end'.[88]

In general there is agreement between the accounts about the extent of the indulgences to be gained, but there was also a steady increase in the number of years granted as time passed. To be present in Rome at the exposition of the Vernicle was to secure 3000 years if one were an inhabitant of the city, 9000 if from outside and 12000 if from overseas. These are figures given in the Vernon manuscript (c. 1370) and reported by Capgrave in 1450.[89] According to the Parkington manuscript of 1460–70, these figures had advanced to 4000, 9000 and 14000 respectively.[90]

Since these lists of indulgences could be long and memories fallible, summaries were prepared, one example being the broadsheet preserved in the Bodleian and printed by Pynson early in the sixteenth century; it simply lists the Roman stations and the amount of indulgences in Latin and English.[91] A little earlier William Brewyn had combined an itinerary and a *liber indulgentiarum* and reported that Boniface, who promoted a demand for the latter by instituting the first Jubilee in 1300, had declared: 'If men knew how great were the indulgences of the church of St John Lateran, they would not cross over to the Sepulchre of the Lord in Jerusalem, nor to St James of Compostela.'[92] This advocacy resulted in the production of many lists relating to Rome, not only in Latin and English but also in German and French. Other pilgrimage centres did not foster so many catalogues but there have been preserved some relating to Bamberg, Compostela, Jerusalem and the Syon monastery in England.[93]

(d) Maps

Armed with itineraries, lists of indulgences and drawing upon the travel diaries of their predecessors, the pilgrims were not ill-equipped, but obviously maps and town plans would have been of great benefit. Indeed a pictorial itinerary was drawn up or copied by Matthew Paris in 1253 to show the route to Rome and the Holy Land.

It is an elaborate strip-map using conventional town symbols and correctly placing rivers, mountains and seas.[94]

However, as early as the fourth century Eusebius of Caesarea had devised a map showing the divisions of the twelve tribes of Israel with a representation of the Temple in Jerusalem. He was followed by Jerome whose version (c. 385) has been preserved in a twelfth-century copy.[95] From Jerome on there is a continuous history of Holy Land cartography, to receive increased stimulus in the thirteenth and fourteenth centuries through the Crusades. Some of the products were quite small, such as the drawing by the Irish scholar-monk (c. 995) that measures only 21 × 18 cms.[96] Others are known to have existed but have been lost, e.g. that of Burchard of Mount Sion, although this particular example did have an effect on the Venetian Marino Sanuti who included three maps in the account of his journey of 1321.[97] These were drawn by Petrus Vesconti on a squared grid for ease of reference and they initiated a new phase in the history of map making and their influence was to extend over three hundred years, e.g. John Poloner, who was probably of German origin, had one divided into numbered squares and this was almost certainly borrowed from Vesconti a century later. Later still in their accounts of the spring voyage to Jerusalem of 1418 both William Wey and Gabriele Capodilista included Holy Land maps.[98] Occasionally one or other of the staging posts was given special treatment, e.g. there is a map of the island of Rhodes of 1534 (Fig. 2) or a closely knit group of sanctuaries could be the subject of a single sketch such as that of Mount Sinai in a fifteenth-century manuscript of the *Liber peregrinationis* written by Giacomo de Verona in 1355 (Fig. 3).

City plans were also issued, there being an example of one of Jerusalem (1150) in the library of Cambrai[99] and another (1160) in a library in Paris.[100] Panoramic views which provided virtually the same information were first used to illustrate an account of a pilgrimage by Bernhard von Breydenbach. He was Dean of Mainz and was accompanied in 1483–4 to Palestine by Erhard Reuwich of Utrecht who was the illustrator. The interest in indulgences, already noted, is clear from these fine woodcuts in that on the one of Jerusalem there appear double and single crosses together with a note that the former indicate a place where plenary remission of sins can be obtained and the latter a period of seven years and the same number of 'lents' (Fig. 4). This work was printed in 1486 and within twelve years had gone through twelve editions: three in German, three in Latin, four in French and one each in Flemish and Spanish.[101]

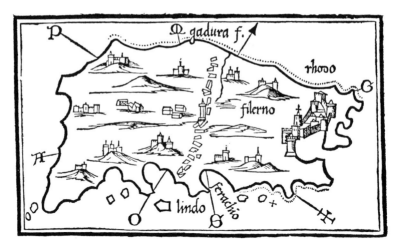

Fig. 2 Map of Rhodes 1534 (from B. Bordone, *Isolario*, N. Zoppino, Venice)

Fig. 3 Plan of Mount Sinai (from Giacomo de Verona, *Liber peregrinationis*, 1355)

Fig. 4 Panoramic view of Jerusalem (from the Latin edition of von Breydenbach, Mainz 1486)

It simply remains to note that in the immediately post-Reformation period not only the Holy Land but all places of biblical interest
were charted, e.g. the exodus route of the Israelites and one of the
journeys of St Paul by Franciscus Haraeus *c.* 1620.[102]

(e) Aids to devotion and their use

In intention a pilgrimage was a protracted spiritual exercise and many of those who took the scrip and the staff carried with them devotional manuals. Those who were clerics of course took their breviaries with them. In addition to these, Frescobaldi reports that he had with him the books of the Bible, i.e. of the Old Testament, the Gospels and the *Moralia* of Gregory the Great written during his stay in Constantinople from 579 to 586.[103] Since Frescobaldi was going via Cairo and Sinai, the first item must have included at least Exodus and Numbers. The third work, which consisted of scriptural meditations on Job, could not have been the entire opus because it was originally issued in six volumes. However, it immediately became a best seller and numerous epitomes were issued; it was probably one of these that Frescobaldi packed in his luggage.

Another devotional handbook is entitled by Felix Fabri *Processional for Pilgrims in the Holy Land*, and he explains: 'these processionals are little books wherein are marked all the versicles, collects, responses, hymns, and psalms and prayers which ought to be said or sung at all the holy places and throughout the course of a pilgrimage beyond the seas'.[104] Examples of at least four of these manuals have been preserved so that Felix's short description can be filled out.

One of these processionals was published in Germany in 1920, another in France in 1940 and the remaining pair in 1957 in Spain being in the Colombina Library in Seville. The earliest in date is the first of the Spanish manuscripts and it is from the fourteenth century. It begins with a simple title: *The Order of Procession in the Church of the Holy Sepulchre when Pilgrims are Present*. There follow ten short offices, after which the scene changes to Bethlehem with another five devotions and the work is completed by an itinerary, including a list of indulgences, in and around Jerusalem and then extending to the Jordan and to Nazareth.[105] The *Reisebüchlein* starts with an itinerary from Venice to Jerusalem, listing mileage and indulgences. There are then ten offices in the Holy Sepulchre after which the itinerary resumes.[106] The second Spanish document (*c.* 1460) begins with the itinerary, indulgences being specified, and reaches its climax with one prayer at Bethlehem and thirteen for stations in Jerusalem and on the Mount of Olives.[107] The fourth processional is included as a separate section, devoted entirely to matters liturgical, within a complete pilgrim guide of 1471. It provides for eighty-six stations covering the entire Holy Land.[108]

Three of these works are in effect versions of the same original: the five offices at Bethlehem appear word for word in the first Spanish manuscript and in the processional of 1471, while the ten for the Holy Sepulchre are reproduced not only in these two but also in the *Reisebüchlein*. It appears that they emanated from the Franciscan monastery on Mount Sion since we are informed that the complete guide book was actually transcribed there on 21 January 1471 – indeed in some books the name of the copyist is even given, e.g. one of 1437 notes that it was 'written on Mount Sion by W. de Gouda'.[109]

The devotions each follow an identical pattern. They open with an antiphon, i.e. a sentence from scripture relating to the place where the pilgrims are gathered. This is followed by a versicle and response and a collect. Where the distance between one station and another warrants it, a hymn is sung as the procession continues. By way of illustration, here is the devotion translated from the Latin for the second station in the Holy Sepulchre which stands in each of the three interrelated documents.

Antiphon. In the morning, on the first day of the week, Jesus rose and appeared first to Mary Magdalene from whom he had cast out seven devils.

Versicle. Mary do not touch me.

Response. I have not yet ascended to my Father.

Collect. Most benign Jesus Christ, the alpha and the omega, who in the morning of the first day of the week did appear to Mary Magdalene as she sweetly lamented you and who in the course of your conversation together did show by your lovable countenance that you are readily approachable, grant to us your unworthy servants that we may be found fit to behold your person full of grace in the heavenly glory of your matchless resurrection, who live and reign unto the ages of ages. Amen.[110]

The character of the fourth independent document, i.e. the second Spanish manuscript, is rather different.[111] Not only does it omit antiphons, versicles, responses and hymns, but its prayers are long and rambling, full of detailed descriptions of what happened in the particular place. It would seem to be the work of an individual who has made up his own devotions rather than copying existing forms. Only one of his prayers conforms to the collect type, but the nature of all the processionals can be most easily grasped by taking it and subjecting it to analysis. It is entitled: *Prayer where the Lord stood before the Governor.*

Most merciful Christ, the King, who on our behalf stood to be judged before a mortal judge and there were even scourged, mocked, crowned with thorns and accepted the sentence of the life-giving cross and of death, grant us for our perfecting always to remember this devotion and so to be prepared by good works that we shall not deserve judgment in wrath but in mercy when you come again from on high, who live and reign unto the ages of ages. Amen.[112]

This is a perfect example of the collect form which has always a more or less unvarying structure, viz. (*i*) An opening address (to Christ as King). (*ii*) A reference to an action or event that is recalled as the ground for the prayer (the scourging etc. and judging of Jesus). (*iii*) The prayer proper – short, simple and definite (that the pilgrims may advance towards perfection, always recalling Christ's devotion, and so be prepared to stand before him at his coming in judgment with the hope of mercy). (*iv*) A concluding doxology.

In this way an event is recalled at the place where it occurred and its significance for now and for the future is drawn out in meditative manner. So the worshippers are reminded that Christ suffered before Pilate (the governor) but that this was in order that they – the pilgrims – may live (the life-giving cross) and the request is made that, recalling Christ's sufferings, the pilgrims may be spared from condemnation when Christ comes again and may be treated with mercy by him who has been addressed at the outset as the merciful one.

This prayer faithfully reflects some of the main senses that exegetes, both of the patristic and mediaeval periods, found in the Bible. Thus there is a reference to the literal fact, i.e. to the judging of Christ as an historical event; next the moral sense is indicated, viz. the advance to perfection, and finally the eschatological dimension is found a place with the mention of the second advent. To appreciate this analysis it is necessary to recall that scholars used to distinguish two principal senses in any scriptural passage: first there is the literal or historical and second there is the spiritual or mystical. This second sense was itself subdivided, as witness this very clear statement by St Thomas Aquinas:

This spiritual sense is divisible into three . . . the allegorical sense is brought into play when the things of the Old Law signify the things of the New Law; the moral sense when the things done in Christ and in those who prefigure him are signs of what we should carry out, and the anagogical sense when the things that lie ahead in eternal glory are signified.[113]

The etymology of the terms used provides important clues to the definitions. Historical derives from *historeo* meaning to narrate and refers to the literal interpretation; allegorical from *allegoreo*, to speak so as to imply other than what is said – this can also be designated typological (*tupos*, type, model or original pattern); tropological from *tropos*, direction or way and so behaviour or character – this is what St Thomas calls the moral sense; anagogical from *anago* to lead up from lower to higher and this is often termed eschatological, i.e. that which is to do with the *eschaton* or final consummation.

A couple of examples will help to illuminate precisely what these distinctions mean when employed in the service of biblical exegesis. Dante supplies the first with his interpretation of the Exodus.

If we consider the letter alone, the thing signified to us is the going out of the children of Israel from Egypt in the time of Moses; if the allegory, our redemption through Christ is signified; if the moral sense, the conversion of the soul from the sorrow and misery of sin to a state of grace is signified; if the anagogical, the passing of the sanctified soul from the bondage of the corruption of this world to the liberty of everlasting glory is signified.[114]

Jerusalem may be taken as another very straightforward example. Literally or historically Jerusalem denotes a city of the Jews; allegorically or typologically it can be referred to the church; tropologically or morally it stands for the human soul; anagogically or eschatologically it indicates the heavenly City of God.

It should now be apparent why the Bible is being considered in this section as a devotional aid and is not being held over for inclusion with guide books. It would only belong to this latter category if it were to be interpreted exclusively as an historical document or series of documents. But the pilgrims of this era were not satisfied simply with reminiscences of past events; it was the contemporary relevance of any scriptural passage and its capacity to nourish their spiritual progress that they had in view. Interpreted according to its mystical sense the Bible was without question a devotional manual, and the processionals, taking their cue from the prevailing method of exegesis, were all of a piece with it.

It would be a mistake to assume that this way of understanding the Bible was a rarefied method known only to schoolmen and doctors. Mention has already been made of the popularity of Gregory's *Moralia*, an epitome of which was in Frescobaldi's baggage, and in his dedicatory epistle to this work the pope made clear his own exegetical method which would therefore be widely known.

> First we lay the foundation in history; then, by pursuing a symbolical sense, we erect an intellectual edifice to be a stronghold of faith; and lastly, by the grace of moral instruction, we as it were paint the fabric with fair colours.[115]

Moreover the technique was made familiar to the mass of mediaeval churchgoers through the homilies to which they listened Sunday by Sunday. Master Robert Rypon, subprior of Durham c. 1400, is but one of many who explained the several senses in great detail to his congregation.[116] Consequently those who went on pilgrimages would be entirely at home with the processionals and they would understand and use their Bibles in like fashion.

But what exactly was their understanding? If they had been taking the circuit that followed the route of the Exodus – and many did – they would have had no difficulty in accepting the exposition of Origen who drew on Jewish and Greek models to become the founder of this school of exegesis. They would have been equally at home with Gregory of Nyssa who used the same method. Indeed, even if completely ignorant of these two patristic commentators, their understanding of their own pilgrimage, enriched as they travelled by meditation on the books of Exodus and Numbers, would have been virtually identical, as was Dante's in the passage quoted above. So by way of entering into their spiritual exploration, let us glance first at Origen's *Homilies on Exodus* and then at Gregory's work.

Origen is quite certain that many of the incidents in the books of Moses 'were not written to instruct us in history . . . What has been written was for our admonition'.[117] What he calls 'the proper understanding of the Exodus' will not necessarily increase one's factual knowledge, but it can lead to growth in virtue.[118] He is convinced of this because he regards the whole of life as a pilgrimage and the wanderings of the Israelites as a commentary upon and illumination of that pilgrimage. They teach us what dangers there are, how they may be faced, and how consequently to advance in spirituality. The way is hard; there are constant struggles against the forces of evil but this never-ending contest tempers the soul. Each halting place teaches something fresh about progress in sanctity, and in his 27th homily on Numbers Origen treats of each station one by one expounding not their literal but their mystical import.

To Gregory of Nyssa, perfection, which is the goal of the human quest, requires one to set out on a never-ending pilgrimage towards God. 'The one limit of perfection is the fact that it knows no limit.'[119] Believing that 'we may be directed in the life of virtue by appropriate examples',[120] he presents Moses as one to be imitated:

> First we shall go through his life as we have learned it from the divine scriptures. Then we shall seek out the spiritual understanding which corresponds to the history in order to obtain suggestions of virtue.[121] Those who emulate their lives cannot experience the identical historical events . . . Since it is impossible to imitate the marvels of these blessed Israelites in their exact events, one might substitute a moral teaching for the literal sequence in those things which admit of such an approach. In this way those who have been striving towards virtue may find aid in living the virtuous life.[122]

Hence Moses' expedition out of Egypt across the desert towards the Promised Land becomes for Gregory the account of the individual's travelling in virtue.[123] It is in keeping with this that like Paul before him (I Cor. 10.2) he finds the 'spiritual' meaning of crossing the Red Sea in baptism: 'Those who pass through the mystical water in baptism must put to death in the water the whole phalanx of evil – such as covetousness, unbridled desire, rapacious thinking' etc.[124] To give a final example of his interpretation:

> The way led through the desert and the people lost hope in the good things promised and were reduced to thirst. Moses again made water flow in the desert for them. When it is perceived spiritually, this account teaches us what the mystery of repentance is.[125]

That this was indeed the way pilgrims understood their endeavours is evident from a guide book of *c.* 1130 that goes under the name of Fetellus, though he was its editor not its author. In this document the wandering in the wilderness is interpreted unhesitatingly in terms of Christian discipleship:

> The Lord detained the people of Israel for forty years in forty-two stations . . . Through them the true Hebrew, who hastens to pass from earth to heaven, must run his race, and, leaving the Egypt of the world, must enter the land of promise, i.e. the heavenly fatherland.[126]

Upon arrival in the Holy Land Christian pilgrims naturally concentrated more on the events in the life of Jesus than upon the doings of the children of Israel, although they were not entirely neglected. Now the Gospels played their part and Gregory of Nyssa may be quoted again to illustrate the way in which historical interpretation could become the stepping stone to spiritual progress. Writing to Eustathia, Ambrosia and Basilissa, Gregory tells them that the 'memorials' of Christ consist not only of holy places but of certain holy individuals who have internalized the spiritual meaning of what was accomplished in those very locations.

> In beholding the saving tokens of the God who gave us life, and in meeting with souls in whom the tokens of the Lord's grace are to be discerned spiritually in such clearness, one can believe that Bethlehem and Golgotha and Olivet and the scene of the resurrection are really in the God-contained heart. For when through a good conscience Christ has been formed in anyone, when anyone has by dint of godly fear nailed down the promptings of the flesh and become crucified to Christ, when anyone has rolled away from himself the heavy stone of this world's illusions and coming forth from the grave of the body has begun to walk in newness of life . . . such a one, in my opinion, is to be counted in the number of those famous ones in whom the memorials of the Lord's love for us are to be seen. When then I not only saw with the sense of sight those holy places but also beheld the tokens of places like them, I was filled with joy.[127]

So the pilgrims too were acting out both the life of Jesus and the Exodus, which, according to Luke 9.30 (where 'departure' in the RSV is actually *exodus* in the original Greek) prefigures his mission, and in this way they made them to happen; the past events became present realities and to accomplish this was an overriding reason for embarking on such an arduous journey.

Finally among aids to devotion should be included what are best described as prayer-cards. A rare example prepared for Christians to Bromholm has been preserved in the Lambeth Palace Library. This depicts Jesus on the cross which has two transverse beams in the Orthodox manner. This refers to the holy Rood which was believed to be pieces of the true cross and it is this relic that the miller's wife invokes in Chaucer's Reeve's Tale.

> 'Help, holy cross of Bromholm,' she said.
> '*In manuas tuas*, Lord, to thee I call.'

On the card itself, there is written in Latin along the top; Jesus of Nazareth the King of the Jews (John 19.19), while an inscription on the sides reads:

> This cross yat here peynted is
> Signe of ye cross of Bromholm is.

Inscribed in the outline of a heart, which itself frames the drawing of the crucifixion, is a prayer for the pilgrims to use. The card in fact is not only an aid to devotion, but a token of a completed pilgrimage to be taken back home.[128]

(f) Guide books

If all the information distributed between the several types of literature surveyed so far is brought together in a single work then the guide book emerges as a genre in its own right and more comprehensive than any of its predecessors. So the guide book transcribed on Mount Sion in 1471, previously mentioned in connexion with devotional aids, consisted of five distinct and self-contained sections dealing successively with historical, geographical, doctrinal, liturgical and linguistic data.[129] Similarly all-embracing was the *Information for Pilgrims unto the Holy Land*, the first edition of which was printed by Wynkyn de Word *c.* 1498. It was based upon a journey a decade previously and also drew upon the accounts of others, such as *The Itineraries of William Wey*,[130] a fellow of Eton who made his first visit to Jerusalem in 1458 and his second four years later. Plagiarism in fact was the order of the day and many a guide is a compilation incorporating extracts from a wide variety of other documents.[131]

A description of the contents of the *Information*, of which a second edition was issued in 1515 (Fig. 5), will show the extent of the practical advice deemed necessary. It begins by specifying a number of alternative itineraries, e.g. 'From Calais to Rome by France' or 'From Dover to the Holy Sepulchre by the Dutch way', the 'Dutch way' being up the Rhine across Bavaria to the Tyrol and over the Alps by the Reschen Pass.[132] There follows information about the rates of exchange from England to France and to Venice, this section being copied from William Wey. Sound advice is given about how to choose a galley (Fig. 6) at Venice and how to select a decent place on board: the pilgrim is warned not to go on the lower deck because it is stinking; he is told to buy a padlock to keep the door of his cabin safe as well as a chest to hold personal items. Various herbs and spices, cookery utensils, crockery and so on are listed – indeed no detail is too insignificant to mention and even the requirement of a barrel in case of sea sickness is stressed.

The advice given about the arrival at Jaffa is to select a mule quickly as the best beasts are soon snapped up. The traveller is further told that when he goes down from Jerusalem to Jericho he should take bread, wine, water, 'hard eggs' and cheese sufficient for two days, 'for

Fig. 5 Title page of the second edition of *Information for Pilgrims unto the Holy Land*, Wynkyn de Worde, 1515

by all that way there is none to sell'. There is then included a brief account of the journey from Venice onwards. From Jaffa distances are given in miles, the holy places are named one by one and those carrying indulgences are indicated. The last few pages are taken up with short vocabularies in Greek and Turkish, with a list of stations at Rome and a final note on the symbolism of the several parts of a church. This was of course in the vernacular, as was also the *Pilgerbüch* from which von Harff copied several pages – this had been printed in Rome by Stephan Planck in 1489.[133] Similar guides have survived and include another to Palestine (c. 1350) which opens its tour at Nazareth because 'it is fitting we should

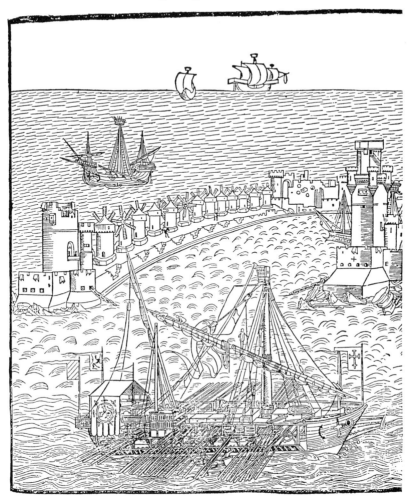

Fig. 6 Pilgrims' galley off Rhodes (from the Latin edition of von Breydenbach)

commence our pilgrimage where were the beginnings of our redemption'.[134]

Many guides are to be differentiated by their destination, the principal one being the Holy Land, then Rome, which could have its own exclusive guide or be included in one to Palestine, and finally Compostela.

Of those devoted to Rome itself the most outstanding were the ones entitled *Mirabilia*. Dating from the mid-twelfth century, they had at first no general title but by the thirteenth some were known as *Graphia Aureae Urbis Romae* and then in the fourteenth and fifteenth centuries simply as *Mirabilia Urbis Romae*. The *Mirabilia* could cover pagan Rome with accounts of such antiquities as the Colosseum and the Pantheon, but when qualified by the words *Romanarum Ecclesiarum* then churches and relics were their subject – such a work was published in 1375.[135] This was widely popular and Martin Luther was but one who made use of it some years before the development of his ideas led to his wholesale repudiation of pilgrimages.[136] The majority of editions were in Latin, but there were also several in German, at least four in French, three in Italian and one in Spanish.[137]

These and similar works have never ceased to have a considerable appeal, witness the one written by G. Franzini in Venice in 1565. This was entitled *Le cosè maravigliose de l'alma città di Roma* and as late as the eighteenth century it was appearing not only in its original version but in Latin, French and Spanish translations.[138] The numerous editions of the itinerary of Burchard of Mount Sion provide another example of the demand: first issued in 1475 at Lübeck, it was published at Lyons in 1486, in Paris two years later and was several times reprinted in the course of the sixteenth century. Other guides were published in Milan by Baptiste da Sessia in 1491 and at Angers by Jean de la Tour two years later.

Besides the Holy Land and Rome, Compostela was of sufficient importance to have its own guide book, produced back in the twelfth century. This is the fifth part of the *Liber Sancti Jacobi* or the *Codex Calixtinus*, the latter name deriving from an apocryphal letter of pope Calixtus II which stands as its preface. Its author, writing c. 1145, was a Frenchman full of devotion for St James and eager to share his enthusiasm with fellow believers and, at the same time, to provide them with help on the basis of his own experiences.[139] The simplest way to convey an idea of what this work is about is to reproduce its table of contents.

I.   The Road to Santiago
II.   The Days' Journeys on the Road of the Apostle
III.   The Names of the Towns on his Road
IV.   The Three Good [Religious] Houses of this World
V.   The Names of the Overseers of St James' Road
VI.   Bitter and Fresh Waters on his Road
VII.   The Characteristics of the Countries and People on his Road

VIII. The Bodies of the Saints to be visited on the Way and the Passion of St Eutropius

IX. The Characteristics of the City and Church of Santiago (Fig. 7)

X. How the Offerings at the Altar of St James are disposed of

XI. How the Pilgrims of St James should be properly received

Since the guide was written prior to the development of the practice of indulgences, they have no place within it, but otherwise it is a very complete *vade mecum*.

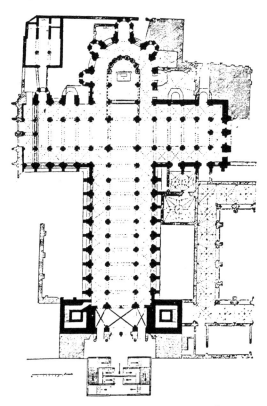

Fig. 7 Plan of a pilgrimage church, Santiago de Compostela

(g) Travel accounts

Not every description of Palestine or Egypt was the end product of a pilgrimage. The very lengthy record of Sir Gilbert de Lannoy based on his tour in 1422 was in fact a report of the situation drawn up at the request of Henry V who was contemplating a crusade and wanted exact information about cities, ports and rivers – there is not a word about holy places.[140]

In the narratives of pilgrims, on the other hand, it is naturally these that occupy the centre of interest. Those indeed who completed their journeys and returned safely to their own countries, especially if they were of a literary turn of mind, often committed their experiences to writing. The number of such authors was considerable and it has been calculated that from 1100 to 1500 some 526 produced narratives of this kind.[141] They strove to make their accounts as accurate as possible: Niccolò of Poggibonsi, for example, who visited the Holy Land in 1346–50, states that he had with him two measuring rods and that all he saw and touched he noted on 'two small tables'.[142]

Some wrote of the places they visited for the sake of those unable to make a similar journey. Abbot Daniel, who travelled from Russia to Jerusalem in 1106–7, says that his account is 'for the faithful, so that, in hearing the description of the holy places, they might be mentally transported to them, from the depths of their soul, and thus obtain from God the same rewards as those who have visited them'.[143] Theoderich (c. 1172) had the same motive, saying that he hoped that by reading his words he who could not go to Palestine

> may learn always to bear Christ in remembrance, and by remembering him may learn to love him, by loving may pity him who suffered near these places; through pity may acquire a longing for him, by longing may be absolved from his sins; by absolution from sin may obtain his grace, and by his grace may be made a partaker of the kingdom of heaven, being thought worthy of him who with the Father and the Holy Spirit lives and reigns for ever and ever.[144]

In similar vein Burchard of Mount Sion, who lived for several years in Palestine (1280), states that he is writing to help others picture the holy places in their minds when they cannot behold them with their eyes.[145]

Others published their journals as alternatives to guide books, so the nun who told of St Willibald's passage to the Holy Land (c. 754) had no hesitation in calling it a *Hodoiporicon* i.e. a book for a journey.[146] Sir John Maundeville (1322) noted in his prologue that he had composed his book 'especially for them that will and are in purpose to visit the holy city of Jerusalem, and the holy places that are thereabout'.[147] Von Harff actually included the names of those whom he hoped would find his work useful: he has penned it (he says) so that if Duke William of Jülich and his wife take the road to Jerusalem they would have in his pages 'a trusty sign-post'.[148]

To make their works as comprehensive as possible, the writers often copied passages from existing guides. As previously noted, von Harff reproduced sections of a *Pilgerbüch* while the *Information for Pilgrims unto the Holy Land* made use of William Wey's *Itineraries*. Similarly Richard Torkington, rector of Mulberton in Norfolk, who set sail from Rye on 20 March 1517, not only repeated pages from the *Information* but also took verbatim the descriptions of Venice, of the voyage to Jaffa and of the sites in the Holy Land from *The Pylgrymage of Sir Richard Guylforde to the Holy Land, AD 1506*, written by Sir Richard's chaplain.[149] Consequently these accounts have a certain uniformity and on occasion identity. This is only to be expected because, quite apart from plagiarism, they were describing the same places, usually in the same order and they were supplying useful information about the very same matters that were of interest to all travellers.

Much of what every pilgrim needed to know was summarized by Niccolò of Poggibonsi in his preface to *A Voyage beyond the Seas* (1346–50).[150] I am going to provide you, he writes, with 'all the indulgences in order, and the distances, and the dimensions of the holy places, and also what things are within them and how they are arranged'. The close link between pilgrimages and indulgences, it will be recalled, was promoted by Boniface in the early fourteenth century and the first table to have survived is that in the *Peregrinationes et Indulgentie Terre Sancte* of Giacomo de Verona, 1335.[151]* From then on they feature regularly; William Wey, for example, devoted six pages to Palestinian indulgences and as many as eleven to those in Rome. Felix Fabri was very meticulous in recording every indulgence that he earned. He marked with a single cross those that secured seven years but used double crosses for plenary indulgences. Since these are travel accounts and not just guide books, it is possible to calculate how many the writers were able to mark up – without going into the complexities of the arithmetic, Felix would appear to have gained something in the region of 2863 years. Associated with these were also relics, which Niccolò calls 'what things are within'. So Sigoli (1384) appended a list both of them and indulgences, using however a single cross for

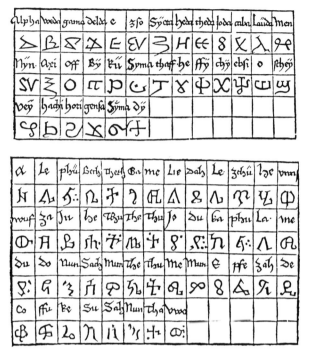

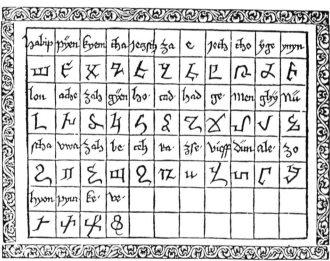

Fig. 8 Alphabets: Coptic and Ethiopic (from the Latin edition of von Breydenbach); Armenian (from Spanish edition of Zaragoza, 1498)

plenary indulgences but employing no special sign for the seven year category.[152]

It was also important to be aware in advance of distances and times; Ludolph von Suchem indicates that travelling by sea to and from the Holy Land is faster from west to east and takes about fifty days at a speed of fifteen mph, while on the way back food is needed for twice that time, i.e. one hundred days.[153] Language difficulties were only to be expected and Wey thoughtfully supplied a Greek vocabulary and the Hebrew alphabet; von Harff even had a word list in Slavonic and Albanian and in various editions of von Breydenbach's narrative Armenian, Coptic, Ethiopic and Syriac were introduced (Fig. 8). So necessary was knowledge of this kind that c. 1483 Caxton printed a phrase book which was a translation of a Flemish-French work compiled in Belgium in the first half of the fourteenth century.

Expenses were clearly a matter to take into account not only in the preliminary planning but also throughout the journey. An anonymous French pilgrim of 1383 therefore noted carefully all the charges imposed by Islamic officials in Palestine;[154] Wey gave the rates of exchange between England and Venice[155] but was also happy to offer advice about all stages of the route. So he suggested that upon arrival in Venice the pilgrim should buy a feather bed, which was to be obtained near St Mark's, together with a mattress, two pillows, two pairs of sheets and a quilt and he recorded that that would cost four ducats.[156] Giorgio Gucci, who was one of a party of Florentines in 1384, went into details about how he and his companions arranged their finances. As far as Alexandria each pilgrim was responsible for paying his own expenses and Gucci noted every item: tolls, guides, hiring of ships, asses, mules and camels, as well as food, utensils and candles to be offered at the several shrines. At Alexandria, however, – they were going to Cairo and then on to Mount Sinai and so to Jerusalem from the south – they made a common purse and this served them until they reached Damascus when once more each had his separate account.[157]

Some of the records of these pilgrims are so terse that they do not rivet the attention; they are informative but nothing more. Others are every bit as lively, attractive and readable as the great travel books produced in the nineteenth century by explorers in Africa and the Middle East. *The Wanderings of Felix Fabri*, for example, constitutes a minor masterpiece, packed with details, the descriptions seasoned with his own comments, often naïve but always frank and illuminating. His energy was such that he must sometimes have been a trying fellow pilgrim; when others were dropping with fatigue, he was still looking into corners that the majority did not bother about and eagerly pressing on to visit areas which few others penetrated. It is a revealing document, amusing and often touching.

These travellers not only put on record what they did and what they saw and what they thought about the places visited, they also sought out other wayfarers to increase their stock of knowledge. Eastern Christians were accustomed to journey to Cologne to venerate the sepulchre of the three Magi and they would diligently enquire of German pilgrims in Jerusalem 'through an interpreter, about the position of the county of Cologne, the size of the city, the cathedral church and the sepulchre of the three kings, and they devoutly write down what they hear in answer word for word in their note-books' – so observed Felix Fabri.[158]

Preparation for Pilgrimage

With some knowledge and understanding of the variety of motives that prompted folk to go on a pilgrimage and of the literature that was generated by it, it is time to pursue the journey, prefacing it with a brief account of the preparations required before setting out. It was regarded as essential to start with as clean a sheet as possible and the Cavalier Santo Brasca has conveniently summarized all that was expected. While his description of his visit to the Holy Land was published towards the end of the Middle Ages (1481), it is equally applicable to any period.

> The pilgrim should prepare himself to pardon the injuries done to him; to restore everything belonging to others; and live according to the law, because without this first and necessary disposition every hope and every fatigue is in vain.[159]

Margery Kempe, setting out in the early 1400s, enlisted the aid of her local parson to ensure the clearing of her debts:

> When the time came that this creature should visit those holy places where our Lord was quick and dead, as she had by revelation years before, she prayed the parish priest of the town where she was dwelling, to say for her in the pulpit, that, if any man or woman claimed any debt from her husband or herself, they should come and speak with her ere she went, and she, with the help of God would make a settlement with each of them, so that they should hold themselves content. And so she did.[160]

Of course Margery, like everyone else who was married, had to obtain the consent of her spouse and wills also had to be duly executed.[161] Nor could any depart before being reconciled with those with whom they were at odds and making amends to any they had injured.[162] These preliminaries reached their climax, after all had made their confessions, with a church service during which they were presented with the tokens of their new profession.

According to Felix Fabri, there are five outward badges of a pilgrim:

> a red cross on a long gray gown, with the monk's cowl sewn to the tunic unless the pilgrim belongs to some order that does not allow the wearing of a gray gown. The second is a black or gray hat, also marked in front with a red cross. The third is a long beard growing from a face that is serious and pale on account of his labours and dangers, for in every land even heathens themselves when travelling let their beards and hair grow long until they return home . . . The fourth is the scrip upon his shoulders containing his slender provisions, with a bottle sufficient not for luxury but barely for the necessaries of life. The fifth, which he assumes only in the Holy Land, is an ass with a Saracen instead of his staff.[163]

Some of these 'badges' could only be obtained en route but the staff and scrip were utilitarian objects essential from the beginning, although their constant employment by all and their associations soon made them symbolic of the pilgrim role (Fig. 9). The staff or bourdon is to help one along, like a walking stick, but can also be a defensive weapon. It recalls Jesus commissioning the apostles who are to take a staff each on his journey (Mark 6.8); this in turn harks back to the Exodus when each Israelite was bidden to be ready with a staff in his hand (Ex. 12.10); it was also linked with Aaron's rod (Num. 17.1–7), while the divine help in adversity is recalled by the Psalmist with the words 'your rod and your staff, they comfort me' (23.4). The scrip or wallet had less symbolic significance but it too recalled the bag in which David had his smooth stones with which, sling in hand, he went to confront Goliath the Philistine (I Sam. 17.40), and the time had now come when Jesus' command to take a wallet was to be obeyed (Luke 22.36).

Pilgrims cherished their scrips and staffs as tokens of their endeavour and many had them buried with them when at death the time came to enter on another stage of their journey. The body of the pilgrim found under the crossing of Worcester cathedral in January 1987 has an ash staff by his right side (Pl. II), but there is no trace of his wallet. His head is missing, having been removed when a trench was

Fig. 9 A pilgrim with scrip, staff and tokens (on a tomb stone in Llandyfodwg church, Glamorgan)

dug sometime in the eighteenth or nineteenth century. His arms, crossed over his chest, are clearly visible as is the remainder of the corpse in a woven garment, complete with the hard worn leather boots on which he had travelled many a mile.

The service for the blessing of pilgrims formed an introduction to the pilgrim mass. Those who were to be commissioned went to their parish church where they prostrated themselves in front of the altar while psalms were said over them; these were chosen from the 'Psalms of Ascent' (120–34) sung by the Hebrews as they went up to the Temple in Jerusalem. The posture was particularly significant for it was that adopted at the profession of a monk or a nun and implied entrance upon a state of life requiring a higher standard of obedience than hitherto. Moreover in many service books the blessing of pilgrims terminates with prayers for those who have come home safely and these are identical with the ones for religious who have returned to their monastery after a period of absence.[164]

After prayers for their safety, the would-be pilgrims stood for the blessing of the scrip and the staff: the former was sprinkled with holy water and placed around the neck of each one with an accompanying

Plate II Mediaeval Pilgrim found buried in Worcester Cathedral

prayer that he or she might be found worthy to reach the destination and travel back in safety; the staff was next presented with a similar formula.

One of the earliest examples of this blessing is to be found in a late eleventh-century pontifical in the British Museum.[165] It has a simple structure, viz. two prayers at the beginning, the formal bestowing of the insignia and a few prayers at the end. The twelfth-century Ely pontifical is much more elaborate and opens with three psalms, a *Kyrie* and a *Pater noster*, versicles and responses and three formulae for the presentation of the scrip and the staff, each followed by a concluding prayer.[166] Some of the meaning of these actions is indicated in the texts by references to Abraham setting out for the Promised Land (Gen. 12.13) and to Raphael who was considered to be the guardian angel of travellers because he had guided Tobias as recounted in the apocryphal book of Tobit. Indeed a special mass of Raphael was produced towards the end of the Middle Ages as well as one of the Three Magi who had in their turn been pilgrims to the stable at Bethlehem.[167]

In the case of those going to Jerusalem, there was an extra ceremony in that a cross was blessed and a special garment marked with one was presented. In the Sarum Missal this is accompanied by the words:

Receive this vestment, marked with the cross of our Lord and Saviour, that through it there may accompany you safety, blessing and strength for a prosperous journey to the sepulchre of him who with God the Father etc.[168]

This same missal follows this prayer with a rubric that 'the branding of a cross upon the flesh of pilgrims going to Jerusalem has been forbidden by canon law under pain of the greater excommunication'. The implication of this is that at one time this practice was common, as indeed it continued to be at the other end of the journey when in Jerusalem crosses were tattooed on the forearms of pilgrims.[169]

In the ensuing mass for travellers the Gospel is Matt. 10.7–15, i.e. the charge of Jesus to the Twelve with its reference to bag and staff. The concluding rubric reads: 'Then shall the pilgrims be communicated, and so depart in the name of the Lord,' fearful perhaps of the dangers ahead but comforted by the possession of episcopal letters of safe conduct.[170]*

The Journey

To depart overseas, as distinct from going to a local shrine like Chaucer's Canterbury pilgrims, could involve so much physical effort and real dangers that it was not to be undertaken lightly. Felix Fabri was speaking out of bitter experience when he stated:

> May God give those who call this pilgrimage an easy exercise the power of feeling its sorrows, that they may learn to have the compassion for pilgrims to the Holy Land which they deserve. It requires courage and audacity to attempt this pilgrimage. That many are prompted to it by sinful and idle curiosity cannot be doubted; but to reach the holy places and to return to one's home active and well is the especial gift of God.[171]

That pilgrims had many fears is apparent from a long prayer transcribed by Giacomo de Verona for daily use. It expresses confidence in Christ as the source of regular succour because at the hearing of his name

> the serpent is brought to a halt, the dragon flies, the viper is still, the restless toad grows stiff, the scorpion is extinguished, the snake is overcome, the scaly creature effects nothing that is noxious and venomous animals, hitherto powerful, and everything that is hurtful are rendered mild.[172]

But over and above these 'injurious adversaries' there was much to be feared from the forces of nature and the character of the terrain to be traversed. To go to Rome from northern Europe meant crossing the Alps and that that was a feat of considerable endurance, especially in winter, may be illustrated from a letter of Brother John of Canterbury writing from the Great St Bernard in February 1188:

> Forgive my not writing. I have been on the Mons Jovis: on the one hand looking up to the heavens of the mountains, on the other shuddering at the hell of the valleys; feeling myself so much nearer to heaven that I was the more assured that my prayer would be heard. 'Lord', I said, 'restore me to my brethren, that I may tell them not to come to this place of torment.' Place of torment it is indeed, where the marble pavement of the rocky ground is ice, and you cannot safely set a foot down; where, strange to say, though it is so slippery that you cannot stand, the death into which you are given every facility to fall, is certain death. I put my hand in my scrip to scratch out a word or two to your sincerity, behold I found my ink bottle filled with a dry mass of ice. My fingers refused to write; my beard was stiff with frost, and my breath congealed in a long icicle. I could not write.[173]

Sea voyages had their own hazards, of which shipwreck was the chief, but those setting out from Britain could not avoid one, whether it was a short trip across the Channel or the five days it took to reach Corunna (for Compostela) from Plymouth.[174] Ports of departure for Alexandria or Jaffa were Marseilles, Bari and Venice. In the case of Venice the sailing times were regulated by maritime law in an attempt to reduce the risks. It was laid down that on the return winter voyage from the Holy Land departure must not be postponed beyond 8 October.[175] Indeed the terrible experiences at sea of Sir Richard Guylforde's chaplain were due to a failure to observe this requirement: the galley should have left Venice immediately before Corpus Christi, 1506, but was delayed for six weeks and so the completion of the pilgrimage was correspondingly postponed.[176]

The foundering of ships with the loss of passengers and crew was not infrequent. On Sunday 12 October 1102 Saewulf arrived off Jaffa; he immediately disembarked, which was fortunate for him because a great storm arose during the night, only seven out of thirty ships survived and more than a thousand people were drowned.[177] A similar disaster is recorded in 1346 by Niccolò of Poggibonsi who tells how, shortly after quitting Venice, a tempest broke and nine ships sank in the Adriatic that night.[178]

There was, however, another threat at sea other than that of inclement weather and that was being boarded by pirates. In 1408, the *Quirina*, homeward bound for Venice, was set upon in the Gulf of Satalia, south of Asia Minor, and many were wounded and killed,[179] while towards the end of the same century in 1497 the *Zorza*, despite damage and deaths, succeeded in repelling a Turkish squadron of nine sail off Modone.[180] One can understand why Felix Fabri thought it necessary to include in his account a description of how to bury persons at sea.[181] Even if death did not ensue, a sea voyage could be an agonizing experience, and a manuscript in the library of Trinity College, Cambridge, from the reign of Henry VI, contains a poem describing the suffering: how they lie with bowls at their sides, have no lust to eat, though some, refusing roast, nibble at 'salted toast', and others cry for hot Malmsey.[182]

On land the circumstances were scarcely less threatening, as may be illustrated from many an account. In the autumn of 1064 a mass pilgrimage, variously estimated to consist of between seven and twelve thousand people, set out from west and southern Germany under the leadership of Archbishop Siegfried of Mainz and Bishop Gunther of Bamberg. They proceeded via Hungary and Bulgaria to Constantinople and thence through Asia Minor into Syria, reaching Caesarea on Maundy Thursday 24 March 1065. The following day they were attacked by a vast horde of Arabs eager for booty. Many of the pilgrims were unarmed and many refused to defend themselves as contrary to the pilgrimage ideal. Those who did resist, using stones and weapons seized from their enemies, were in fact anticipating a new concept, viz. that of the warrior pilgrim that would reach fruition in the crusading era soon to begin. Hearing of what was taking place, the local Saracen governor, fearful of losing a lucrative source of revenue through the collection of tolls, came to their rescue and the survivors were able to continue their journey, reaching Jerusalem on 12 April. Of those who originally set out, it was reported that only two thousand returned to their homes.[183]

Many pilgrims died of sickness or of sheer exhaustion; this was the fate of eleven out of twenty French pilgrims, the survivors of whom met Frescobaldi and his fellow Florentines on their way through the desert from Cairo to Mount Sinai in 1384.[184] One final example: in 1459 the monks of Mont-Saint-Michel petitioned Pius II to be allowed to bury in consecrated ground the many whose corpses lay along the roadside; such permission was necessary because these interments could not take place without certificates from the parish priests of the victims. Pius granted the request.[185] In Jerusalem itself, where many pilgrims died before they could leave on their return journey, a special cemetery was provided for them on the lower slopes of Mount Sion close to the Franciscan monastery.

Those who remained at home were not unmindful of the perils to which their relatives and friends were subject and so petitions on their behalf were a normal feature of the 'Bidding of the Bedes', i.e. of the vernacular intercessions before the sermon in the mediaeval mass. In a form printed by Wynkyn de Worde in 1532 we read:

> Also ye shall pray for all true pilgrims and palmers, that have taken their way to Rome, to Jerusalem, to St Catherine's, or to St James, or to any other place, that God of his grace give them time and space well for to go and to come, to the profit of their lives and souls.[186]

Yet another risk was that of losing one's valuables by theft, and Frescobaldi tells how he and his companions opened a cavity in the bottom of a small chest with a bodkin and hid therein 600 ducats.[187] John Maundeville also provides the information that a verse from Luke was employed as a kind of anti-thieving spell;[188] it was the custom to repeat frequently the words: 'But passing through the midst of them he went away' (Luke 4.30) and then Ex. 15.16 was said three times:

> Terror and dread fall upon them;
>   because of the greatness of your arm,
>   they are as still as stone,
>   till your people, O Lord, pass by,
>   till the people pass by whom you have
>   purchased.

Since there is some safety in numbers, as time passed there were few individual pilgrims, usually they went in groups for mutual assistance and spiritual comfort. Each company devised its own rallying cry: those on the way to Compostela were accustomed to shout *Deus adjuva* (God help) or *Sancte Jacobe* (St James).[189]

Even when relatively free from trouble, the journey was exceedingly strenuous. Overland the well-to-do went on horseback; others might only afford mules; some walked, though barefoot was unusual except as an extra act of penance at the final stage of the journey within sight of the end. Camels could be hired and were *de rigueur* in the desert, though this required protracted negotiations and it was wise to secure a signed contract before starting. Von Harff provides an example, so charming that it is worth reproducing, but he adds that such a certificate would be insufficient without 'secret presents'.

> I, N. Mokarij, will carry N., this Frank [so they call us who come from our countries] from here in Cairo to the monastery lying below Mount Sinai on a good camel, on which he shall sit on one side in a wooden box covered with a thick pelt and carrying on the other side his provisions and the camel's food. I shall also carry for him two udders, namely goat-skins, full of water for him, myself and the camel. In addition I will assist him to get on and off the camel, and will stay by him by day and night and attend to his welfare. This Frank, N., is to give me two seraphim, namely two ducats, one at Cairo and the other when we reach the monastery below Mount Sinai.[190]

Whatever the mode of travel, each day had its complement of invocations, prayers and other devotions, including pious jingles that fitted their steps and served as a kind of marching song.

E ultreia	et outre	Onwards
E sus eia	et sus	Take courage
Deus aia nos!	Die nous aide!	God help us![191]

Psalms were frequently chanted and the ones entitled 'Songs of Ascents' were particularly suitable in seeking protection against dangers and in fostering hope and confidence. 'In my distress I cry to the Lord' (120); 'I will lift up my eyes to the hills. From whence does my help come?' (121); 'Blessed is every one who fears the Lord, who walks in his ways'! (128). Roberto de Sanseverino (1458) also found the seven penitential psalms[192] of great help and litanies too proved to be an appropriate corporate form.[193] More individualistic was the use of rosaries which by the late fifteenth century had become such a familiar attribute of pilgrims that they were often depicted carrying them.[194] Specially composed prayers were also available, such as this one preserved in the *Rituale* of the abbey of Sant Cugat del Valles:

> O God, who required Abraham to leave his country and preserved him safe and sound throughout his travels, grant to your children the same protection; uphold us in perils and lighten our journey; be unto us a shade against the sun, a covering against the rain and the cold; support us in our weariness and defend us against every danger; be unto us a staff to prevent falling and a port to welcome the shipwrecked: so that, guided by you, we may attain our goal with certitude and may return home safe and sound. Amen.[195]

Many pilgrims intensified the penitential aspect of their journey by fasting, some wore hair shirts, others travelled more or less naked but with chains on their arms and legs.[196] Some observed a self-imposed silence and passed their time in meditation, and others again deliberately travelled alone to deny themselves companionship.[197] Priests, of course, were expected to say mass regularly, while the laity were encouraged to attend, to hear sermons and to pay their respects at the many shrines and memorial buildings that came to mark the pilgrimage routes, whether to Compostela, Rome or the Holy Land. Hence Fabri reported that 'it is the custom of all pilgrims that whensoever they pass by any holy place, even when they have no set purpose of visiting those holy places, they kiss the place and go their way'.[198] As for those going to Jerusalem, this, he says, 'is what is done by all respectable pilgrims, namely, that at whatever towns they stop on the way, they straightway make enquiries about the churches and the relics of the saints, and visit them'.[199] This, for example, is what von Harff did on his way back from Palestine when passing through Vienne: he went to the church of St Anthony where the saint's body was kept above the high altar in a silver gilt shrine and had 'red wine to drink which has run through the holy body of St Anthony'.[200]

The pilgrims' guide to Compostela gives very full and typical advice about appropriate devotions on the way and where they are to be offered. At Saint-Gilles they are recommended to kiss the saint's altar and then his tomb, and listen to readings from his *Libellus*, which included, in addition to an account of his life and miracles, an office and sermon together with texts for his feast day.[201] The saint should then be invoked in the certain faith that 'on the very day that you pray to him with all your heart, your request will be granted without any doubt'.[202] Taking communion is also prescribed, although this did not apply to those on a penitential pilgrimage: they had to complete their journey before receiving absolution.[203] They were also encouraged to join in the devotions of the monks who guarded the wayside shrines, as at Angeby where the head of John the Baptist was to be seen: there 'it is venerated night and day by a choir of a hundred monks'.[204] The guide in fact lists thirty-two martyrs and confessors by name, indicates where their relics are preserved, and adds three other items of special merit: a fragment of the true cross, the knife used at the Last Supper and the Baptist's head already mentioned.

As for sermons, Torkington's account may be taken as typical, although the preacher does seem to have been somewhat advanced in his audio-visual presentation.

At Chambéry there I heard a famous sermon of a doctor which began at 5 of the clock in the morning and continued till it was 9 of the clock. In his sermon at one time he had a chalice in his hand, another time a scourge, the third time a crown of thorns, the fourth time he showed the people a picture painted on a cloth of the passion of Our Lord. And after that he showed them the image of God crucified upon a cross, and then all the people both young and old, they fell down upon their knees and cried with lamentable voice. Amen; the preacher, the people, they wept, marvel it was to see.[205]

The pilgrims originally left home with a blessing and they sought further blessings as they went along, particularly at those places which were in a sense new points of departure. In Rome, for example, a papal blessing was the norm, especially as the pontiff's permission to go on to the Holy Land was required. This was based on the idea that he alone, having declared Palestine excommunicate when it fell under the control of the Sultan, could allow church members to swell the coffers of the anti-Christ; however, those who failed to obtain a license could receive absolution from the guardians of Mount Sion.[206]

It was at Milan that Pietro Casola asked for a benediction. He attended the service in the cathedral on 14 May 1494 and, as it reached its end, he went up to the high altar where the archbishop was about to pronounce the blessing and asked him 'to bless the emblems of my pilgrimage that is, the cross, the stick or pilgrim's staff, and the wallet and to bestow his blessing on me, according to the order and the ancient institution to be found written in the pastoral': this the archbishop did and kissed him and sent him onwards with the peace of God.[207]

Venice (Fig. 10) was another important staging post, since there one took ship for the eastern Mediterranean, and special services were arranged in St Mark's. Torkington reports how on Corpus Christi Day, 1517, they were invited to sit on the left side of the choir. A procession then entered consisting of the Venetian nobles and the wayfarers were assigned one to each grandee, taking a place at his right hand. They next received candles and went in procession to the Ducal Palace, going no further on that occasion because it began to rain.[208]

Once on board a regular round of services was arranged. According to Fabri there was formal worship three times a day. The first service was at sunrise when a sailor blew a whistle and erected a board having on it a painting of the Virgin and Child. Everyone knelt and said the

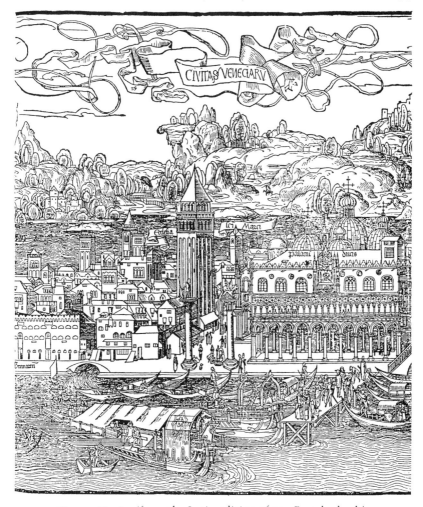

Fig. 10 Venice (from the Latin edition of von Breydenbach)

Ave Maria with other prayers. 'About the eighth hour before midday,' the whistle was blown again and all gathered on the upper deck near the mast where a chest had been placed and covered with a cloth; it had on it two candelabra, a crucifix and a missal and then a dry mass was celebrated. At sunset, again around the main mast, all knelt and sang together *Salve Regina*. This was originally an eleventh-century anthem much used by Italian fishermen, especially in stormy weather; it was eventually incorporated into hymns of which there are several different versions. This song was preceded by some litanies, by the exposition once more of the picture of the Virgin and Child and by the repetition of three *Ave Marias*. The pilgrims then retired to their cabins for the night.[209]

On occasion a priest would deliver a sermon and Pietro Casola reports one on the eve of John the Baptist's Day (23 June 1494). The galley had become completely becalmed and so one of the clerics invited everyone to come on deck.

> He took his text from the Gospel for St John's Day, i.e. 'What manner of child should this be' (Luke 1.66), and divided his address into nine meditations to be made on the saint. As all, however, were not suitable on the day before his nativity, he said a great deal suitable for the vigil, that is, of the prophecies of the said saint made by the prophets and of the annunciation of him made by the angel, and in what place.[210]

On the day following, Casola notes, 'several dry masses were said, as is the custom at sea,' i.e. masses without the canon and communion. Fabri, according to his own admission, had previously abhorred the very thought of these, but his experience of life before the mast soon altered his view. His ready pen transcribed at length fifteen reasons for justifying them, including such common sense observations as that on a heaving deck the bread and wine could soon be scattered to the four winds, while a heaving priest could find his act of communion coinciding with a violent fit of vomiting.[211] Hymn singing was however frequent and Fabri mentions one favourite of the German speaking pilgrims, viz. *In Gottes Namen fahren wir*:

> In God's name we are sailing,
> His grace we need:
> May his power shield us
> And his holy sepulchre protect us.
> *Kyrie eleison.*[212]

The crew added its contribution and he notes that in fair weather the steersman and the one watching the compass continually chant antiphonally in praise of God, the Virgin and the saints.[213]

The devotional climax of any journey is undoubtedly reached when the destination hoves in view, whether that is Compostela or Rome or the coast of Palestine. Fabri recorded his 'earnest longing for the joyful sight', comparing himself with Moses on Mount Pisgah surveying the Promised Land (Deut. 3.27). Indeed so eager was Fabri not to miss it when it appeared over the horizon that the day and night beforehand he could scarcely eat or sleep.

Ach mein Gott, he declares, how sweet the love of a heavenly country can be to the devout and contemplative, when undevout, wretched, sinful, and wandering pilgrims feel so pleasant, so deep and so keen a longing for an earthly one.

Very fittingly they responded, as soon as they could descry the outlines of the coast, by singing the *Te Deum,* weeping for joy and offering prayers.[214] This would appear to have been the normal reaction for both Guylforde[215] and Roberto de Sanseverino[216] can be cited as two among many who made the identical devotional gesture as their journey neared completion.

The Mini-Pilgrimage or Devotions at the Holy Places

To arrive at the planned destination was not to complete a pilgrimage and most reached their climax in what may be best termed a mini-pilgrimage. After entering Rome, for example, there was still the round to be made of the many churches housing relics. To land at Alexandria was first to go to the place where St Mark was believed to have been beheaded; then on to Cairo where the Pyramids were mistakenly identified with the storehouses of Joseph (Gen. 41.56). The stopping places of the Holy Family, fleeing before Herod, were then to be visited before leaving for Sinai in the wake of Moses and the Israelites, and so eventually into Palestine. At Joppa (or Jaffa, now a suburb of modern Tel Aviv), if that was one's port of entry, the entire Holy Land had still to be traversed to see the sites made sacred by mention in the Old and New Testaments. While Jerusalem itself had its own pilgrimage circuit, or rather circuits, with, for example, a day set apart for the sites on the Mount of Olives, another to go to Bethlehem and a protracted series of services and processions in the Church of the Holy Sepulchre.

If the climax was delayed, the arrival itself was an occasion for joy. In fact this experience was such a feature that the place, usually a hill, from which the first glimpse of one's goal could be obtained was called Mountjoy – there was one close to Compostela and another near to Jerusalem. Of the latter John Maundeville (1322) remarked: 'two miles from Jerusalem is Mount Joy . . . and it is called Mount Joy because it gives joy to pilgrims' hearts, for from that place men first see Jerusalem.'[217]

Having reached their destinations, the habitual way for pilgrims to express both their delight and their gratitude was to salute the ground with a kiss. Kissing in fact was but one of many physical ways of manifesting devotion. Consequently before describing the practices at the holy places it is important to be aware of the extent to which Christians of this period did not accept a rigid division between the material and the spiritual. Touch and sight, as well as hearing and speech, were all equally valid ways of relating to God and worshipping him. Just as from the earliest days of the church the sign of the cross was both a profession of faith and a prayer and yet at the same time was entirely non-verbal, so devotions at any shrine could take many forms, and pilgrims record a variety of postures, gestures, movements and prayers which are so many equivalent or complementary expressions of piety.

Kissing is one of the most sensitive modes of touching. It was the favoured method for venerating the cross when it was exposed near Golgotha; Egeria is the first to describe this simple ceremony and the Piacenza pilgrim also records it.[218] According to Arculf, whose pilgrimage to Jerusalem some time between 679 and 688 provided the substance of Adomnan's book *On the Holy Places*, the same salutation was given to the lance that was believed to have pierced the side of Jesus hanging on the cross.[219] When the relic was not so accessible, as was the case with the cup of the Last Supper kept in a reliquary with an opening in its door, touching with the outstretched hand, and no kiss, had to suffice.[220] Adomnan was also told that within the cup was the sponge offered to Jesus on the cross[221] but, a hundred years before, the Piacenza pilgrim had actually imbibed water from it – or so he said.[222] Indeed drinking as a physical/ spiritual exercise was common: Arculf had a draught from Jacob's well,[223] while Felix Fabri drank out of the cistern from which he was told water had been taken for the Last Supper.[224] Alternatively, instead of consuming the liquid, pilgrims would wash in it. The Piacenza pilgrim dipped 'in a spring to gain a blessing' at Cana[225] and Arculf refreshed his face from a pool at Bethlehem.

The supreme instance of such ceremonial cleansing took place where Jesus had been baptized in the Jordan by John. A visit there was deemed essential for all Holy Land pilgrims. They sang a hymn, removed their clothes and, according to Fabri, 'in the name of God immersed ourselves in its waves.'[226] Sigurd of Norway, who reached there in the year 1109, bathed in the normal fashion and it is easy to understand how this came to be regarded almost as a second baptism because, in the words of a Nordic bard who recounted Sigurd's journey,

All sin and evil from him flings
In Jordan's wave: for all his sins
(which all must praise) he pardon wins.[227]

Despite the swirling current and the drownings that were not
infrequent, even those who could not swim took the plunge, clinging
to logs or bundles of reeds. On the far bank some made wreaths from
the willow trees[228] and all offered further prayers and chanted the *Te
Deum* before swimming back.[229]

While seeking in this way to regain innocence and to progress in
sanctity, the pilgrims would also take the initiative against evil. This
is quaintly revealed in the Piacenza pilgrim's reference to Mount
Gilboa.

> Goliath's resting place is there in the middle of the road, and there is a
> pile of wood at his head. There is also a heap of stones – such a
> mountain of them that there is no pebble left for a distance of twenty
> miles, since anyone going that way makes a gesture of contempt by
> taking three stones and throwing them at his grave.[230]

In this way, by a symbolic but effective gesture, it was believed that
evil could be kept at a distance. It was, however, the positive aspect of
holiness that impressed the travellers most and this led them to
remove their footwear whenever they were drawing near to a place
deemed especially sacred. Frescobaldi and his friends may be taken as
typical of this imitation of Moses at the Burning Bush (Ex. 3.5) – so in
sight of Jerusalem they took off their sandals 'and we proceeded with
great devotion: for the place invites to devotion'.[231] Likewise, about
two miles from Bethlehem, Gucci, a member of the same party, tells
us how they unlaced their boots and 'so barefoot as far as the said
place we went the way reciting the penitential psalms and the
litanies and the *Te Deum* and other prayers. The approach to that
place awakens in everybody's soul the greatest devotion.'[232]

Like the Magi of old, who were seen as exemplary pilgrims, they
came bearing gifts and their presentation was very much a part of the
ceremonial at each shrine. When these oblations were made in
fulfilment of a vow they were known as ex-votos or votive offerings.
All the donations can be divided into four groups: inanimate,
animate, exuvial and replicative.[233] To the first category belong alms
which were not simply for the enrichment of the shrine but to
provide the means of dispensing charity to the many needy folk who
reached there. So Arculf told Adomnan that at Jerusalem, between
the Martyrium and Golgotha, 'there stands the large wooden table on

which the alms for the poor are offered by the people'.[234] In certain sanctuaries there was a special gift ceremonial, e.g. at Compostela. At the first mass of the day, the *arqueyro* or treasure of the cathedral was carried in in a large coffer. A sacristan read out a list of the relics and the indulgences available; next a priest uttered a prayer for forgiveness and the pilgrims were bidden to come forward and place their gifts in the box.[235]

Also to be included in the inanimate category of gifts are such objects as crutches, gratefully presented by those healed of their lameness. Some shrines were literally festooned with offerings; in the Holy Sepulchre, for example, according to the Piacenza pilgrim, 'there are ornaments in vast numbers, which hang from iron rods: armlets, bracelets, necklaces, rings, tiaras, plaited girdles, belts, emperors' crowns of gold and precious stones, and the insignia of an empress'.[236] Perhaps more poignant were the chains attached to the walls both inside and out. These were presented by three different groups of pilgrims: those who had worn them on a penitential pilgrimage as symbols of their state of sin; those who had been condemned to a judicial pilgrimage and those who had been held in captivity – to this last category belong those seized by the Saracens who gave their shackles as ex-votos to St Foy at Conques in the belief that he had arranged their liberation.[237] At Corbigny, according to the *Guide to Compostela*, in the church dedicated to St Leonard of Limoges, 'thousands upon thousands of iron fetters, more barbarous than can be told, were hung around . . . iron manicles, fetters, chains, hobbles, shackles, traps, bars, yokes, helmets, scythes and divers instruments'.[238]

Animate gifts – the second category of donations – include birds and animals, such as the pig specially fattened for the poor by a farmer of Abellas who took it to the nearby shrine of St Felix at Nola, as reported by Paulinus in one of his poems.[239]

Exuvial offerings comprise such remnants of past illnesses as diseased bones and stones ejected from the urinary system. However the largest group consists of the replicative, i.e. models in wax or silver of parts of the body cured, e.g. limbs, or of goods lost and found such as the two figures of bulls presented at Rocamadour by a farmer to whom they had returned after he had vowed to go on a pilgrimage. Sometimes a candle equal to the height or weight of the pilgrim was presented, to be melted down later for the provision of lights for the shrine. Offerings in precious metals were not uncommon: amongst many at Rocamadour may be noted a silver anchor promised by sailors from Boulogne when in peril on the sea; a silver falcon from the Duke of Lorraine who had nearly lost his favourite bird and a chalice from a merchant of Caen in thanksgiving for the preservation of his cargo in a shipwreck between La Rochelle and Normandy.[240]

What at first sight may appear to be a peculiar offering was that of the Piacenza pilgrim who, upon arrival at Mount Sinai, cut off his hair and his beard and threw them on the ground.[241] That he should have long hair was normal; in fact Felix Fabri counted it as the third outward badge of five by which a pilgrim can be identified – 'a long beard growing from a face that is serious and pale on account of his labours and dangers, for in every land even heathens themselves when travelling let their beards and hair grow long until they return home'.[242] The explanation of its removal by the Piacenza pilgrim and at that stage of his journey is probably to be sought in the prescriptions for a Nazirite in Numbers 6. 'All the days of his vow of separation no razor shall come upon his head; until the time is completed for which he separated himself to the Lord, he shall be holy; he shall let the locks of hair of his head grow long . . . When the time of his separation has been completed . . . the Nazirite shall shave his consecrated head at the door of the tent of meeting' (6.5, 13, 18). It was of course on Mount Sinai that the tent of meeting was first constructed by the Israelites (Ex. 35.10). The place was therefore fitting but also the time in the sense that the pilgrim, like the Nazirite, had come to the end of 'the days of his vow of separation', i.e. of his pilgrimage and so offered his hair to God.[243]*

If many of the gifts just catalogued were returns for services rendered, others were part of a transaction on the basis of *do ut des*, i.e. I am giving in order that you will give in your turn. Health was much sought after and healing was an important motive for a large number of pilgrims. One of the principal methods adopted in the belief that it would lead to a cure was incubation; this involved the sufferer sleeping in the shrine all night with the hope of awakening whole or at least being instructed in a dream about the remedy to be taken.[244] If one night was insufficient, a patient would stay for days, weeks and even months awaiting the desired result. The Piacenza pilgrim witnessed an example of this practice when he visited Gadara.

> Three miles from the city there are hot springs called the Baths of Elijah. Lepers are cleansed there, and have their meals from the inn there at public expense. The baths fill in the evening. In front of the basin is a large tank. When it is full, all the gates are closed, and they are sent in through a small door with lights and incense, and sit in the tank all night. They fall asleep, and the person who is going to be cured sees a

vision. When he has told it, the springs do not flow for a week. In one week he is cleansed.[245]

For those with infected bodily parts there were often constructed special 'limb holes' (Fig. 11). Such a device, with three openings, still survives from the thirteenth century in the church of St Wite, Whitchurch Canonicorum, Dorset, in the north transept. The invalid inserted the limb into the cavity in order to reach as close as possible to the saint's relics. If a healing did occur, then a wick of the length and breadth of the restored part was made into a candle, but if the entire body was made whole then the wick was wound into a coil or 'trindle' before being coated with wax.

To see and if possible to touch relics was every pilgrim's hope, especially as the Middle Ages advanced, but above all they wanted to gain possession of some in order to carry them home. Few seem to have restrained themselves in seeking to fulfil this desire. At the ceremony of adoring the cross in Jerusalem, in which Egeria participated, the sacred wood was guarded by two clerics to avoid a repetition of the unfortunate incident when a man actually bit off a piece and concealed it in his mouth.[246] Burchard quite unashamedly tells of working 'much with iron tools' in a vain attempt to remove some of the rock in Gethsemane,[247] and some two hundred years later the same conduct can be seen in the case of von Harff. He visited the Golden Gate, through which Jesus entered on an ass on the first Palm Sunday, and, he says, 'we broke and cut off many pieces of wood and copper which I carried back with me'.[248] Fabri collected 'holy pebbles from holy places' and he regarded them as infinitely preferable to 'new relics brought from parts beyond the seas'.[249] Indeed Fabri, like many pilgrims of the day, was by no means entirely credulous. He did believe that certain places were to be regarded as holy and he did wish to convey back home some of this holiness in the form of a genuine relic. At the same time he was not prepared to accept every tale he was told, nor every relic presented for his veneration. At Bethlehem, visiting the Milk Grotto, so-called because its walls oozed a white liquid believed to be the milk of the Virgin, he says, 'I learned by experience that it is nothing more than moisture which drops from a rock', but he hastens to add: 'far be it from me to take away by these words any of the honour, praise and reverence due to the blessed Virgin Mary'.[250] Von Harff was scandalized to be shown near Damascus a stone on which it was said St George had stood to mount his horse before setting out to kill the

Fig. 11 Pilgrims burrowing into limb holes in a thirteenth-century shrine. Measuring wicks for 'trindles' are in the foreground

dragon. If anyone with a bad back rubbed it against this object they were believed to be cured. 'What pitiful superstition is this,' he comments, 'of which we have many in our country.'[251] He was equally sceptical of those who claimed to have viewed a sunken city beneath the surface of the Dead Sea and the pillar of salt into which Lot's wife had been transformed; he himself was unable to find any trace of either and comments: 'Many say they have seen these things, for a fine lie well adorns a tale.'[252]

Contact-relics were preferable to nothing if one was thwarted in obtaining the genuine article. Von Harff at St Catherine's monastery on Sinai rubbed the limbs of the saints 'with our jewels',[253] while Casola 'touched with the rosaries and other objects of devotion' the footprints of Jesus in the Church of the Ascension.[254] At the Jordan many baptized in the name of the Trinity little bells they had bought expressly for this purpose before leaving Venice and they treasured them in the belief that they would afford protection against hail and lightning.[255] Fabri had been loaded by his friends with beads, rings, silver crosses and so on and requested to bring them into contact with every relic he saw and every holy place he visited in order 'that they may perchance derive some sanctity from the touch'.[256]

Earth was scattered daily in the Holy Sepulchre and then 'those who go in take some as a blessing',[257] and in the Church of the Ascension 'some of the grains of the holy dust' could be obtained by reaching through a hole in the railing.[258] 'Measures' were also welcome, i.e. ribbons that had been wrapped around relics such as the pillar of scourging,[259] though here again Fabri shows his critical approach to the primary relic. The pillar was dotted with red spots about which he remarks: 'This is due either to the nature of the stone, or, as Jerome and Bede appear to think, to a miracle.'[260] The earth and dust, together with wine or water that had circulated through a sarcophagus (all designated as blessings, *eulogiae*) were enclosed in small flasks frequently decorated with scenes from the gospels – such were the Monza ampullae[261] – and these were then tiny packages of holiness. Oil too from the sanctuary lamps was treasured; alternatively one could take one's own supply to the shrine and, reports the Piacenza pilgrim, 'when the mouth of the little flasks touches the wood of the cross at Golgotha, the oil immediately boils over, unless it is closed very speedily it all spills out.'[262] To make doubly sure that flasks and contact-relics were fully sanctified, some pilgrims, like Luchino del Campo in 1413, took them to a mass in the Holy Sepulchre and had them blessed.[263]

To describe what pilgrims did at the shrines is necessary in order to arrive at some understanding of their devotion because the outward acts express the inward reality, but something also has to be known about their feelings and their total response to the sacred environments. Emotional reaction was certainly very much evident; so intense could it be that when Phocas, the Cretan, came to record his pilgrimage in 1185, his recollection of entering the Cave of the Nativity was still so vivid that

> I leap for joy as I write, and am altogether in the spirit within that holy grotto. I see the cloth which covered our Lord at his birth, the laying of the new-born babe in the manger, and I am thrilled by the thought of the saviour's love for me and his extreme poverty through which he made me worthy of the kingdom of heaven. Yet I think the grotto is a palace, and that the king sat upon the Virgin's bosom as on a throne, and I see choirs of angels encircling the grotto, and the Magi bringing presents to the king. I am filled with all manner of delight, and rejoice to think what grace I have been thought worthy to receive.[264]

In many particulars this is reminiscent of another statement, written eight hundred or so years previously by Jerome, regarding one of the earliest Holy Land pilgrims, the Roman matron Paula.

> In visiting the holy places so great was the passion and the enthusiasm she exhibited for each that she could never have torn herself away from one had she not been eager to visit the rest. Before the cross she threw herself down in adoration as though she beheld the Lord hanging upon

it: and when she entered the tomb, which was the scene of the resurrection, she kissed the stone that the angel had rolled away from the door of the sepulchre. Indeed so ardent was her faith that she even licked with her mouth the very spot on which the Lord's body had lain, like one thirsty for a river he has longed for. What tears she shed there, what groans she uttered, and what grief she poured forth, all Jerusalem knows; the Lord also to whom she prayed knows well . . . After this she came to Bethlehem and entered the cave where the saviour was born . . . When she looked upon these things she protested to me that she could behold with the eyes of faith the infant Jesus wrapped in swaddling clothes and crying in the manger, the wise men worshipping him, the shepherds coming by night.[265]

Such fervour at pilgrimage centres, so Burchard suggested,[266] is increased by being with hundreds of others so that the zeal of all augments that of the individual. The beating of the breast, the weeping, the sighing and so on show the depth of the religious feeling being experienced. It is however Brother Felix Fabri who most tellingly speaks of his reaction when he entered the court of the Holy Sepulchre for the first time.

O my brother! If you had been with me in that court at that hour, you would have seen such plenteous tears, such bitter heartfelt groans, such sweet wailings, such deep sighs, such true sorrow, such sobs from the inmost breast, such peaceful and gladsome silence, that had you a heart of stone it must have melted, and you would have burst into a flood of tears together with the weeping pilgrims. I saw there some pilgrims lying powerless on the ground, forsaken by their strength, and as it were forgetful of their own being by reason of their excessive feeling of devotion. Others I saw who wandered here and there from one corner to another, beating their breasts as though they were driven by an evil spirit. Some knelt on the earth with their bare knees, and prayed with tears, holding their arms out in the form of a cross. Others were shaken with such violent sobs that they could not hold themselves up, and were forced to sit down and hold their heads with their hands, that they might endure their thick coming sobs. Some lay prostrate so long without motion, that they seemed as they were dead. Above all our companions and sisters the women pilgrims shrieked as if in labour, cried aloud and wept. Some pilgrims out of excess of devotion lost all command of themselves, forgot how they should behave, and out of excessive zeal to please God, made strange and childish gestures. It was indeed pleasant to behold the very earnest and yet different behaviour of the pilgrims as they prayed at the holy places, which places have a wonderful power of moving to tears, groans and sighs, men who in any other place could not be moved by any other speech, advice or passage of scripture, by any painting or carving, examples, promise or threats, by prosperity or adversity.[267]

The pilgrims responded not only with physical manifestations but also verbally and in particular with spontaneous prayers especially of the exclamatory kind. So Burchard, leaving Bethany and coming up over the Mount of Olives within sight of Jerusalem:

> O God, how many devout tears have been shed at this place by those who have there beheld the joy of the whole earth, the city of the great king! O what delight will it be to see the place of your glory, blessed Jesus, when we see the place of your shame and confusion with such exaltation![268]

Brother Felix combined both the physical and verbal in the Garden of Gethsemane when he recalled the agony of Jesus.

> With what gestures, what movements, what postures shall we pray? Surely with no other than those with which he who hallowed this place showed himself to his heavenly Father. It is clear to one who reads the gospels with care that in his three prayers Christ used three different postures. First, he fell upon his face, prostrating his whole body, according to Matthew. The second time he fell upon the earth, leaning upon his elbows, according to Mark. The third time he prayed more at length, resting upon his knees, according to Luke. He then, fourthly, rose to his feet, repeating that sweetest of prayers, when raising his eyes to heaven he said: Father, the hour is coming; glorify your Son . . . Wherefore using these gestures, the pilgrims prayed for a longer while in this most holy place.[269]

The Lord's Prayer was frequently on their lips and often, but especially on penitential pilgrimages, there were petitions for pardon, nor were travellers in the later Middle Ages unmindful of the number of indulgences their presence was securing for them. Meditation was yet another form of prayer that was strongly recommended and many accounts reproduce the subjects or the actual meditations that were stimulated by and were appropriate to the places being visited. Jerome reports that Paula took the old road from Bethlehem to Gaza and meditated silently on the Ethiopian eunuch (Acts 7.27–39), while on the way down to Jericho she chose to concentrate on the parable of the good Samaritan.[270] At the foot of the cross Fabri says: 'In this place we reflected upon the immeasurable sorrow of the blessed Virgin, because we knew that there she suffered all the pangs of every bodily suffering.'[271] Again, at the site of the pedilavium, he comments: 'I beg you, beloved pilgrim, not to leave this place, any more than the others, without previous meditation.'[272] He was in fact entirely convinced that meditation lies at the very heart of a pilgrimage.

> Prayers avail but little, and indulgences have small value, nay, the whole labour of pilgrimage is in vain, if a man in these holy places does not meditate upon the examples he meets and takes them to heart for the amendment of his own life.[273]

Indeed despite his zeal for pilgrimages – he himself went twice to the Holy Land – Felix emphasized that mere physical presence was insufficient for spiritual progress.

> Good and simple Christians believe that if they were at the places where the Lord Jesus wrought the work of our redemption, they would derive much devotion from them; but I say to those men that meditation about these places and listening to descriptions of them is more efficacious than the actual seeing and kissing of them. Unless a pilgrim has before his eyes some living examples of devotion, the place helps him little in the matter of true holiness.[274]

Felix therefore was all the more concerned to promote in those who were actually in Jerusalem the right spirit, and of the Holy Sepulchre he declares: 'Here, then, I pray you, let us lay aside our pious plaints of sorrow, our clouds of grief, and let us draw a quiet breath in happiness: let us who have followed our redeemer to his tomb with sorrow, now take part in the joy of his glorious resurrection.'[275] For an example of an actual meditation within the tomb we may turn to Niccolò of Poggibonsi.

> The one who has been in the tomb should thank our Lord Jesus Christ, for verily there is none so hard who can here withhold his tears, who cries not aloud, when he enters inside this most holy chapel; for this is a holy place, and it is a holy tomb, for here was placed the benign body of the blessed Jesus Christ. This is the place of remission, for whoever here will pray with devotion, all his sins are forgiven. This is a devout house, which no man can leave without weeping more bitterly when parting than when entering. Here would he remain, who thinks of where he is, without food or drink. Let each think what it is to stand where was the Son of God, living and dead; where stood his mother with so great sorrow, who saw placed in the most holy tomb her most precious Son. Blessed be he ever who well considers that in that place was shed that precious blood of Jesus Christ.[276]

Singing was not omitted from the pilgrims' devotions; they could even be greeted by it on arrival. At Compostela, according to William

Wey, it was the custom of children, in the hope of receiving alms, to dance while chanting the following refrain.

> *Sancte Jace a Compostel da vose leve a votir tere*
> St James give you welcome to Compostela from your land.
> *Sancte Jace bone baron de vose da de bon pardon,*
> St James, your good lord, give you a good remission,
> *Bona tempe, bona vye, bona vente, bon perpassi,*
> Good weather, good journey, a good wind, and a good return,
> *Do istys kee synt assen vna brank a vowse curtese,*
> Of your courtesy grant a coin to those who are here.[277]

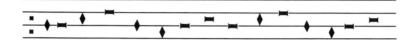

Both when approaching and at the holy places the pilgrims sang psalms and canticles as well as favourite hymns, especially those which had a direct reference to the events which the shrines had witnessed. The *Magnificat* was sung at the place where Elizabeth greeted Mary;[278] on the way to Bethlehem *Puer natus in Bethlehem, unde gaudet Jerusalem* and *Resonet in laudibus, cum jucundis plausibus,* as well as *In dulci Jubilo nu singent und sind fro,* with, 'in chorus', the angels' hymn, i.e. *Gloria in excelsis.*[279] In the Cave of the Nativity a Christmas hymn was obviously suitable[280] and Ludolph von Suchem records that all the canonical hours there and all the masses, even requiems, began with *Gloria in excelsis* which was also very fittingly repeated in the Shepherds' field.[281] At the Jordan a *Te Deum* was intoned.[282] On the way to the Sepulchre German pilgrims united in singing *In Gottes Namen fahren wir*[283] and inside the chapel itself a large repertoire included *Salve Regina, Pange lingua, Vexilla Regis,* and an Easter hymn – *Ad cenam Agni providi* with many Alleluias – while in the church of the first Pentecost *Veni Creator Spiritus* was rendered 'very merrily'.[284]

However, much that took place at pilgrimage centres was not spontaneous; it was carefully planned by the custodians, devotions being provided and supervised. At Rome, for example, it was customary to mount the *scala santa* – so von Harff:

> We came to a marble staircase, eight and twenty steps high, which stood in Jerusalem at Pilate's house, upon which staircase Christ was led to Pilate and was judged there. We crawled up these steps on our knees, saying a *Pater noster* on each step, and on one step is a cross

enclosed within an iron grating. This is the place where Christ fell swooning on his knee. We were told that whoever climbs the steps receives for each step indulgences for nine years and whoever crawls up on his knees redeems a soul from purgatory.[285]

Nearly fifty years before, John Capgrave had performed the same penitential act but also noted that he was expected to kiss each step.[286] Thirteen years after von Harff's visit, Martin Luther, in 1510, undertook the same exercise.

If Rome in this way contrived to attract those who wished to follow in the steps of Jesus, without the labour of going to Palestine, in the last analysis it could not compete with Jerusalem, and Abbot Daniel spoke for many when he gave the motive for his journey as the desire to venerate the places 'which Christ our God pressed with his feet'.[287] Indeed to kiss the footprints of Jesus in the Church of the Ascension was the next best thing to kissing his very feet like the woman in the house of Simon the Pharisee (Luke 7.38). Pilgrims therefore sought to pace out Jesus' movements in and around Jerusalem, doing as he did and pausing at significant locations where one or other of the gospel events was said to have occurred. So Gucci tells how he and his friends went to Bethphage, where Jesus mounted the ass, on what he calls 'Olivet Sunday', and 'we travelled the same way on which Christ went when he entered Jerusalem'.[288] Some devotees saw themselves as fulfilling the roles of the gospel characters, as did Theoderich when visiting the crypt in which Peter was incarcerated; his prayer was: 'I wish to be imprisoned with Peter, that with him I may be taught by Christ not to deny him, but to pray.'[289]

The number of sites to be visited multiplied apace, sometimes relating to legend rather than to fact, as when pilgrims were taken to the spot where the Apostles' Creed was supposed to have been composed. Indeed the precision claimed in identifying exact locations could be absurd, with stations where Matthias was chosen by lot, James was consecrated bishop of Jerusalem and even exactly where in the Upper Room the water was warmed to wash the disciples' feet.[290] With such an abundance of stations, newcomers to the holy city obviously needed some assistance to find their way about, otherwise they could lose themselves. Some had guide books to which numerous signposts and placards were a useful adjunct. The wording of these notices was faithfully recorded by a number of pilgrims. The inscription relating to the Dome of the Rock on the Temple Mount, for example, was preserved by John of Würzburg:

> The king of kings, of Virgin Mother born,
> Was here presented. This is holy ground.
> Here Jacob saw the ladder; here he built
> His altar. Well may we hang gifts around.[291]

By the tomb there was the following wording:

> Here Christ was laid within his sepulchre of rock,
> His burial heaven's gates to mortals does unlock.[292]

But since the sepulchre also witnessed his rising from the dead, Theoderich, who was there in 1172, two years after John, copied this down:

> The place and guardian testify Christ's resurrection;
> Also the linen clothes, the angel, and redemption.[293]

At the same time some of the inscriptions indicated the relevance of the gospel events in the past to the pilgrim in the present, e.g. on the door of the cloisters to the Holy Sepulchre:

> You that this way do go,
> 'Twas you that caused my woe;
> I suffered this for you,
> For my sake vice eschew.[294]

In general, however, most did not venture to make a circuit on their own until they had first been conducted on an official tour, i.e. they followed a carefully designed itinerary 'making the visits according to the usage of pilgrims', as Frescobaldi expressed it,[295] or, in the words of Fabri:

> Pilgrims are led through the localities of Christ' passion in such an order that they meet their Lord, and go to meet him as he comes towards them.[296]

From the last quarter of the fourth century, as Egeria makes plain, a liturgical structure of considerable complexity had been devised, probably under the influence of Cyril of Jerusalem.[297] As the mini-pilgrimage in and around the city became even more organized and the number of visitors increased, additional observances were introduced and guides had to be authorized. Ultimately this task was officially committed to the Franciscans (from 1384) and so in the later Middle Ages the initial encounter of visitors was with them. They came in procession bearing candles and led the travellers to their guest house on Mount Sion. After the pilgrims' feet had been washed, they were conducted to the monastery chapel where they were addressed and exhorted to repentance and confession.[298]

The warm welcome accorded by local Christians at all the pilgrimage centres was remarked upon by many. The monks of Mount Sion in particular are frequently commended for their hospitality. The Piacenza pilgrim records how 'they greeted us with great respect, falling on their faces to the ground'.[299] Nine hundred years later, Frescobaldi was similarly impressed by the monks of St Catherine's who, he says, 'received us with joy . . . and did us great honour.' His companion, Gucci, noted that 'they honour the guests with all they have and they see them with pleasure and they give them a great reception'.[300]

The next stage was, of course, the organized visit or mini-pilgrimage and what this could involve is best illustrated by concentrating on one centre, Jerusalem being the obvious choice because of the very full information about it that is available. Depending partly upon what hour the pilgrims reached the city, a start was made early next morning before daybreak at a time when the relative freedom from hustle and bustle would allow concentration. What ensued has been conveniently summarized in Guylforde's account:

> Whensoever they come to any holy place, there they make a station, and declared unto us the mysteries of the same, we all bearing lights in our hands . . . and they sang anthems, hymns, versicles and collects appropriate to the said holy place right solemnly and devoutly.[301]

For the most important circuit, viz. that in the Holy Sepulchre, they assembled in the evening before the main doors, were eventually allowed access and were locked in. The one deputized to lead them then issued a series of instructions: they were to buy each a wax taper to carry in procession; they were to join in matins; everyone was to make his or her confession; each was to communicate at mass; priests would be provided with altars for their individual celebrations, and so on. Finally, according to Fabri,

> he besought us that each would rouse himself to a spirit of lively devotion, and that we would profit by those most holy places, showing them that honour and reverence that is due to them.[302]

For a complete picture of what happened at each station the brief summary given by Guylforde and quoted above needs to be filled out and the invaluable Felix Fabri provides a clue where to turn for the necessary details. Repeatedly, as he describes the circuit, he remarks that 'we said the customary prayers appointed in the processionals of the Holy Land'.[303] Four of these processionals have previously been introduced when reviewing the 'aids to devotion' available to mediaeval pilgrims. Here is information enough to recover vividly the spiritual exercises in which they engaged.

The *Ordo processionis* in the Church of the Holy Sepulchre opens with a note to the effect that, when all have assembled, each with a cross and candle, a cantor shall begin in a loud voice to sing the anthem *Salve Regina* (Queen of heaven). The procession is then to move to the chapel of the Virgin.

> *Antiphon:* Pilate had Jesus arrested and he was tied to a column and severely scourged.
> *Versicle:* Surely he has borne our griefs
> *Response:* And carried our sorrows.
> *Collect:* Be present to us, Christ the saviour, by the torment of your scourging and by your precious blood which was shed so that you might destroy all our sins, grant us your grace, protect us from every peril and every adversity and lead us to the joys of eternal life, you who live and reign world without end. Amen.[304]

Other anthems, antiphons, etc. provide themes for meditations on the appearance of Jesus to Mary Magdalene in the garden, Jesus' arrest, the pilgrimage of St Helena to the holy city and so on. The sequence of these subjects is not that found in the gospels, but has obviously been determined by the plan of the building and the need to promote circulation. On other pages of these manuscripts extra devotions are suggested e.g. a litany of the saints and numerous traditional hymns.[305]

To complete this illustration of the character and contents of these processionals, here is the station at Calvary.

> *Antiphon:* Behold the place where the salvation of the world hung: come let us adore.
> *Versicle:* We adore you, O Christ, and we bless you,
> *Response:* Because by your cross you have redeemed the world.
> *Collect:* Lord Jesus Christ, Son of the living God, who, for the salvation of the human race by your precious blood, did consecrate this most holy place, to which you

willed to be brought at the third hour, and then permitted yourself to be despoiled by the soldiers, and at length, at the sixth hour, having hung on the cross for our sins, did entreat your Mother and commend the sorrowing Virgin to a virgin [i.e. Mary to John], and finally at the ninth hour, crying aloud, praying and weeping, commended your spirit into the hands of the Father, and in this very place sustained in your most sacred body a piercing from the lance, grant, we pray, that we and all who have been redeemed by your most precious blood and celebrate the memorial of your passion may deserve to receive the benefits of that same passion, who live and reign world without end. Amen.[306]

The next action was indeed to 'celebrate the memorial of the passion', i.e. the mass, but before coming to this a word would be in order about the extent to which these devotions were based upon the current exegetical approach to the Bible. The transition from the literal or historical to the spiritual or mystical is very evident, so that what is happening as they gather at Calvary is not simply a pious remembering but the experiencing of the contemporary relevance and reality of Jesus' crucifixion and, further, passing on to the anagogical or eschatological reference, there is a looking forward to receiving 'the benefits of the same passion', not only here and now but unto the ages of ages.

The celebration of mass was a truly dramatic affair. The pilgrims presented the crosses they were carrying – these were later burned on Easter Eve.[307] Then, according to von Suchem, 'they read all the chief matters in the gospel with gesticulations'.[308] What these movements were is made plain by a passage in *The City of Jerusalem* (1220), an English translation of the old French text *La Citez de Jherusalem*.

In chanting the mass of the resurrection, the deacon, when he comes to the gospel, turns towards Mount Calvary at the word *crucifixum*; after which he turns to the tomb, then he says *Surrexit, non est hic*. Then he points with a finger at *Ecce locus ubi posuerunt eum*: and then, returning to the book, finishes the gospel.[309]

The climax was of course the act of communion and in Guylforde's words:

We were houseled at the high mass which was sung at Calvary with right great solemnity, and that ended about seven of the clock in the morning.[310]

The celebration of the mass was undoubtedly the highlight of any visit to a sacred place; at Compostela, for example, there were morning masses for pilgrims at the altar of St Mary Magdalene,[311] but at Jerusalem they would go again and again to the Holy Sepulchre and they were encouraged to do so by other organized events. John of Würzburg reports a procession every Saturday night from Easter to Advent at vespers. The respond was *Christus resurgens*, and then, according to his cryptic note:

> The precentor begins, 'but in the evening etc.', with the psalm 'My soul doth magnify the Lord', and the collect for the resurrection, 'Almighty and everlasting . . .' prefaced by the versicle 'From the sepulchre the Lord arose'.[312]

Other itineraries in and around Jerusalem embraced the Mount of Olives or extended as far as Bethlehem and Jericho; the processionals were once again in use. The prayer in Gethsemane from the second Spanish manuscript takes up Jesus' petition that his Father's will, and not his own, should prevail; this is applied to the pilgrims to the effect that it was not the Son's will that differed from that of his Father but that by using these words he was giving them a sign of the need to bend their wills to that of their heavenly Father. The prayer continues by contrasting Jesus' refusal to seek divine assistance, or indeed help of any kind since he ordered Peter to put up his sword, with the pilgrims' need of continual help and the continual forgiveness of their sins.[313] In this text there is a noticeable transition from the literal to the moral, while the prayer at Bethlehem in the first Spanish manuscript illustrates how the eschatological could be founded on the historical.

> O God, who revealed your Only-begotten Son to the Gentiles by the leading of a star, grant that we who know you now by faith may be led to contemplate your countenance on high, through the same Christ our Lord. Amen.[314]

These processionals, despite overlaps, were not always identical; where, for example, the same station was described different prayers could appear in each, so variety was possible. Yet on occasion they were not used at all and this led Pietro Casola to complain.

Many itineraries, both Italian and Ultramontane, written in the vulgar tongue and in Latin, mention that formerly antiphons and prayers appropriate to the place visited were said. I can only say that in fact this was not done. I can well believe that as the friars were in such a hurry to show us those places, they omitted some of the usual ceremonies.[315]

Yet this was not the norm according to the witness of most travellers. From the days of Egeria on, they frequently stress how valuable the readings were in that the narratives came to life when heard in the physical context of their original occurrences. This prayer, transcribed by John of Würzburg when present on the Temple Mount to celebrate the Presentation of the Virgin Mary on 21 November, is yet another example of how the 'literal' event, although in this instance derived from the apocryphal *Book of James*, can become the ground for the petition that grows out of it.

O God, who after three years was pleased to receive the presentation in the Temple of the holy Mother of God, who is the temple of the Holy Spirit, have respect unto the prayers of your faithful people, and grant that we, who now keep the feast of that presentation, may ourselves be made into a temple meet for you to dwell in, through our Lord, etc.[316]

To speak of these devotions as spiritual exercises, especially if one assumes an anti-biblical dichotomy of body and spirit, is something of a misnomer; they were physical too in the sense that they could take the form of role-playing. Theodosius speaks of 'eating food' in the room of the Last Supper[317] and later in the same century the Piacenza pilgrim relates how they reached Cana 'where the Lord attended the wedding, and we actually reclined on the couch'.[318] Similarly in Gethsemane 'where the Lord was betrayed, there are three couches on which he reclined and where we also reclined to gain their blessing'.[319] The devotions were physical also in the sense that they required considerable stamina and perseverance, which many, including Brother Felix, had to a remarkable degree.

No one should think visiting the holy places to be a light task; there is the intense heat of the sun, the walking from place to place, kneeling and prostration: above all, there is the strain which everyone puts on himself in striving with all his might to rouse himself to earnest piety and comprehension of what is shown him in the holy places, and to devout prayer and meditation, all which cannot be done without great fatigue, because to do them fitly a man should be at rest and not walking about. To struggle after mental abstraction whilst bodily walking from place to place is exceeding toilsome.[320]

Sensibly, therefore, the Franciscans arranged shortened circuits for those who were zealous but were not endowed with superhuman strength. The friars of Mount Sion made nightly circumambulations, additional to the ones described previously, and whereas they did visit some specific shrines, they made several stops facing in different directions, e.g. towards the Mount of Olive's, 'and worshipped all the holy places in one brief prayer'.[321]

Although most pilgrims were individually motivated, this did not mean that they were selfish, caring solely for their own spiritual welfare and indifferent to that of others. On the contrary, many a one speaks of regular acts of intercession, and this was certainly one of the objectives of Abbot Daniel who notes that in the Holy Sepulchre he celebrated fifty masses for the Russian princes and all living Orthodox believers as well as another forty for the dead. 'I did not forget,' he affirms, 'the names of the Russian princes, princesses, and their children; of the bishops, abbots and nobles; nor of my spiritual children and all Christians.'[322] Felix Fabri was equally mindful of others. Not only did he carry back a multitude of *eulogiae* for those at home but he fulfilled his promise to remember them at the holy places, especially his fellow friars and the benefactors who had helped to defray his expenses.

> I went up to the holy hill of Calvary, lighted a candle, and sat down with ink in front of me close by the holy rock wherein the cross once stood bearing him crucified, and there I wrote down the names of all whom I had especially promised, and all for whom I was in duty bound to pray. Having written down all the names as in litanies, I went with the paper to the holy rock, and there, kneeling on my knees, I laid the paper on the holy rock, and offered a prayer for each person whose name was written thereon, and for others whose names occurred to my memory.[323]

Whether the Piacenza pilgrim can be said to have gone one better or whether he is not rather to be censured may be questioned: at Cana he actually wrote the names of his parents on the couch. Perhaps this was a little more disinterested than the graffiti of the knights who incised their coats of arms and sometimes crosses, thus prolonging their presence in the sanctuaries by leaving behind some sign of their passing.

Before setting off on the return journey, some pilgrims in the late Middle Ages engaged in a novena, i.e. nine days of prayer in the principal sanctuaries, and all, without exception, sought tokens, the great period of their use being from the thirteenth to the fifteenth centuries. These badges were proof positive that the task had been accomplished and the goal reached. They could take many forms: flasks or ampullae, broaches, pins and medallions. They were displayed fastened to hats or on cloaks or they hung round the neck on a cord. That there should be no doubt about the identity of the holy place visited, they bore signs or pictures that associated them with a particular saint or locality.[324]

To go to the tomb of Edward the Confessor at Westminster Abbey was to secure a long pin surmounted by the king's head; at Amiens, where the severed head of John the Baptist was believed to be preserved, his portrait was obtainable; at Walsingham the Annunciation was the subject of the design. At Boulogne the badge showed the Virgin erect in a crescent-shaped vessel, recalling the miraculous arrival of a ship without visible means of propulsion bearing her statue.

The four great mediaeval centres – Jerusalem, Rome, Compostela and Canterbury – had each its special design. In Palestine pilgrims obtained a palm gathered 'in the garden of Abraham' at Jericho; originally carried on the back and hung between the shoulder blades, a small metal facsimile was later in use. It was soon interpreted to signify victory and to proclaim that the 'palmers', like the martyrs before them who had entered heaven in triumph, were now purified of their sins.[325]

A visitor to Rome – a 'roamer' according to Dante[326] – could procure a medallion showing the keys of St Peter or an engraving of the Vernicle. A badge depicting Peter and Paul side by side was also on offer.[327] At Compostela, so von Harff informs us, 'in front of the church you see countless great and small shells, which you can buy and bind on your cloak and say that you have been there'.[328] In origin this badge was simply a shell gathered on the nearest beach where many of the pilgrims landed. The next stage was for some enterprising metal worker to reproduce it in lead or pewter, its popularity perhaps owing something to the fact that it resembles the liturgical comb and so could symbolize purity. Not that the scallop was exclusive to Santiago; it was also handed out at Mont-Saint-Michel, but this was probably suggested by its proximity to the sea. The significance of the shell as a pilgrim token was widely recognized; it

Plate III Cockleshells decorating a capital of Saint-Hilaire, Melle

even had an influence on the details of church buildings, e.g. the capital by the south door of Saint-Hilaire, Melle, reproduces the form (Pl. III). In addition to the cockle sheils, the Compostela guide lists a wide variety of objects on sale: 'wine flasks, sandals, deerskin pouches, purses, straps, belts, and all sorts of medicinal herbs and other balms, and many other things'.[329]

Canterbury had numerous tokens all referring naturally to Thomas à Becket (Fig. 12). There were flasks containing 'Canterbury Water', which was water having had a remote contact with the blood he had spilled in the cathedral when he was martyred, and these containers were stamped with the scene of his death. The simplest token was a leaden dish with a 'T' upon it. More refined were the brooches showing either his head or a full length portrait in robes. He was also represented on horseback because he was a famous rider and had fought under Henry II in southern France and even after his elevation continued to take daily exercise in this manner.[330] A particular favourite was a small metal bell, a number of which have been recovered from the Thames mud and are now in the London Museum.[331] These bear the inscription *Campana Thome*, i.e. the bell of Thomas, and it is a suitable symbol because at that period small bells were sometimes appended to priestly garments to recall the bells on the high priest's robe of Ex. 28.33. Such bells were attached to the bridles of horses or, if they were on foot, to the pilgrims' hats and cloaks, and so, tinkling gently, they would set out on their return journey, possibly having prayed, as at Compostela, that they 'should not again wander from the paths of the Lord'.[332]

The Return Home

When the camels were loaded, and asses chosen and saddled, we went over to the Church of Sion and received the pilgrims' blessing from the venerable Father Guardian of Mount Sion, who embraced each one of us, blessed him, and dismissed him with a kiss ... Not without sadness of heart, nor without tears did we depart.[333]

With these words Felix Fabri recorded his feelings at the start of his homeward journey – a journey which, like the one in the reverse direction, was not to be undertaken without trepidation because the same dangers and fatigues attended both. Bertrand de la Brocquière, counsellor of the Duke of Burgundy (1432), was so certain that he would not be safe without special assistance that he went to the tomb

Fig. 12 Canterbury pilgrims' tokens

of the Virgin 'to implore her protection for my grand journey home and I heard divine service at the Cordeliers'.[334] Indeed it would not have been impossible to have found oneself engaged in an endless chain of pilgrimages as fresh perils were encountered and new vows made in the hope of being preserved, though often, rather sensibly, the vows were related to sanctuaries still ahead on the route home or to the provision of money to finance a substitute.

Sir Richard Guylforde's chaplain was particularly unfortunate in being caught in two fierce storms at sea. Off the island of Milos in the Cyclades they were subject to 'a marvellous great tempest, with exceeding rain and with the greatest rage of wind that ever I saw in all my life'. They lowered two anchors which began to drag and there was fear that the ship would be driven on to the rocky shore. The pilgrims huddled together and 'devoutly and fearfully sang *Salve Regina* and other anthems, with versicles and collects appropriate for such effect, and we all gave money and vowed a pilgrimage in general to our blessed Lady dei Miracoli at Venice'.[335] Later he was happy to record the fulfilment of the vow on 31 January 1507. However, within a few days of the first storm, they ran into an even more terrifying one off the island of Sapientza. 'We all by one assent avowed a pilgrimage to be made on our behalf to our blessed Lady of Loreto, besides Ancona in Italy, and deputed certain pilgrims to gather the money in our names with our offerings for a good speed and deliverance of all perils and dangers.'[336]

Life and limb were at risk in a storm, but it could bring an added peril in the shape of the sailors' wrath because they believed that tempests were aroused by the misdemeanours of pilgrims, as had been the case with Jonah when he was disobedient to the divine will (Jonah 1.4f.); in particular the mariners were fearful of the theft of relics and the bringing on board of Jordan water.[337] It must have been therefore with a great feeling of relief that pilgrims from the Holy Land arrived off Venice, heard the bells pealing a welcome and saw the large number of small craft that came out to meet the galley.[338]

If they survived their ordeals and eventually reached home – not neglecting to visit other shrines as they journeyed thither – the pilgrims were full of gratitude to God for preserving them and were accustomed to visit a local sanctuary to give thanks.[339] They would present their scrips and staffs to their parish churches; ampullae from Canterbury and shells from Compostela were hung up and other relics were carefully cherished to be placed in their coffins when death came to claim them. In the case of a person of substance, quite a ceremonial of greeting could be celebrated, although no set form was laid down. William de Mandeville, for example, was met by a solemn procession singing: 'Blessed is he that cometh in the name of the Lord.' He was then escorted with great joy into the church and up to the high altar where he prostrated himself and received a blessing. Rising, he genuflected and proceeded to offer the precious relics he had acquired in Jerusalem and a solemn *Te Deum* was then sung.[340] He, and many both before and after him, felt that they had come to the end of a truly remarkable spiritual exploration.

It must be admitted that the preceding account of Christian pilgrimage is somewhat of an idealized one. Nothing has been said of the adverse criticisms of the entire concept which began in the fourth century and were continuous thereafter. What may be called the seamy side of pilgrimage has not so far been mentioned. The decrease in the number of pilgrims towards the close of the Middle Ages has been passed over in silence. But all these are so many signposts towards the Reformation condemnation and are indeed essential to understanding it. They are consequently best left until the next chapter where they will receive immediate attention before the Protestant case is surveyed and analysed in detail.

2

Criticisms of Pilgrimage and the Protestant Condemnation

Pre-Reformation Criticism

(a) From within the ranks of the faithful

Pilgrimage was to become more and more popular from the Peace of the Church onwards, but even in the fourth century it was not without its critics. Both Gregory of Nyssa and Jerome questioned certain features, although they were not entirely of one mind about the subject. The former was quite certain that going on a pilgrimage was not something required by Christ,[1] but the latter was prepared to state: 'It is still your duty as believers to worship on the spot where the Lord's feet once stood and to see for yourselves the still fresh traces of his birth, his cross and his passion.'[2] However this recommendation did not prevent Jerome from agreeing with Gregory in several particulars. He acknowledged that God's omnipresence was not to be denied: 'I do not presume to limit God's omnipotence or to restrict to a narrow strip of earth him whom the heavens cannot contain. Each believer is judged not by his residence in this place or that but according to the deserts of his faith.'[3] To the same effect, Gregory affirmed that 'the grace of the Holy Spirit is not more abundant at Jerusalem than elsewhere'.[4]

Gregory was also sure that 'change of place does not effect any drawing nearer to God, but wherever you may be God will come to you'.[5] This is precisely the same point made by Jerome: 'Access to the court of heaven is as easy from Britain as it is from Jerusalem.'[6] So, concluded Gregory, 'you who fear the Lord, praise him in the places where you are now.' Both were equally convinced that the Christian's task is to interiorize that to which the holy places are witnesses – so Jerome, as the more succinct: 'The places which witnessed the crucifixion and the resurrection profit those only who bear their several crosses, who day by day rise again with Christ.⁷ Yet Gregory remained hesitant; while he was prepared to call the holy places 'memorials of the immense love of the Lord for us men', he thought the best tokens of the divine grace were holy people. Moreover he considered that pilgrimage could lead into temptation, and what he had seen in Jerusalem itself, when present not as a pilgrim but on official ecclesiastical business, filled him with scorn: 'Rascality, adultery, theft, idolatry, poisoning, quarreling, murder, are rife.'⁸

All these various points were to be raised again and again over the next millennium. Thomas à Kempis (c. 1379–1471), whose friend Frederick of Heilo actually wrote a treatise entitled *Contra peregrinantes*, shared Jerome's hesitation to suppose that God is more present in one place than in another.⁹ Others repeated Gregory's condemnation of the misbehaviour at pilgrimage centres. There was much competition as each person upon arrival sought to be the first to reach the shrine – a spirit of rivalry that was apparently justified by an appeal to the case of the sick man at the pool of Bethesda who had not been cured of his blindness because 'when the water is troubled, and while I am going another steps down before me' (John 5.7). There was consequently much jostling, so intense that in one single year, 1318, thirteen pilgrims were crushed to death at Mont-Saint-Michel; there were quarrels and blows too. The vigils were often not devoted to spiritual exercises but to sleeping, to idle conversation, to the consumption of picnics, to the singing of popular ballads or the playing of musical instruments.¹⁰ Nor was Gregory of Nyssa's reference to adultery applicable only to his day. In fact in 1372, when the Knight of La-Tour Landry compiled a book of instructions for his daughters, it was the immoral side of pilgrimages that provided the subject of one of his cautionary tales. This tells of a certain young wife who had become enamoured of a squire and they both went on a pilgrimage to a shrine of the Virgin Mary, not stirred by devotion but in order to be together without the husband suspecting the affair. Being a cautionary tale, the lady falls ill and is only restored to health when she confesses and repents. Here, admonishes the Knight,

> is an example that nobody should go on holy pilgrimages for to fulfil no folly, pleasance, nor the world, nor fleshly delight. But they should go entirely with heart to serve God; and also that it is good to pray for father and mother, and for other friends that be dead, for they obtain by petitions grace for them that be alive. And also it is good to give alms.¹¹

Not surprisingly there was a mediaeval proverb to this effect: 'Go a pilgrim, return a whore.'[12]

Chaucer's Wife of Bath, interested in 'dauliance', was therefore not untypical (Fig. 13). Indeed, with but few exceptions, such as the Clerk, the Knight, the Parson and the Plowman, most of his characters were prompted by a desire to have a good time, and the merchant in the Shipwright's Tale even saw the outing as a way to avoid his creditors. Consequently the church authorities, while happy to encourage pilgrimages, sought to institutionalize and regulate them. One of the most determined attempts to achieve this was made at the Council of Châlons in 813. Its 45th canon condemns numerous categories of so-called pilgrims who are very precisely defined:

1. Clerics who think they will be able to purge their sins by going on a pilgrimage and at the same time escape from their pastoral duties.

2. Laity who think they can sin with impunity simply by frequenting such places of prayer.

3. Powerful folk who exact payment from the rest of the company under pretence of protecting them.

4. Poor people whose motive is solely to have better opportunities for begging.

5. Wanderers who go on one pilgrimage after another in the belief that simply to *see* a holy place will purge their sins.

The canon concludes by defining those whose devotion is to be commended, viz. the ones who have confessed their sins to their parish priests and have received advice about the penance to be performed, whether unceasing prayer, generous almsgiving, emendation of life and morals or travelling to the threshold of the apostles.[13]

This insistence on proper motives led one divine to make a statement that could well have been acceptable to Martin Luther, with only slight modification. This was Maurice of Sully, Bishop of Paris from 1160 to 1196.

> God has no regard for the works of a bad Christian, for neither he nor his works please him . . . What profit can it be to go on pilgrimages and travel far from his village if he does not travel far from sin and vice?[14]

In the fifteenth century the Dominican John Bromyard could press the point most vigorously.

> There are some who keep their pilgrimages and festivals not for God but for the devil. Those who sin more freely when away from home or who go on pilgrimage to succeed in inordinate and foolish love – those

Fig. 13 Chaucer's Wife of Bath (from *The Canterbury Tales*,
William Caxton 1484)

who spend their time on the road in evil and uncharitable conversation
may indeed say *peregrinamur a Domino*: they make their pilgrimage
away from God to the devil.[15]

Then there were those who considered that pilgrims were reprehensible in so far as they ceased to fulfil their responsibilities to their
families and dependants. The financial outlay on the journey was
deemed excessive, while the offerings at the shrines were simply used
to manufacture more statues. To Honorius of Autun, 'it is better to
spend money on the poor than to use it for travel' – this was later to be
an argument advanced by the Lollards – such money ought to be
employed for the redemption of captives, for feeding the hungry and
clothing the naked.[16]

All these criticisms could be and were directed at every form of
pilgrimage, but those whose objective was the veneration of relics
and images were the objects of other attacks. As early as the fourth
century, Vigilantius, a Protestant before his time, had posed the
question: 'Why do you kiss and adore a bit of powder wrapped up in a
cloth?'[17] This was to disparage the adoration of sacred remains and
the standard reply was that contained in Jerome's letter to Riparius:

> We honour the relics of the martyrs that we may adore him whose
> martyrs they are. We honour the saints that their honour may be
> reflected on their Lord who himself says, 'He that receives you,
> receives me' (Matt. 10.40).[18]

In general this response was held to be sufficient to dispose of the
matter, but when Guibert de Nogent treated of relics some seven
hundred years later, while not condemning their veneration, he

stressed hearing sermons and confession as preferable activities,[19] and he did take the view that much of the advocacy of the importance of relics originated in the profit motive.[20] He argued further that some alleged saints were not real ones and that not all relics are genuine.[21] Of course the more people travelled, the more they came to question what was displayed to them since they could not fail to notice the occurrence of duplicates. Von Harff was but one of many to remark on the situation, anticipating Calvin's attack, and noting that in the cathedral of St Denis, in the outskirts of Paris, one could see the hand of St Thomas which he thrust into the side of Jesus, whereas he himself had already seen it in India and it was also on display at Maastricht.[22] This was sufficient to raise some misgivings in the minds even of the most credulous who were also subject to a general change in popular devotion. This approach, already present in the early patristic era, developed most rapidly from the eleventh century and involved a movement away from local saints in favour of universal ones such as the Virgin, and from a hagiocentric spirituality to one focused on Christ.[23] In Finucane's vivid phrase there was a shifting away from 'the spiritual middle-men'.[24]

The centrality of Christ is also evident from the emphasis upon his Real Presence at the eucharist, and the way in which this told against the practice of pilgrimage is indicated by Thomas à Kempis' meditation on the communion service.

> Many run to divers places to visit the memorials of saints departed, are full of admiration at hearing of their deeds, behold with awe the spacious buildings of their temples, and find their affections moved by whatever is connected with their memory.
>
> But, behold, thou art thyself here present with me on thine altar, my God, Saint of saints, Creator of men, and Lord of the angels.[25]

The practice of benediction, i.e. of the adoration of Christ present in the consecrated host exposed to view, belongs to the same realm of thought and led also to a displacement of the saints, especially noticeable as the monstrances containing the host assumed the form of the earlier reliquaries in which their bones had been displayed. The centrality of Christ in Reformation thought was already being anticipated and at the same time pilgrimages to honour his followers were to that extent being discouraged.

Images too, another attraction to pilgrims, were coming in for their fair share of opposition. It is true that preachers sought to promote imitation of the saints as patterns for right conduct and hence declared that images were acceptable because they brought them most vividly before the eyes of the unlettered, but there were those who feared they could lead to idolatry. So Archbishop Fitzralph of Armagh, preaching on All Saints' Day, 1356, referred to

> a certain danger from the veneration of images which some frequently and wrongfully call by the names of those they are intended to represent . . . Wherefore those who venerate such images for their own sake and make offerings to them to procure healing or benefits of some kind appear to be true and potent idolaters.[26]

Hence the need for those who respected statues to come to their defence; one such was the English mystic Walter Hilton who argued that they help to concentrate a wandering mind and that they are 'commemorative tokens of the departed . . . When they kneel before the images that are as it were a reminder, they forget them and utter their prayers to God and his saints.'[27] Not all were convinced, and the ease with which the Reformation attack on the cult of saints and on pilgrimages was to succeed is in part understandable because of the late mediaeval devaluation of both.

There was another aspect of early mediaeval thought that had always created a certain suspicion about the legitimacy of pilgrimages and that was the concept of *curiositas*. *Curiositas* had been condemned by such writers widely separated in time as Augustine, Bernard and Aquinas; they did so because they held that curiosity about the universe could prevent concentration upon the world to come. To pursue knowledge under the impetus of curiosity was indeed to be like Adam in the garden and his knowledge was disastrous. Further, curiosity was related to instability, aimlessness, restlessness and so to wandering about. Since to travel could be regarded as succumbing to *curiositas*, pilgrimage was questionable. Many held that pilgrimage can never be more than a religiously sanctioned way of curiously exploring the world.[28] So for an Augustine, since the human condition is one of restlessness, the heavenly city will be free from pilgrimages which are its product,[29] and Honorius, in a passage already quoted, could condemn 'rushing about the holy places either for curiosity or for the praise of men'. This view was constant. This is à Kempis' verdict:

> Often, in looking after such memorials, men are moved by curiosity, and by the novelty of fresh sights, whilst little or no fruit of amendment is carried home; particularly when they go from place to place with levity, without a true penitent heart.[30]

Right up to the eve of the Reformation this attitude remained unchanged. The Cavalier Santo Brasca, drawing on the experience of his visit to Jerusalem in 1480, gave this advice:

> A man should undertake this voyage solely with the intention of visiting, contemplating and adoring the most holy mysteries, with great effusion of tears, in order that Jesus may graciously pardon his sins; and not with the intention of seeing the world, or from ambition, to be able to boast 'I have been there' or 'I have seen that' – in order to be exalted by his fellow men, as perhaps some do, who in this case from now have received their reward.[31]

But the cavalier was fighting a losing battle and expressing a largely outdated opinion. At the time he was writing, *curiositas* was ceasing to be regarded as a vice; a desire to know the world was emerging and travel could be undertaken as a proper human pursuit for those concerned to learn more about God's creation. While this removed one of the grounds for objecting to pilgrimages, the new view was equally inimical because travel was now undertaken specifically for the exercise of curiosity and the religious aspect ceased to be central. Already John Maundeville, *c.* 1322, while still providing a pilgrimage itinerary, could combine it with an account of worldly exploration, signalling the shift in motivation that was to distinguish the Renaissance voyager from the mediaeval pilgrim.[32]

Amongst other factors that had an effect on pilgrimages was a way of understanding discipleship that was never entirely absent from Christian thought but began to receive very considerable emphasis from the twelfth century onwards: this was the stress on the need to internalize religion. A form of asceticism that had manifested itself previously in physical displacement now began to be replaced by the inculcation of a set of inner attitudes. The important thing was not to leave one's country but one's self. Emphasis was laid upon the value of dying with Christ, of undergoing the crucifixion of the self, rather than on actively assuming a cross and travelling to the earthly Jerusalem.[33] God's true place of habitation was now held to be within the individual and to pursue the perfect pilgrimage was to engage in an interior journey.[34] Anticipating this attitude a mid- ninth century Irish poet could write: 'To go to Rome, much labour, little profit: you will not find the King whom you seek there unless you bring him with you.'[35] A document from the same country, the eleventh-century *Codex Boernerianus*, is quite condemnatory: 'To go on a pilgrimage to

Rome means going to one's death and calling down upon oneself the wrath of the Son of Mary.'[36]

Of course all this could and did result in the playing down of pilgrimage in the literal sense of going to holy places. Active pilgrimage became devalued because of a revaluation of the concept in terms of an inner process. Pilgrimage could be used as an allegory of the whole of life and a devotion to its inner dimension. A sustained interpretation on these lines is represented by such a work as *Ayenbite of Inwyte*, a translation from the French, completed in 1340 by Dan Michel of Northgate, Kent.[37] By the fifteenth century this had become a commonplace among all preachers, typified by Richard Allerton speaking in London in 1406. He used the palmer's tokens as the framework for his sermon: the staff is to defend oneself against the dangers of hell; the mantle is the cloak of charity without which no one can enter the heavenly Jerusalem and the scrip points to the necessity of giving alms and engaging in works of mercy.[38]

This shift in meaning and application corresponded to the disregard for the literal meaning in favour of the spiritual in biblical exegesis. This is very evident in the mediaeval plays based upon the Emmaus story and variously called *Officium* or *Ordo Peregrinorum* or simply *Ad Faciendum Peregrinum*.[39] Usually performed at vespers on Easter Monday, these have a ritualistic aspect in that they 'act out' an experience and in so doing 'make it to happen'. In this way those in the church, beholding the characters dressed in cloaks, with scrip and staff, were moved to make fresh efforts to pursue the pilgrimage of life (Pl. IV). While these presentations were undoubtedly dramatic, they were not historically conceived since the incident was primarily interpreted not as an episode from Luke's account of Christ's resurrection but as relevant to one's own journey there and then.[40] In similar fashion, the original production of the Second Shepherd's Play in the Wakefield cycle was not about the finding of Christ at a specific historical moment, but about the discovery of him by any of those present as they followed the spectacle.[41] This use of drama as a means to devotion was not an isolated phenomenon: the last centuries of the Middle Ages were those that saw the development of the practice of meditation and the invention of spiritual exercises such as the Stations of the Cross. Clearly while the Stations were a boon to those quite unable to make the journey to Jerusalem, for whatever reason, they could easily become a substitute.

Not only the resort to alternative devotional practices and also the objections and the adverse arguments but the figures too tell a tale of

Plate IV Jesus as a pilgrim on the Way to Emmaus (San Domingo de Silos
near Burgos, 1085–1100)

waning interest. From the Venetian registers listing permission granted to pilgrims to embark for Palestine, it is possible to detect a steady decline in applications: 1385 – 380; 1386 – 340; 1387 – 323; 1388 – 310.[42] The decline was to continue. In 1496, to give but one instance, von Harff was told by the monks of St Catherine's that for the previous ten years not a single pilgrim from a Latin country had come to Mount Sinai.[43] It is not surprising therefore that William Wey, who was an inveterate pilgrim (twice to Jerusalem and once to Compostela), should feel it incumbent on him to set out ten reasons why one should go to the Holy Land. He appealed to the authority of Jerome and of Leo, previously quoted;[44] he asserted that Jesus himself motivates people to go thither and that, according to a reliable tradition, he did so particularly in the cases of St Paul and St Brigitte. Wey twice stressed the value of the indulgences to be gained, pointed to the familiarity to be acquired with the biblical place-names and sites and concluded by calling attention to the opportunities to venerate relics.[45] But by this time his fellow countrymen had been hearing the strictures of Wyclif and the Lollards and the Reformation was looming on the horizon.

(b) *Wyclif and the Lollards*

Neither pilgrimages nor the veneration of images had a primary place in the thought of John Wyclif (*c.* 1329–84). He did however regard the former as 'blind' because Christ is everywhere ready to take away sin. He further considered that while pilgrimages may obtain centuries of pardon for the rich, they did little or nothing for the poor, and he condemned the lechery which often accompanied them.[46] His attitude to images may be labelled reserved, although he rejected as idolatrous any idea that particular images have special merit or are indwelt by some divine power.

> It is evident that images may be made both well and ill: well in order to rouse, assist and kindle the minds of the faithful to love God more devoutly; and ill when by reason of images there is deviation from the true faith, as when the image is worshipped.[47]

In Bohemia, John Huss (*c.* 1369–1415), who owed much to the teaching of Wyclif, was also relatively conservative in his stance about these matters. He deemed many relics to be spurious; he did not reject indulgences but opposed their sale, and he sought to dissuade folk from going on pilgrimages.[48] Wyclif's English followers – the Lollards – were prepared to go much further.

The Lollards did object to indulgences, thus questioning what had become one of the prime motives for becoming a pilgrim. They even specified particular examples, condemning, amongst others, a papal grant of 1223 to the Porziuncola at Assisi which was the first centre of the Franciscan order. Honorius III had decreed that those who entered the chapel after being shriven on August 2 each year and were present from first vespers to sunset would obtain full remission of sins from the day of their baptism to that of their visit.[49]

They also mounted a sustained attack on the veneration of images and relics which they held to be synonymous with idolatry, and consequently they repudiated the practice of going to shrines where these were to be found.[50] They maintained that *latria* belongs to God alone and that *dulia* is appropriate towards men and angels but 'to no other creature'. They ridiculed the adoration of relics, contending that if the lance that pierced the side of Jesus on the cross is to be held in special honour, equally the lips of Judas, were it possible to recover them, would deserve the same honour, since they, like the lance, had come into contact with the Lord.[51]

The Lollards had no hesitation in holding that believers should honour the image of God in man not those made of wood and stone, and the way to do this is to give alms. Indeed money is not to be wasted in the form of gifts at shrines nor spent upon pilgrimages: it can be better spent on the poor.[52] Furthermore, they took the view that God is everywhere present and so no place can be regarded as more holy than another 'and no image is holier than another like image. Wherefore it is a vain waste and idle to trot to Walsingham rather than to each other place in which an image of Mary is.'[53] To suppose also that the saints will hear our prayers and do something about them is erroneous because the best saint in heaven has enough to do to intercede for himself.[54] As for calling to mind the lives of both Christ and the saints, neither images nor pilgrimages are needed for that purpose but the reading of the Bible and other devout works.[55]

This last contention may seem to rule out going to the Holy Land, but the Lollards never addressed themselves specifically to that issue. Their prime target was image worship and the veneration of relics and travelling to those places where they were to be found. Nevertheless, in keeping with the contemporary movement towards the interiorization of religion, they spoke of the whole of life as a pilgrimage in such a way as to imply that travel was unnecessary. This is quite evident in a Lollard tract entitled *The Lanterne of Light* (1409/10).

According to this work, 'true pilgrimage is done in six manners' and these are then listed. We are pilgrims from the moment of birth on the way to the heavenly city; we are pilgrims when we go to church, when we visit the poor and distribute alms; studying holy writ and then going to proclaim it is another manner of pilgrimage; so is going away from a place where there is no priest at the direction of God as did Abram; the sixth pilgrimage is that upon which we enter at death 'to bliss or pain'. The comment is then made: 'There is no other pilgrimage that may please God ... as holy writ bears witness.'[56] This in itself certainly intimates that going to the earthly Jerusalem is to be ruled out.

The effect of this campaign by the Lollards was twofold: it provoked a counterblast by the supporters of the veneration of images and of pilgrimages and it led to an attempt to stamp out Lollardy by arresting its adherents and charging them with heresy.

In 1391 John Devereux felt the need to put the counter-case[57] and others followed in his wake. Roger Dynmok was prompted to do so when early in 1395 some Lollards nailed up on the door of St Paul's a broadsheet consisting of twelve articles specifying certain beliefs and practices that they rejected. These included the veneration of saints and images and the pilgrimages associated with them. Dynmok replied at length and in particular argued that pilgrimages were obviously approved by God since he worked miracles at all these shrines.[58] However it was Reginald Pecock who was the most doughty defender of the traditional practices.

Pecock, who was successively Bishop of St Asaph and of Chichester, wrote his *Repressor* c. 1449 against those whom he calls 'Bible-men'.[59] While condemning the idolatrous adoration of images, and making it plain that he holds it false to think that a divine power resides in statues, he sees value in them as 'reminding signs'.[60] Pilgrimages too can be 'reminders' of the life of Christ and of the example of his saints.[61] Indeed to go on a pilgrimage may be deemed meritorious because it provides an example to others of penitence and devotion.[62] As for the Lollard contention that the Bible together with accounts of the saints are sufficient for calling Christ and his holy ones to mind, Pecock states that pilgrimages are far more effective for achieving this end. He instances the annual pilgrimage to the College of St Catherine's in London on 25 November, and declares that this turns one's thoughts to the saint far more surely than if there were ten thousand books about her available.[63] He was prepared to admit that some may venture forth from vainglory but he was convinced that there are three entirely valid reasons that justify the practice. First, it recalls the benefits, punishments, holy life and passion of the Saviour and the conduct of his saints without the distractions that inevitably arise at home. Second, it sets a good example and moves others to seek sanctification. Third, it both renews and maintains one's remembrance of what God had done on our behalf.[64] Indeed to embark on a pilgrimage is to imitate the three women who went to the sepulchre of Christ: 'They made a bodily pilgrimage, even like to the bodily pilgrimage which of devout and well governed pilgrims now wont to be done.'[65]

These arguments did not dissuade the Lollards from continuing their opposition and so the ecclesiastical courts were brought into operation. The recorded cases are numerous and that of William Colyn will serve as a typical illustration of what was happening. He was a skinner of South Creake, Norfolk, who had apparently refused to pray before a statue of the Virgin, and, what is more, had spoken disparagingly of Walsingham.[66] It is, however, the case of William Thorpe that is among the most fully documented. He appeared before Thomas Arundel, Archbishop of Canterbury, in 1407, charged with heresy. In his own account of the cross-examination, Thorpe records how he was accused of denying the propriety of venerating images and of objecting to pilgrimages. On the first count, he admitted that he thought the adoration of statues to be idolatrous and that the miracles said to be wrought at the shrines were the work of the devil, who, in this way, turned folk away from hearing and knowing God's word. As for pilgrimages, Thorpe distinguished between the true and the false. The former, for him as for the author of the *Lanterne of Light,* refers to the Christian way of life, involving obedience to the divine commandments, avoidance of the seven deadly sins, performing works of mercy, and so on, whereas the latter – actually travelling to a so-called holy place – is reprehensible. The Archbishop, who had very little time for Thorpe and was constantly addressing him as 'lewd losel', countered by listing the beneficial effects of pilgrimages, but Thorpe would have none of this. On the basis of his own experience, he claimed to know that the majority of pilgrims are ignoramuses, incapable of saying the *Pater noster,* the *Ave Maria* or the creed. Their motives are of the worst. 'It is more for the health of their bodies than for their souls; more for to have riches and prosperity of this world than for to be enriched with virtues in their souls; more to have here worldly and fleshly friendship, than for to have friendship with God, and of his saints in heaven.' Pilgrimage indeed is not pleasing to God, especially as for most people it is simply a pretext for diverting themselves.

> They have with them both men and women that can sing wanton songs, and some other pilgrims will have with them bagpipes; so that every town that they come through, what with the noise of their singing, and with the sound of their piping, and with the jangling of their Canterbury bells, and with the barking of dogs after them, that they make more noise, than if the king came their way, with all his clarions and many other minstrels.

The money they spend is declared by Thorpe to be a blasphemous waste of God's goods which should have been used for works of mercy.[67] Many of these arguments were to be taken up again and re-echoed a century later when the Reformation began to gather momentum, but its most immediate herald, without question, was Erasmus of Rotterdam.

The Barbed Wit of Erasmus of Rotterdam

One of the most distinguished scholars of his day with a reputation that was European wide, Erasmus (*c.* 1466–1536) lent his name and support to the movement to internalize religion which was developing throughout the Middle Ages. As early as 1503, in his *Enchiridion* first published in Antwerp, he contrasted the outward physical activity of travelling to shrines with the internal spiritual cultivation of the Christian character. So clearly does he bring out this distinction, which was to play a major part in forming the Reformation attitude, that he is worth quoting at some length on the issue.

> You venerate saints; you are glad to touch their relics. But you condemn what goods they have left, namely the example of a pure life. No worship of Mary is more gracious than if you imitate Mary's humility. No devotion to the saints is more acceptable and more proper than if you strive to express their virtue. You wish to deserve well of Peter and Paul? Imitate the faith of the one, the charity of the other – and you will thereby do more than if you were to dash back and forth to Rome ten times . . . You may embrace the ashes of Paul with the highest veneration – I do not condemn it – if your religion conforms to his. If, however, you venerate dead, dumb ashes, and neglect his living image, which shines forth, speaking and even breathing, in Scripture, is not your religion a preposterous thing? You worship the bones of Paul, preserved in nooks and niches, but you do not worship the mind of Paul, hidden in Scripture? You make much of

the fragment of a body, seen through glass, yet you do not marvel at the whole mind of Paul, shining through Scripture. You worship ashes to which the vices of the body are ever reduced; why not rather worship the Scriptures, by which the vices of souls are cured? . . . You give homage to the image of Christ's countenance, delineated in stone or wood, or painted in colours; much more religiously ought you to honour the image of his mind, which the Holy Spirit as artificer expressed in the words of the gospel . . . You gaze in dumb amazement at the tunic or sweat cloth reputedly Christ's, yet half asleep you read the utterances of Christ. You believe it much more important that you possess a small piece of the cross in your house. Yet this latter is nothing in comparison with bearing the mystery of the cross fixed in your breast . . . Is it a great matter that you visit Jerusalem in the flesh, when inwardly you are a veritable Sodom, an Egypt, a Babylon? It is not great to have trod in Christ's footsteps with carnal feet, yet it is the greatest thing to follow in Christ's footsteps in the affection. If it is a wonderful thing to have touched Christ's sepulchre, will it not be wonderful also to have expressed the mystery of the sepulchre? You reproach your sins before a human priest: see how you will reproach them before God! For to reproach before him is to hate within. Perchance you believe that by wax seals, or trifling coins, or paltry little pilgrimages, your guilt can be washed off all at once. You have wandered completely from the path. Within, the wound has been inflicted; within, it is necessary to attack the poisoner . . . That you may be absolved from guilt, you dash to Rome, you sail to the shrine of St James, you buy the most ample indulgences. Certainly I do not condemn what you do, but that you do all things; yet there is no more useful method by which after the offence you may be reconciled to God than if you, offended, are reconciled to your brother. Pardon the neighbour for a light sin (for whatever man sins against man is a light sin) that Christ may forgive you your countless thousands of sins.[68]

Within eight years, Erasmus returned to the attack in a work which became immensely popular and was consequently very influential; this was *The Praise of Folly*, which used ridicule as a weapon.

What should I say of them that hug themselves with their counterfeit pardons; that have measured purgatory with an hour glass, and can without the least mistake demonstrate its ages, years, months, days, hours, minutes, and seconds, as it were in a mathematical table? . . . Several countries avouch to themselves their peculiar saint, and as every one of them has his peculiar gift, so also his particular form of worship. As, one is good for the toothache; another for groaning women; a third for stolen goods; a fourth for making a voyage prosperous; and a fifth to cure sheep of the rot; and so of the rest, for it would be too tedious to run over all. And some there are that are good for more things than one; but chiefly the Virgin Mother to whom the common people do in a manner attribute more than to the Son . . . Among all those offerings that are so frequently hung up in churches, nay up to the very roof of some of them, did you ever see the least acknowledgment from anyone that had left his Folly, or grown a hair's breadth the wiser? One escapes a shipwreck and gets safe to shore. Another, run through in a duel, recovers. Another, while the rest were fighting, ran out of the field, no less luckily than valiantly. Another, condemned to be hanged, by the favour of some saint or other, a friend to thieves, got himself off by impeaching his fellows . . . All these hang up their tablets, but no one gives thanks for his recovery from Folly . . . How many are there that burn candles to the Virgin Mother, and that too at noonday when there is no need of them! But how few are there that study to imitate her in pureness of life, humility and love of heavenly things, which is the true worship and most acceptable to heaven . . . What of he who leaves his wife and children at home, and goes to Jerusalem, Rome, or in pilgrimage to St James, where he has no business.[69]

Incisive though the criticisms of Erasmus were, he never contemplated joining the Reformers. He was essentially a moderate, wanting to correct abuses from within the church and so his condemnation was often qualified. He could grant that 'it is possible for someone to gain spiritual benefit from going to Jerusalem' and at the same time insist that there are 'other things more conducive to true godliness'.[70] He denied that 'the essence of true holiness is to have visited Jerusalem'[71] but acknowledged that such a journey may be out of devotion.[72] He respected the saints but feared that constantly to seek favours from them might lead people to suppose either that they were more compassionate than God or even that Christ himself were dead.[73] As he frequently used humour to drive home his arguments, he attracted much opposition and criticism, as when he contended that it is better to address oneself directly to the Father rather than to a saint because, heaven being a very large place, the saint could take so long to encounter God that the petitioner could well have died in the meantime.[74]

Erasmus' extensive influence was instrumental in creating a critical and untraditional form of mind, especially with such popular works as his *Colloquies* (1526). In these he scoffed at the making of vows to go on a pilgrimage during a storm at sea[75] – thus condemning the practice of one such as Sir Richard Guylforde's chaplain who had happily recorded making two vows under identical circumstances as the natural response of piety to dangerous situations.[76] In his *Pilgrimage for Religion's Sake*, Erasmus also questioned the motives of pilgrims by telling of the man who found himself on the road to Rome and then to Compostela because while under the influence of drink he had rashly declared his intention to go there .[77] He reproached both those who would throw all images out of churches, such as the followers of Zwingli at Zurich, and those who were 'crazy' about pilgrimages, and at the same time he raised the issue of the genuineness of the relics exposed to view.[78] His position *in via media* often found expression, as when he declared 'I do not condemn papal indulgences or briefs; but I do reprove the utterly frivolous man who, without a thought of amending his life, puts his whole hope in human pardons.'[79] He was consequently not prepared to go to the extremes of Martin Luther, however much he played a major role in creating the climate within which Luther was to make so great an impact.

Martin Luther and the Reformation Condemnation of Pilgrimages

It was in fact a year before the publication of *The Praise of Folly* that Luther himself went to Rome as one of two emissaries on behalf of his order. Many years later he told how at his first sight of the city he threw himself to the ground, saying: 'Hail, sacred Rome, sanctified in truth by the sacred martyrs with whose blood you were drenched.' In fact he conducted himself exactly like multitudes of mediaeval Christians before him and like them too, making use of the *Mirabilia Urbis Romae*, he visited the seven great basilicas and climbed the *scala santa* in pursuit of indulgences.[80] However after another nine years, Luther had come to share Erasmus' questioning of indulgences, had embraced the concept of the internalization of religion, particularly in the form of the doctrine of justification by faith, and was adversely criticizing both devotions to the saints and pilgrimages to their shrines.

Luther had his own explanation, which is not lacking in credibility for it derives from his personal experience, of the development of the cult of the saints. He summed it up succinctly in one of his sermons on the Gospel of John by remarking that in the past Christ had been represented as an awesome judge rather than a loving saviour and so 'all the pilgrimages and all the invocations of the saints stem from this view of Christ'.[81] However his understanding is more fully set out in his commentary on Psalm 110.

Christ's exacting and serious wrath was impressed on the people to such a degree that they had to flee from him. This view was driven so deeply in the hearts of people that I and others were terrified when we heard the name of Christ. They taught us to call upon the dear Mother of Christ and to urge her, for the sake of the breasts which she gave her Son, to plead against his wrath over us and to obtain his grace. And if our dear Lady did not suffice, we enlisted the help of the apostles and other saints . . . Pilgrimages were organized in their behalf, masses were endowed, and the pope added his indulgences and blessing.[82]

Visual evidence supporting the accuracy of Luther's account of the mediaeval attitude is provided by the bas-reliefs, completed in 1130, on the façade of Saint-Jouin-de-Marnes (Pl. I). Christ, flanked by two angels, has descended from the cross which towers behind his throne, having thus exchanged his role of mediator for that of judge. Below him a long line of suppliants, including the naked figures of Adam and Eve but with the majority in pilgrim garb, advance towards the Virgin Mary; in this way she has been accorded a mediatorial role as more humane and approachable than her fearsome Son.

Luther was convinced that Jesus was the sole mediator, that he alone exercises an eternal highpriesthood and that he is the only advocate with the Father. Consequently he disparaged the saints in so far as they appeared to be his rivals. In fact they not only appeared to be, they had become so and this can be simply illustrated. In one year alone at Canterbury the shrine of Becket attracted £832 12s 3d, while the high altar received only £3 2s 6d; the year following the Becket offerings had risen to £954 6s 3d and those of the high altar had declined to nil.[83] Other evidence from the Middle Ages does support the view that Christ was being replaced by one saint or another, however little this may have been intended by those who reverenced them. Sulpicius Severus, for example, could describe Martin of Tours as another Christ who 'emulates the miracles performed by the Saviour'.[84] He was of course able to appeal to John 4.12 – 'greater works than these will he do' – but to the simple believer it suggested a certain equality if not superiority. Similarly Gregory of Tours sought to prevent Winnock, a Breton pilgrim, from continuing to Jerusalem as if to live near the shrine of St Martin dispensed him from going to seek Christ.[85] But Luther would have none of this. '"There is no other name under heaven given among men by which we must be saved" (Acts 4.12). Thus there is no analogy between Christ and James of Compostela. Therefore I reject James as an idol.'[86] Since he held that pilgrimages were 'organized on their behalf' i.e. on behalf of the saints who were regarded as effective intercessors, he had no time for such journeyings.[87] Nor indeed was he happy about images, although he had to admit that he was 'not bold enough' to advocate their destruction. In a sermon at Wittenberg on 1 March 1522 he had this to say:

> Now we must come to images, and concerning them also it is true that they are unnecessary, and we are free to have them or not, although it would be much better if we did not have them at all. I am not partial to them . . . We must not worship them.[88]

In entire keeping with this, Luther left out the invocations of the saints and the intercessions for the departed from his *Latin Litany Corrected* and his *Germany Litany*, both of 1529.[89] He also replaced references to Mary, for whom he had a profound respect, with the name of God. Instead of 'Virgin Mary be with us' in a hymn dating back to 1480, Luther's version of 1524 reads 'God the Father be with us'.[90]

That visitors to the shrines of saints or to the Holy Land could secure a reward in the form of indulgences was another cause for Luther's opposition. Indeed his 95 Theses of 1517, nailed to the Castle Church door of Wittenberg at noon on 31 October, were one prolonged attack on the sale of these pardons. It is true that pilgrimage is not specifically mentioned but that Luther considered it to be directly related to them is made plain in his *Explanations of the Ninety-Five Theses* that were published not quite a year later. With his customary directness Luther asserted:

> Since indulgences are voluntary, have not been commanded, and therefore have no merit, surely those who make pilgrimages only for the sake of indulgences merit nothing at all. Moreover, those people are to be justly ridiculed who neglect Christ and neighbour at home, in order to spend ten times as much money away from home without having any results and merit to show for it. Therefore he who would remain at home . . . would be doing far better – indeed he would be doing the only right thing – than if he were to bring home all the indulgences from Jerusalem and Rome.[91]

Only two years later, as *To the Christian Nobility* reveals, his attitude was hardening.

> All pilgrimages should be stopped. There is no good in them: no commandment enjoins them, no obedience attaches to them. Rather

do these pilgrimages give countless occasions to commit sin and to despise God's commandments.[92]

He followed this by listing many pilgrimage churches and saying that they 'should be leveled',[93] and also included in his rejection of existing practices and beliefs were masses for the dead and purgatory 'with its torments and satisfactions which let the dead neither sleep nor rest'.[94]

> We have removed from our churches and completely abolished the papish abominations, such as vigils, masses for the dead, purgatory, and all other hocus-pocus on behalf of the dead.[95]

This wholesale excision necessarily included pilgrimages because they had come to be so closely bound up with indulgences which were also deemed to have an effect on the condition of the deceased. In the case that Luther built up there were both cohesion and logic. While acknowledging that some few people, such as the patriarchs, may be required by God to become pilgrims, the journeyings of his day, he was convinced, were 'works' devised by men.[96] Consequently they were to be regarded as a means of seeking merit and so a denial of grace.[97] The practice was therefore in conflict with the doctrine of *sola gratia*;[98] justification is by faith not by pilgrimages.[99] 'The Spirit does not come through fasting, praying, pilgrimages, running to and fro through the country; no, only through faith.'[100] Salvation is indeed through Christ 'and not by means of visiting holy places;[101] pilgrimages do not procure eternal life.[102] Forgiveness of sins in fact is made available through baptism and the eucharist and nothing else, pilgrimage included, is needed.[103] Rather it is an outward show that turns the believer away from his true vocation.

> In former times saints made many pilgrimages to Rome, Jerusalem and Compostela in order to make satisfaction for sins. Now, however, we can go on true pilgrimages in faith, namely, when we diligently read the psalms, prophets, gospels and so on. Rather than walk about holy places we can thus pause at our own thoughts, examine our hearts and visit the real promised land and paradise of eternal life.[104]

At every turn Luther castigated pilgrimages, and to remarkable effect as Erasmus himself testified. In *A Pilgrimage for Religion's Sake*, he refers to St James of Compostela and remarks:

> This new-fangled notion that pervades the whole world results in his being greeted more seldom than usual. And if people do come, they

merely greet him; they make no offering at all, or only a very slight one, declaring it would be better to contribute money to the poor.[105]

Those who responded to Luther in this way understood his message to be a call to freedom. They were eager to be liberated from dependence upon works, merit-theology, pardons, pilgrimages and so on. Now, stimulated by him, they were ready to repudiate all these practices as idolatrous, magical or irrelevant, as pagan or, at best, semi-pagan. This corresponded to a 'shift from a religion that often went out of doors on pilgrimages and processions to an indoor one'.[106] The aural was displacing the visual; the Word was to be heard within the church building and had to be internalized within the hearts of the faithful – a view of Christian discipleship and spiritual endeavour previously promoted by many of the mediaeval divines that the Protestants were apt to scorn.

Calvin was at one with Luther in his attitude to pilgrimages. Among 'the faults contravening the Reformation', he listed the behaviour of those who have been 'on pilgrimages and voyages'.[107] In general, however, it was not a subject to which he returned with much frequency. His main centre of attack, which had of course implications for pilgrimages though they are not specified, was the cult of the saints. He would accept them neither as protectors nor intercessors; images he scorned and relics he ridiculed, considering the latter to present such an evil temptation that he published a treatise entirely devoted to them. In the *Catechism of the Church of Geneva*, he affirmed:

> If we throw ourselves on the protection of saints or angels, when God calls us to himself alone, and transfer to them part of that faith which ought to reside entirely in God alone, we fall into idolatry, since we share with them what God claimed for himself alone.[108]

In his reply to Sadolet, it was the usurpation of the role of Christ by saints, previously objected to by both Erasmus and Luther, that he had in his sights:

> Regarding the intercession of the saints . . . these innumerable superstitions were to be cut away, which had arisen to such heights, that the intercession of Christ was quite erased from men's thoughts; saints were invoked as gods; the offices peculiar to God were distributed among them; nor was there any difference between this worship paid to them and that ancient idolatry which we all rightly execrate.[109]

Veneration of images was in his view certainly to be described as idolatrous.

> When God is worshipped in images, when fictitious worship is instituted in his name, when supplication is made to the images of saints, and divine honours paid to dead mens' bones, and other similar things, we call them abominations as they are.[110]

This last passage comes from *The Necessity of Reforming the Church* in which he also ridiculed the honouring of relics, most of which he regarded as spurious,[111] and in the same year (1543) that that appeared he published his *Traité des reliques*. He was prepared to grant it proper to meditate on the lives of the saints in order to follow their good examples, but since devotion to their relics took the same form as devotion to God – prostration, kneeling, lighting torches and candles, seeking aid etc. – he believed it would lead inevitably to idolatry.[112] Moreover most relics, he held, were not genuine. He contended that some are demonstrably not what they are claimed to be and he cited an arm of St Anthony which examination showed to be the leg of a deer. He further argued that some are most unlikely to be authentic and he instanced the foreskin of Jesus removed at his circumcision. What is more, there are those whose identification must be wrong and he specifically considered the table of the Last Supper displayed in St John Lateran. In relation to this, he pointed out that the house where the supper was celebrated was a borrowed one and so the table would not have been removed nor is there any mention in the gospels of the apostles having taken it; moreover Jerusalem was later destroyed and, in any case, the shape of the table does not conform to those in use in Jesus' day.[113] His final contention was that the number of relics in existence was too great for all to be genuine and, among many examples, he enumerated fourteen nails in named churches throughout Europe, whereas only three were used at the crucifixion;[114] and he was able to record three bodies of Lazarus: one at Marseilles, another at Autun and a third at Avalon – some mediaeval pilgrims, it will be recalled, had similarly noted the multiplication of the same relics. Not surprisingly, Calvin regarded all acts of veneration of such objects as no more than pagan superstition.[115] Pilgrimages, therefore, to the shrines that housed them, were in vain.

The views of churchmen in England are less easy to disentangle, partly because of the vicissitudes of the Reformation in that country, now vigorously pressing forward, now in retreat, now on the march again. Even those who were convinced of the need for reform were uncertain how far to go – whether the removal of abuses was sufficient or whether something more radical was required. Royal injunctions and episcopal articles followed each other in rapid succession, sometimes contradicting one another in a way that must have been bewildering. But there was growing distaste for the veneration of relics, as in the case of the Dean of St Paul's, John Colet, who was the friend of Erasmus and his companion on the visits to Walsingham and Canterbury.

Colet had read Wyclif's works and as far as relics were concerned was 'less respectful towards this side of religion' than Erasmus liked.[116] Moreover according to Erasmus, when an arm with blood-stains upon it was produced at Canterbury, 'he shrunk from kissing this, looking rather disgusted'. Apparently Colet also suggested that the money given to the shrine and spent on treasures would be better given to the poor. On their way back to London, the Dean was sprinkled with water by some beggars and presented with what was claimed to be St Thomas' shoe; he thereupon demanded of Erasmus: 'What, do these brutes want us to kiss all good men's shoes? Why not, in the same fashion, hold out spittle and other excrements to be kissed?'[117] Yet as late as 1527 Thomas Bilney of Cambridge was to preach against images, relics and pilgrimages and be arrested for heresy; he recanted, but four years later, having returned to the attack, he was burned at the stake.[118] While in 1533 one Sir John Gifford obtained permission to go on a pilgrimage to Amiens[119] and only a year previously a Somerset gentleman named James Hadley had left money to twelve shrines 'in as much as I have been negligent to visit holy places and going on pilgrimages'.[120] However, with the suppression of the monasteries, prompted above all by Henry VIII's desire to replenish his coffers, the dislike, of which Colet was an early representative, was given free rein and in his injunctions of 1535 Thomas Cromwell instructed those whom he had appointed to visit these establishments as follows:

> Item, that the religious shall not show no relics or feigned miracles for increase of lucre; but that they exhort pilgrims and strangers to give that to the poor that they thought to offer to their images or relics.[121]

The voluminous correspondence that resulted demonstrated the extent to which these commissioners were opposed to all that in their eyes smacked of superstition or idolatry, in particular images and relics, and they sought to end all pilgrimages associated with them.

Whatever pecuniary motives the king may have had in authorizing their activities, it is clear that this was not a primary concern of the visitors. Thomas Wriothesley reports how he has removed many items from the shrine of St Swithin in Winchester cathedral, many of them of gold and silver, but he adds: 'We intend, both at Hyde and St Mary's, to sweep away all the rotten bones that be called relics; which we may not omit, lest it be thought we came more for the treasures than for the avoiding of the abomination of idolatry.'[122] The letters, in fact, dating in the main from August 1535 to October 1538, show how frequently they were scandalized by what they found and they seasoned their reports with acid comments. The claim that many of the relics on display were genuine seemed to them to surpass rational belief.

Dr Richard Layton to Cromwell from St Augustine's Abbey, Bristol:

I send you reliquaries; first, two flowers wrapped in white and black sarcenet that on Christmas Eve, in the hour in which Christ was born, will spring and burgeon and bear blossoms, which may be seen, saith the prior of Maiden Bradley; ye shall also receive a bag of relics, wherein ye shall see strange things, as shall appear by the scripture, as God's coat, our Lady's smock, part of God's supper on the Lord's table, part of the manger stone in which was born Jesus at Bethlehem; belike there is in Bethlehem plenty of stones and some quarry, and maketh their mangers of stone.[123]

John ap Rice to Cromwell concerning the Abbey of Bury St Edmunds:

Amongst the relics we found much vanity and superstition, as the coals that St Lawrence was toasted withal, the parings of St Edmund's nails, St Thomas of Canterbury's penknife and his boots, and divers skills for the headache.[124]

Bishop Ingworth of Dover, on his way from Shrewsbury to North Wales, writes that he now has in his possession 'Malchus's ear that Peter struck off as it is written and a 1000 as true as that'.[125]

Others relics were demonstrably not what they were claimed to be. The Holy Blood of Hayles attracted huge crowds in the Middle Ages; it had been presented to the convent in 1270 by Edward, Earl of Cornwall, no doubt in good faith, but when Hugh Latimer, Bishop of Worcester, examined it at Cromwell's behest, he had to report as follows:

Sir, we have been sifting the blood of Hayles all this forenoon. It was wondrously and craftily enclosed and stopped for taking of care. And it cleaves fast to the bottom of the little glass that it is in. And verily it seemed to be an unctuous gum, and a compound of many things. It hath a certain unctuous moistness, and though it seems somewhat like blood while it is in the glass, yet when any parcel of the same is taken out, it turneth to yellowness and is cleaving like glue[126] – the final verdict was that it was a liquid coloured with saffron.

Perhaps even more striking was the trickery that was brought to light, the most glaring example being the Rood of Grace at Boxley in Kent. Geoffrey Chamber described to Cromwell exactly what he had discovered:

In that image of the Rood called the Rood of Grace, the which heretofore hath been held in great veneration of people, certain engines and old wire were to be seen, with old rotten sticks in the back of the same, that did cause the eyes of the same to move and stare in the head thereof like unto a living thing; and also the nether lip is likewise to move as though it should speak.[127]

All Cromwell's officers were convinced that these objects promoted superstition and encouraged pilgrimages. Ellis Price indeed reported daily pilgrimages to the image of David Gatheren at St Asaph and he gave the figure of five to six hundred 'enticed to worship' upon one day alone (6 April 1538).[128] Bishop Barlow was speaking for all when he referred to 'devilish delusions' and 'feigned relics to allure people to superstition', and he issued his own injunctions to the effect that ignorant people were not to be encouraged to 'pilgrimage idolatry'.[129] A policy of removal and destruction was therefore initiated. Sir William Bassett impounded the ex-votos in Buxton and in Burton-upon-Trent, including crutches, shirts and sheets.[130] Similarly Dr John London defaced all the lights, shrouds, crutches and images of wax hanging about the chapel in the church of the Grey Friars in Reading and successfully recommended that the building be turned into the town hall.[131]

The final indignity meted out to the most important images was to put them on public display and then to destroy them. The image of David Gatheren was burned at Smithfield, while the Rood of Grace was first shown at Maidstone on market day and then taken to London where it was broken up and committed to the flames at St Paul's Cross on 24 February 1538, after an address by the Bishop of Rochester to declare its iniquity.[132] The following year on 24 November, the same bishop showed the blood of Hayles, again at St Paul's Cross, declaring how fraudulent it was.[133] There is no question that such a sustained campaign, so rigorously pressed home, was bound to have its effect on popular devotion.

To follow the steadily continuing campaign against the closely knit quaternity of relics, images, saints and pilgrimages would be tedious, especially as the many injunctions and articles often repeat each other verbatim. What is needed is a clear picture of what was being attacked and why as a basis for appreciating the case against a form of spiritual exercise that within Christianity was already nearly 1400 years old. Much of the case elaborated in England had been fashioned by Erasmus and further sharpened by Luther; indeed the influence of both of them is unquestionable if unacknowledged.

The case for and against relics was not long debated in England – the general atmosphere and the discoveries of Cromwell's men had fatally compromised these objects of devotion. Nevertheless, as late as 1541, 'The King's Letter for Taking away Shrines and Images' expressed concern that many relics had not been removed and so it ordered a search 'for those things, and if any shrine, covering of shrine, table, monument of miracles, or other pilgrimage do there continue, to cause it to be taken away'.[134]

The attitude to images was at first more favourable. There were many, including King Henry himself, who could see some value in them, while granting that they may have been misused in the past. The *Ten Articles* of 1536 declared that they 'were representors of virtue and good examples, that they also be by occasion the kindlers and stirrers of mens' hearts'.[135] To similar effect the *Bishops' Book* of 1537 referred to them as 'books for unlearned people', a description taken up in the more or less identical *King's Book* of 1543.[136] However both documents hasten to warn against abuse. People are not to pay honour to images and they should be mindful of the second commandment that forbids bowing down or worshipping them. Nor is one image to be preferred to another because none can accomplish anything.[137]

They also offend that so dote in this behalf that they make vows and go on pilgrimages even to the images, and there do call upon the same images for aid and help, phantasying that either the image will work the same, or else some other thing in the image, or God for the image's sake, as though God supernaturally wrought by images carved, engraven or painted, brought once into churches, as he doth work by other his creatures. In which things, if any person heretofore hath or yet doth offend, all good and learn'd men have great cause to lament such error and rudeness, and to put their studies and diligence for the reformation of the same.[138]

In any case, according to the *King's Book* from which this quotation derives, money spent on embellishing these figures would be better given to the poor who are 'the quick and living images of God' – a sound Wyclifite and Lutheran sentiment. Veneration too was declared illegal and accordingly the second *Royal Injunctions* of Henry VIII, in 1538, forbade candles, tapers or images of wax (i.e. ex-votos) being set before any image. Moreover the seventh injunction was to the effect that

> such feigned images as ye know of in any of your cures to be so abused with pilgrimages or offerings of anything made thereunto, ye shall, for avoiding that most detestable sin of idolatry, forthwith take down and delay.[139]

Shaxton's injunctions for Salisbury diocese expand on this since he banned not only candles but also oats, oat-cakes, cheese and wool.[140]

Not all images were specifically prohibited, although Cranmer himself would have been only too pleased to see them entirely rooted out. In conference with his cathedral clergy on Trinity Sunday, 1541, he was emphatic that *idolum* and *imago* are identical: 'They are all one,' he asserted.[141] Yet without exception all those were condemned who had been 'abused with pilgrimages, offerings or censings.'[142] However many survived into the reign of Edward VI, whose *Royal Articles* of 1547 extolled 'the true use of images'.[143] Nevertheless the tide was turning, as is evident by Hooper's injunctions for Gloucester and Winchester, 1551–2, which embraced both relics and images under the heading of idols.[144] Some nine years later Bencham's injunctions for Coventry and Lichfield (1561) spoke of even the 'stones or blocks whereupon images were set' as monuments of superstition.[145] Parker's articles for Winchester (1575) represent a mere sweeping-up operation, 'whether all images, altars, shrines, and other monuments of idolatry and superstition be utterly defaced and put out in your parishes'.[146] When the 'Homily Against Peril of Idolatry' came to be written, its author had no hesitation in affirming that images lead inevitably to idolatry and should be suppressed.

The saints received even shorter shrift and less attention than the images that represented them. Henry, in this particular like Luther despite his previous opposition to him, was convinced that 'all goodness, health and grace' are to be looked for from God and not from the saints. He allowed that they may be honoured but this does not mean that they can be given what belongs to God alone. Indeed the only proper form of devotion towards them is 'to laud and praise

Christ in them for their excellent virtues which he planted in them'. Yet whereas grace, remission of sins and indeed salvation can only be obtained from God, saints may be asked to act as intercessors.[147] This was in 1536 – the view was not to persist. In 1550 Ridley ordered invocations or prayers to the saints to be blotted out[148] and the following year Bulkeley repeated the same for the diocese of Bangor.[149] Hooper was in effect voicing the consensus of opinion when he said that

> the veneration, invocation and worshipping of saints or images, is contrary and injurious to the honour of Christ our only Mediator and Redeemer, also against the doctrine of the first and second commandments of God.[150]

This speedy demise of the cult of the saints within sixteenth century Anglicanism is only understandable in the light of the late mediaeval devaluation; this accelerated their repudiation so that, according to J. Huizinga, 'they fell without a blow being struck in their defence'.[151]

Although the unrelenting repudiation of relics, images and the veneration of the saints would have led logically and eventually to the rejection of the fourth of the quartet, i.e. of pilgrimages, they had in fact also been under attack from the earliest years of the English Reformation. On the afternoon of 9 June 1536, in a sermon before the Convocation of the clergy, Hugh Latimer denounced them as superstitious and without scriptural warrant.[152] Two years later Henry required all those who had extolled pilgrimages to make public retractions,[153] and Nicholas Shaxton ordered his diocesan clergy to denounce them.[154] The bishop further declared that Christians should not go on such journeys.[155] Some of the arguments deployed in condemnation are already familiar from their use against relics and images – e.g. the money should be spent on the poor.[156] Cranmer would have nothing to do with them because of their association with the invocation of the saints.[157] He was also of the view that they were evidence of false doctrine and superstition. 'Never had the Jews in their most blindness so many pilgrimages unto images, nor used so many kneelings, kissings, and censing of them, as hath been used in our time.'[158] He had no need to press his opinion; by 1559 one of the principal motives for going to holy places had been totally undermined by the 35th of the Queen's injunctions: 'that no person keep in their houses any abused images, tables, pictures, paintings, and other monuments of feigned miracles, pilgrimage, idolatry or superstition'.[159] In the same year Archbishop Parker issued a statement about some proposed articles of religion and asserted that he himself utterly disallowed 'wanderings on pilgrimages'.[160] From this it is evident what is implied in Article XXII of the Church of England, although pilgrimages are not specifically mentioned.

> The Romish Doctrine concerning Purgatory, Pardons, Worshipping and Adoration, as well of Images as of Relics, and also Invocation of Saints, is a fond thing, vainly invented, and grounded upon no warranty of Scripture, but rather repugnant to the Word of God.

Now the way was open for the full interiorization of the concept of pilgrimage and this was to attain its full flowering in Bunyan's *Pilgrim's Progress*, but long before him Hugh Latimer had followed the same path. In one of his sermons preached in Lincolnshire in 1552 he discoursed on what he called 'the Christian man's pilgrimage'. In effect this was a rhetorical device to present an exposition of the beatitudes, but he was quick to say at the outset:

> Ye shall not think that I will speak of the popish pilgrimages, which we were wont to use in times past, in running hither and thither to Mr John Shorn [whose shrine was near Gravesend] or to our Lady of Walsingham. No, no; I will not speak of such fooleries.[161]

Aspects of the Catholic Response

A Catholic rejoinder to the Protestant attack on the so-called 'popish pilgrimages' was not long in forthcoming; in fact in England it predated the actual Reformation by several years in the *Dialogue* of Sir Thomas More. More was well aware of the criticisms being advanced, because not only was he the friend of Erasmus and Colet but he was also conversant with the writings of Luther. The actual occasion of his entry into the fray was the circulation of copies of William Tyndale's New Testament which was printed in 1525. More had no objections to vernacular renderings of the scriptures, but he regarded Tyndale's version as Protestant, and indeed Lutheran, propaganda. The full title of his rejoinder, which was first published in 1528, reveals both its scope and intent: *A Dialogue of Sir Thomas More Knight: One of the council of our sovereign Lord the King, and Chancellor of his Duchy of Lancaster. Wherein be treated divers matters, as of the veneration and worship of images and relics, praying to saints, and going on pilgrimage. With many other things touching the pestilent sect of Luther and Tyndale by the one begone in Saxony, and by the other laboured to be brought into England.*

There are two parties to the discussion: the Messenger, who acts as the mouthpiece of Thomas Bilney, recently charged with heresy,[162] and voices criticisms of these devotions, and More himself, who seeks to defend them. It must be said that More is scrupulously fair to his opponent; the case put forward by the Messenger is a very powerful one and More comments on the vigour with which it is pressed;[163] here then is no straw man to be blown away with a mere puff.

Against relics, the Messenger, anticipating Calvin by some fifteen years, contends that many are not genuine: some have been shown to be nothing but sheeps' bones and the claims of more than one centre to house the body of the same saint at least mean that all but one must be fraudulent.[164]

More replies that existence of counterfeit relics does not mean that no relics are to be honoured, that souls suffer no harm if through no fault of their own they reverence ones that are not genuine and that the case for the falsity of most is not proven. As for there being more than one body, he very plausibly remarks that they are often unavailable for scrutiny and that upon examination the reliquaries might well contain only parts of one, other parts being housed elsewhere and equally described, though mistakenly, as 'bodies'. Nor is More above making the debating point that it is by no means impossible for there to have been several holy persons with the same name living in different countries with the likelihood of genuine confusion between them.[165] He also appeals to the miracles said to have been wrought through inanimate objects in the New Testament to show that relics may mediate spiritual power, viz. Jesus' garment touched by the woman with the issue of blood and the handkerchiefs that had been in contact with the body of Paul and were taken to the sick (Mark 6.56; Acts 19.12).[166]

As regards images, the Messenger feels himself on strong ground when he quotes Ex. 20.4: 'You shall not make for yourself a graven image.' He also regards it as clear evidence of idolatry that some pay the same devotions to images as to God and he holds that preference for one image above another – of, say, our Lady of Walsingham above our Lady of Ipswich – indicates trust in the image itself.[167]

More counters by saying that the commandment does not preclude each and every image since the Jerusalem Temple had sculptured figures of cherubim. Jesus himself sanctioned their use when, according to Eusebius of Caesarea, he sent his portrait to king Abgar and allowed his likeness to be preserved on the Vernicle. Images in fact are most useful in that they are 'but the laymens' books'.[168] The similarity in devotions to images and to God only applies to the outward gestures not to the inner intent. Just as bowing to a bishop or kissing his hand does not mean to worship him, so similar actions towards images do not identify what is done with that *latria* that is to be offered to God alone.[169] Quite as emphatically as any Protestant, More rejects the worship of images. No man is to fix 'his final intent in the image, but refer it further to the honour of the person that the image represents, since in such reverence done unto the image there is none withdrawn neither from God nor good man, but both the saint is honoured in his image and God in his saint'.[170] More would not allow the ascription of absolute credulity to every lay man and woman. When someone says they are going to the King's Head for wine, they do not mean they will be seeing an actual portion of the royal anatomy, but a sign.[171]

> The flock of Christ is not so foolish as those heretics bear in hand, that whereas there is no dog so made but he knoweth a very coney from a coney carved and painted, Christian people that have reason in their heads, and thereto the light of faith in their souls, should ween that the image of our Lady were our Lady herself [172]

As for preferring Walsingham to Ipswich, that is simply to recognize that God may perform more miracles in one place than in another.[173]

But to honour the saints, represented by the images – so the Messenger urges – could be said to detract from the honour due to God alone. As for invoking them, it is doubtful if (*i*) they can hear us; (*ii*) they can help us, especially as God himself is our best help, for, according to James 1.17, 'every good endowment and every perfect gift is from above, coming down from the Father of lights'. Further, while the schoolmen distinguished between *dulia, hyperdulia* and *latria*, in practice the *hyperdulia* of saints does not differ from the *latria* of God, viz. praying, kissing, offering incense and setting up candles.[174] In any case neither God nor the saints are in need of lights. Finally there is Matt. 23.29 to be borne in mind; in this verse Jesus calls down woe on the scribes and Pharisees who 'build the tombs of the prophets and adorn the monuments of the righteous'.

Blow by blow More seeks to demolish his opponent; honouring the saints is not dishonouring God any more than obeying the commandment and honouring one's parents; indeed the honour due to the saints 'redoundeth principally to the honour of their Master'.[175] The invocation of saints is defended on the grounds that, having immortal souls, they are alive and must therefore be able to hear us; they are consequently able to give assistance as they did while on earth, nor is it to be supposed that they are more restricted after death. In no sense does this make them rivals of God because they can do nothing of themselves, God being the ultimate source of all blessings.[176] More then deals with the possibility of confusing *hyperdulia* and *latria* in the same way as he did when speaking previously of devotions to images; as for the remark about candles, this is properly dismissed as mere facetiousness. The verse in Matthew has nothing to do with the propriety of erecting tombs; it is a condemnation of those who would kill Jesus as they slew the prophets while pretending to honour them with monuments.[177] That the discovery of the bodies of saints has frequently been the direct result of revelation shows the divine will that they should be honoured.

Step by step More has sought to remove the objections to pilgrimages but he still has further arguments to deploy. Granted that God is everywhere present, this does not mean that he is absent from the shrines to which pilgrims wend their way. However, if it were to be suggested that the divine omnipresence precludes going to any particular locality, this would result in non-attendance at one's parish church.[178] In fact, so More argues, God is especially to be sought in some places rather than others and this he has shown by performing miracles in specific localities. In other words, pilgrimage centres have been authenticated as places where God may be encountered – miracles demonstrate that God approves of pilgrimages[179] and this was an argument already advanced by Roger Dynmok in 1395. More would therefore have none of the repeated demand to divert money from shrines and travel to the poor. God is to be served with the best we can afford and certainly no expense was spared in constructing and enriching the Temple at Jerusalem in the divine honour.[180] Let those who object first dispose of the gold and silver objects they have about the house and even then the quantity of precious metal available to charity would be insufficient to relieve much suffering.

More, like Erasmus, was not blind to the misconduct often associated with pilgrimages[181] nor would he condone the substitution of idols for God, but he was equally sure that it would not be right that

all worship of saints and reverence of holy relics and honour of saints' images – by which good devout folk do much merit – we should abolish and put away because some folk do abuse it.[182]

His defence was a powerful one; some of his arguments are undeniably valid, although some are weak. It is not likely that he would have made much impression upon his opponents because he supported his appeal to reason with the assertion of the paramount authority of the church, while those, such as Tyndale, rested their case upon the Bible with an ultimate resort in individual judgment. This More found unacceptable; he was sure that the church could not be wrong:

> God will not suffer his whole Church to agree in any damnable error, and fall into a false faith . . . He would never suffer the Church to consent so fully in the worship of saints and reverence of relics if it were a thing, such as some men would have it seem, that is to wit damnable, false and feigned.[183]

Equally More refused to allow arguments from the Bible, as understood by Protestants, to sway him to the contrary because he held that 'the Church cannot misunderstand scripture'.[184] The heretics both misinterpreted it and misapplied it. Hence it was his abiding conviction that

> The Church in that it believeth saints to be prayed unto, relics and images to be worshipped, and pilgrimages to be visited and sought, is not deceived nor doth not err, but the belief of the Church is true therein.[185]

There were few of the calibre and consistency of More during the era of the English Reformation and to turn next to Stephen Gardiner is to present something of a contrast. Gardiner shared with More a concern for Catholicism but he combined this with anti-papalism. He supported Henry unfailingly, resisted the extreme Protestantism of Somerset in Edward VI's reign and then served as Lord Chancellor under Queen Mary when the allegiance to Rome was reaffirmed. He was sufficiently reformist to oppose indulgences, 'wherein,' he said, 'heaven is sold for a little money,'[186] but he defended the veneration of images which was one of the key factors promoting pilgrimages. In a tract, probably issued in 1544, he distinguished between worship on the one hand and godly honour or reverent behaviour on the other and he castigated extreme Protestants because 'they would have all teaching, they speak so much of preaching, so as all the gates of our senses and ways to man's understanding should be shut up, saving the ear alone.'[187] He took Ridley to task for his denunciation of images, declaring them to be perfectly acceptable – 'all the matter to be feared is excess in worshipping'.[188] When reports reached him of rioting in Portsmouth leading to the pulling down of images, he wrote to Edward Vaughan, captain of the town, on 3 May 1547, asking if a visit from him to deliver a sermon on the subject would be of any help;[189] he did go there but could find no evidence that images had been idolatrously used but much that they had been sacrilegiously treated.

Gardiner's middle-of-the-road policy did not commend him to everyone and on St Peter's Day 1548 he was required to preach on certain prescribed topics as a test of his support of the new Protestant orthodoxy. He declared that what is non-essential in religion may be either reformed or abolished and he included the veneration of images within this category. He further admitted that he had preached against the despisers of images and 'have said that images might be suffered and used in the church as laymen's books,' but now that they have been removed he did not think that the Christian faith had been adversely affected.[190] This was insufficiently advanced for the powers that be and he was consigned to the Tower, not to be released for five years, well before the Counter Reformation, as expressed through the Council of Trent, had turned to consider the subject.

At its twenty-fifth session, on 3 and 4 December 1563, the Council reviewed the invocation, veneration and relics of the saints together with sacred images – not raising, it will be noticed, directly the question of pilgrimages, although its pronouncements on these topics were bound to have an effect. The Council was somewhat reticent but was much concerned to stamp out abuses. 'Every superstition shall be removed, all filthy lucre be abolished'.[191] The remainder of the statement shows sensitivity to Protestant arguments together with great care to preserve what the bishops deemed to be of value in the practices.

There is, they said, need for right teaching on these subjects. They declared that it is good and useful to invoke the saints and seek their aid, but this is 'for obtaining benefits from God, through his Son, Jesus Christ our Lord, who is our alone redeemer and saviour'.[192] They repudiated the idea that this involves idolatry or that the practice 'is opposed to the honour of the one mediator of God and man, Christ Jesus'. They were prepared to affirm that the bodies of saints, having been temples of the Holy Spirit, were to be venerated and they condemned those who objected to this or to the honouring of relics. As for images of Christ, the Virgin and the saints, they affirmed that no divinity nor virtue is to be supposed to reside in them so that they should be worshipped. 'The honour which is shown them is referred to the prototypes which those images represent, so that kissing of images, the uncovering of the head and prostrating before them are ways to adore Christ.' Here are More's views given official backing; his use too of scripture found its way into the Catechism of the Council. This, usually called the Roman Catechism, which had been requested by the members at the 24th session, was completed by 1564 and published in 1566.

This Catechism affirms that the invocation of saints and the veneration of their relics serve to excite and confirm the hope of men and to encourage the imitation of the said saints. Relics, it is stated, have virtue as is evident from the miracles they have wrought. 'But why multiply proofs? If the clothes, the kerchiefs (Acts 19.12), if the shadows of the saints (Acts 5.15), before they departed life, banished disease and restored strength, who will have the hardihood to deny that God wonderfully works the same by the sacred ashes, bones, and other relics of the saints?'

The Catechism then comments on the commandment about not making graven images, admitting that there is a risk of idolatry and arguing that to counteract this a priest must instruct his flock that the honour and respect should be directed to the prototypes.

> He will also inform the illiterate, and those who are ignorant of the purpose of images, that they are intended to instruct in the history of both Testaments, and occasionally to renew the remembrance of those events which they record, that thus excited by the recollection of divine things, we may be the more intensely inflamed to adore and love God himself. He will also show that the images of the saints are placed in churches to be honoured, and also in order that, admonished by example, we may conform ourselves to their lives and virtues.[193]

Thus reassured, the Catholic faithful could continue to go on pilgrimages, as and when they felt ready and able to do so; their Protestant counterparts discontinued the practice.

3

The Death and Resurrection
of Protestant Pilgrimages

The Aftermath of the Reformation

Sixteenth-century Europeans were convinced that for the unity and well-being of any realm one form of religion only was to be allowed within its borders: *cujus regio, ejus religio*. To be an Englishman therefore meant to be a member of the Church of England and anyone of a different persuasion – a papist for example – was regarded as unpatriotic, a potential traitor and to that extent not a proper citizen. In those countries where allegiance to Rome was preserved local pilgrimages continued unabated, but where the Reformation had prevailed they came to an end. The wholesale destruction of relics and images, quite apart from the unrelenting attack on the practice of pilgrimage itself, meant that there was little point in going to the former shrines where they had been housed and had functioned as foci for devotion. Other centres which might have been retained intact outside one's homeland, such as Rome and Compostela, had little attraction for Protestants, although they continued to draw faithful Catholics (Fig. 14).

Not that Protestants were welcome. Fynes Moryson, who was in Rome in 1594, was not prepared to venerate relics and so studiously avoided them, because 'it is not safe for him to inquire after relics, who will not worship them'.[1] What the danger was is made plain by William Lithgow who was a visitor in 1603. According to him he 'hardly escaped from the hunting of those blood-sucking Inquisitors' and he only did so because a friend hid him for three days and he then scaled the wall in the middle of the night and set off for Naples.[2] Those who were unfortunate enough to be apprehended did not have a happy prospect before them. Such, for example, was John Mole,

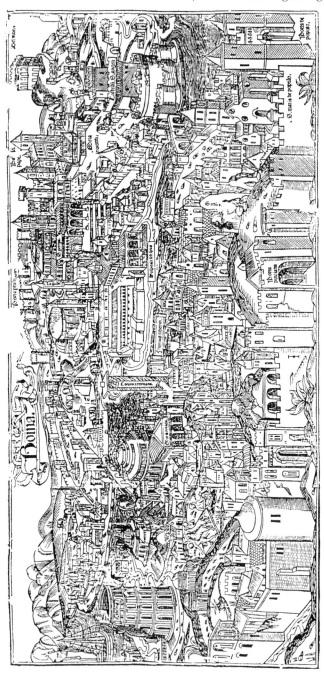

Fig. 14 Rome (from the Spanish edition of von Breydenbach)

tutor to Lord Roos, who died in the prison of the Inquisition in Rome in 1638 at the age of eighty after thirty years' imprisonment.[3] When this was their possible fate, travellers did not flock to St Peter's from Protestant countries and they were also discouraged by the rising cost of travel as well as by the fear of crossing the alps which was felt, even by some of the Catholics, to be a kind of purgatory preliminary to reaching the paradise of Italy.[4]

Sound Protestants, like Lewis Owen (1624), were delighted that not many were now making the journey. Indeed it is with obvious pleasure that he reports how 'very few Pilgrims, whether English or Welsh, resort to Rome', and he adds the explanation that it was because at the accession of Elizabeth 'it pleased God of his infinite goodness and mercy to disperse and scatter those thick clouds of ignorance and superstition that had a long time bedimmed the eyes and understanding of our forefathers'.[5]

Superstition was, of course, a frequent charge of the Reformers and it was often on the lips of their heirs as they witnessed the devotional practices at the several shrines. Anthony Munday (1582) is typical. He lists the seven principal basilicas at Rome to which all pilgrims went and then goes on:

> In all these churches there be divers relics which make them haunted of a marvellous multitude of people: whereby the lazy lurden friars that keep the churches get more riches than so many honest men should do. For either at the coming into the church, or else at the altar where the relics be, there standeth a basin, and the people cast money therein with very great liberality. And there standeth a friar with a forked stick in his hand, and thereupon he taketh everybody's beads that lays them on the altar, and then he wipes them along a great proportioned thing of crystal and gold, wherein are a number of rotten bones which they make the people credit to be the bones of saints; so wiping along the outside of this tabernacle, the beads steal a terrible deal of holiness out of those bones, and God knows, the people think they do God good service in it: O monstrous blindness![6]

In true Protestant fashion Munday pours scorn on these contact relics; he will have none of the *Agnus Deis* (wax medallions with the impress of a lamb) nor the *grana benedicta* (rosary beads) nor the girdles for women, all blessed by the pope.[7] In any case, according to his view, most relics are spurious, e.g. the 'above dozen nails' from the crucifixion on show when there could only have been three originally in use.[8] Munday therefore condemned a practice that meant that 'the worship which we ought of duty to give to God is bestowed on a rabble of rascal relics'.[9] Many Protestant travellers simply ignored them. John Sanderson was one such; he set out in 1584 and eventually included in his narrative an itinerary from Venice back to Dover; he listed days, distances and places but does not mention a single church *en route* let alone their contents.[10] Similarly, while his account of the Holy Land is detailed, with all the sites he visited named and the biblical events associated with them duly noted, there is no reference to sacred objects – he was a pilgrim, but not one motivated by a desire to venerate relics.

All these 'roamers' of the seventeenth century ring the changes on the same list of charges. What they see is 'horrible and indeed heathenish pomp . . . unimaginable superstition' – so the diarist John Evelyn who spent Holy Week in Rome in 1645. It is idolatry – so William Lithgow[11] – and the identical verdict is submitted by Lewis Owen when he describes how those at the English College are granted leave 'to visit some holy Image of our Lady, or some other Saint, and to mumble over their beads upon their knees before some wooden or stone god or goddess . . . They go to see a dumb Image, or some rotten bones; which they hold to be holy Reliques.'[12]

The least hint of possible idolatry made these travellers react violently, yet one of them, Fynes Moryson, does provide evidence of the concern of the church authorities to prohibit it. In 1594 he visited St Mark's, Venice, and read some verses written above the altar of St Clement:

> That which the Image shows, is God, itself is none,
> See this, but God here seen, in mind alone adore.

He remarks that these lines indicate how 'they worshipped images in a more modest though superstitious age'.[13] The relics on show, however, were usually deemed to be fraudulent – so Munday previously quoted – so also Lithgow who declared that in addition to the Vernicle exposed in Rome, a second could be seen at Palermo and a third in a town in Spain.[14] To Mortoft (1658) the claim that the bodies of Shadrach, Meshach and Abednego were preserved in St Adrian's is 'without doubt a grievous lie'.[15] Equally he questioned the footprint in St Sebastian's said to have been made by Christ when he met Peter fleeing the city and asked him *Quo vadis?* Mortoft comments: 'Whether this is true I know not, only it must be taken as a narration of papists, who will not spare some time to tell bouncers, especially if it may advance their Romish Church.'[16] He was ready too to speak satirically of certain pious practices. On 17 January 1659 he was in St Peter's for the feast of the apostle's 'pretended' chair and described how the people brought their beads into contact with it – 'I dare affirm truly there were more beads touched the side of the chair this day than could load a cart!'[17] In the same church there is the apostle's statue 'to which every person that comes in shows great reverence, and, very ridiculously, kiss his brass toe and put their heads under his foot, as a token that he and his successors, the popes, are heads of the church'.[18]

Indulgences too inevitably attracted the scorn of Protestants – Mortoft again:

> Whensoever the heads of Peter and Paul are shown in St John Lateran, there is a general pardon given for 3000 years to those people which are present; and to those who come out of far countries, and are present when they are shown, there is pardon for them for 12000 years, and the remission of the third part of their sins; and, if so, who will not come out of their countries to obtain so many years out of purgatory? but basta![19]

Hardly a century later, Samuel Pepys' nephew described in a letter to his uncle an audience with the pope whose right toe projected from under his robe, 'which we that would kissed on our knees, and, in return had indulgences granted ourselves and our friends for a 1000 years'.[20] It is true that John Jackson neither approves nor condemns the action but it is difficult not to suppose that a simple description by a staunch Protestant would be understood as anything other than a demonstration of its absurdity. Some, however, when compiling their narratives, were not content just to chronicle; they went out of their way to exhort their readers not to make the journey to Rome; their expectations would certainly be dashed,[21] and they would find themselves mingling with the dregs of humanity – 'the High-Dutch Pilgrims, when they bed, do sing; the Frenchmen whine and cry; the Spaniards curse, swear and blaspheme; and the Irish and English steal. Whereby you may see, what a credit or benefit it is for a man to be a Pilgrim.'[22]

Lewis Owen, from whom these views are derived, can describe the city in this fashion:

> *Equit mundi*; I would have said, *Caput omnium malorum*, the head and source of all evil. For what treason, villainy, or conspiracy was here ever invented or pretended in later times against this land by the devil, and his impious instruments, but hath been commended and ratified here *sub annulo Piscatoris*? under the Fisherman's signet? or, to say

the truth, *sub sigillo peccatoris*, under the Seal of that man of sin, II Thess. 2.3.[23]

Patriotism and Protestantism combine to make him almost splutter with righteous indignation. No wonder he had no time for pilgrim tokens, dismissing them as 'trash'.[24]

All whose accounts have been preserved were evidently of one mind. This is very clear from the impressions of those who visited Loreto. Mortoft thought that the claims that Mary's house had been transported thither from Palestine were 'great lyes and as foolish to be believed'.[25] Lithgow delivered himself of a diatribe on the iniquities of Mariolatry which derogates from the glory of God.[26] Moryson considered the sanctuary to be 'famous for men's superstitious worship . . . I abhorred it and hastened from it much as I might'.[27] This did not prevent his going inside for he was not so much a pilgrim in Italy as a curious traveller anxious not to miss anything of possible interest. Once within, he found some coins on the grating of an iron chest behind the altar; these he transferred quickly to his purse 'and got that clear gain by that idol. God forbid that I should brag of any contempt to religion; but . . . it appears that such worship is unpleasing to God.'[28]

Different people, whatever ideas they may have in common, react differently to the same situations. In Rome Lithgow would not observe the usual act of devotion at the *scala santa*. He and his companions 'slipped into the next church, and going in at one door, and out of the other, escaped the worshipping of those holy stairs, and at fit time came to take our horses with the rest'.[29] Mortoft, on the other hand, since he could not see the stairs without climbing them on his knees, did so and found it 'a great trouble . . . and so suffered for my curiosity'.[30] Here is no hint of devotion but then Mortoft and the others had not made the journey for religious motives; pilgrimage for them, at least to these shrines, was a dead concept. They were tourists, abroad to gaze and record for the delectation of others strange and fascinating things in distant places. Mortoft has no pretences in this respect. He has come to Rome because it is 'so much renowned for those rare antiquities that are here to be seen, more than in any other place . . . Here is to be seen those rare curiosities that no city in the world can afford the like.'[31] This did not prevent him from doing the rounds of the usual pilgrimage centres nor even from kissing the pope's foot and receiving a candle.[32] This was because he did not want to miss anything and his chief declared interests were to admire the paintings and statues and enjoy the music which he much appreciated. Owen, it will be recalled, actively sought to discourage anyone from following in his footsteps, and while Moryson did write for those who might come after him, his itinerary was not arranged for pilgrims but 'for the use of unexperienced travellers passing those ways'.[33]

Of the six Protestants who visited Rome between 1582 and 1658, whose writings have just been drawn upon to illustrate something of the post-Reformation attitude, two went on to the Holy Land where they then regarded themselves as pilgrims, viz. Moryson who reached there in 1596 and Lithgow seven years later. There had in fact been a steady falling off in numbers throughout the closing decades of the Middle Ages which continued into the post-Reformation era. This was in part due to the Turkish domination of the eastern Mediterranean but also to waning interest. So from 1581 to 1586 no pilgrim galleys left Venice, and after 1586 sailings were few and irregular.[34] Indeed when two German pilgrims arrived in Venice on 26 March 1625, they discovered that none of the ships that used to embark about Corpus Christi had done so for over twenty years.[35] However in 1603 Henry Timberlake and John Bunel(l) had noted in the Holy Sepulchre that

> even unto this day it is much resorted to, both by Pilgrims from all parts of the Romish Church, and by divers Gentlemen of the Reformed Churches; partly from curiosity and partly for the Antiquity of the place. It is farmed from the Turks, and kept by the Popes Creatures.[36]

Some idea of the numbers of these 'divers gentlemen' may be obtained from the report of fourteen Englishmen who went to Jerusalem from the factory in Aleppo in 1669. They discovered that the Franciscans kept a visitors' book and that from 1601 to the date of their arrival 158 pilgrims from their home country had been noted in it.[37] Over a century later, in 1784, M. C.-F. Volney was to record that Western pilgrims had been 'reduced to a few Italian, Spanish, and German monks, but the case is different with the Orientals'; there were in fact two thousand present, but even this represented a decline since 'formerly ten or twelve thousand annually made their pilgrimage'.[38] Yet there continued a steady trickle of Protestants. How did they understand their journey?

It is to be expected that Moryson and Lithgow at least would be consistent and not give an impression of their visit to Jerusalem that was markedly different from that of the Italian part of their journey.

Just as Moryson had avoided what to him were superstitious practices at the *scala santa*, so when he was locked in the Church of the Holy Sepulchre over night he pleaded bowel trouble and was allowed to lie undisturbed on a camp bed and did not become involved in any activity that might have offended his Protestant conscience. This, he cheerfully acknowledges, might perhaps be called 'honest dissembling',[39] but in Bethlehem he did accept a lighted candle to visit Jerome's grotto, remarking 'let them place what religion they will therein, I am sure the Cave was so dark, as we could not have passed it without a light'.[40] Lithgow, a more blunt character, did not hide his Protestant convictions but roundly informed the monks who gave him lodging that he was 'no Popish Catholic',[41] yet when he was requested by his hosts not to mock their devotions, he 'promised to give no occasion of offence, seeing our outward carriage in going along with them to their customs tended no way to hurt the inner dispositions of our souls'.[42] In similar vein John Bunel and Henry Timberlake were prepared to say the Lord's Prayer in the Church of the Ascension but would not repeat the five *Ave Marias* as instructed by the Franciscans.[43] In the Church of the Holy Sepulchre they were presented 'every one a Book of Holy Songs, for every place in Latin'[44] – probably copies of the mediaeval processionals[45] – but they do not say if they used them. Nevertheless when Bunel loudly declared he was not an Orthodox nor a Roman Catholic, because 'I would neither deny my Country nor Religion',[46] he was put in prison, while Sanderson was convinced that because of 'my disowning Papal superstition' the Franciscans fired some shots at him from a distance, and in any case they denied him access to the tomb itself.[47]

All these Protestants had a highly critical attitude towards what they were shown. Lithgow was typical when he doubted that a house he was taken to visit was actually that of Dives, since, as he pointed out, this rich man was not an historical person but a character in a parable.[48] In the Church of the Ascension he mused to himself: 'Who can think our Saviour trod so hard at his ascension as to have left the impression of his feet behind?'[49]

Lithgow saw himself as on a voyage of discovery of the biblical past. In Jerusalem his intention was to provide descriptions of what he saw, 'not much condemning, neither absolutely qualifying them, but shall (as it were) neutrally nominate, and recapitulate these places'.[50] Throughout the Holy Land his account is mainly historical and topographical: here Jesus turned water into wine, there Elijah ascended into heaven. Yet at Jacob's well he did have a drink 'for Jacob's sake',[51] and when he caught his first glimpse of Jerusalem he could not hide his emotions nor the extent to which he was stirred.

At last we beheld the prospect of Jerusalem, which was not only a contentment to my weary body, but also being ravished with a kind of unwonted rejoicing, the tears gushed from my eyes for too much joy. In this time the Armenians with whom we had joined began to sing in their own fashion Psalms to praise the Lord: and I also sang the 103 Psalm all the way, till we arrived near the walls of the City, where we ceased from our singing for fear of the Turks.[52]

Moryson was also emphatic that he was not going on a pilgrimage as understood by the mediaeval palmers or by contemporary Roman Catholics; neverthless he too had to confess that there was something special about it all:

I think it good to profess that by my journey to this City I had no thought to expiate any least sin of mine; much less did I hope to merit any less grace from God . . . Yet I thought no place more worthy to be viewed in the whole world than this City, where howsoever I gave all divine worship to God, and thought none to be given to the places, yet I confess that (through the grace of God) the very places struck me with a religious horror, and filled my mind prepared to devotion with holy motions.[53]

Both Moryson and Lithgow, although reticent about their own devotions and not mentioning a single prayer while in Italy, do indicate that they regarded that part of their journey that was in Palestine as in some sense a spiritual exercise. On board ship, Moryson noted that the Catholics prayed publicly in Latin and on some days celebrated mass and that he and his companions also prayed daily, but 'each man prayed privately after his own manner'[54] – the mediaeval trend towards the complete internalization of the spiritual life was here exemplified. Yet when Lithgow came to the Sepulchre with his friends, 'we prostrated ourselves in great humility, every man according to his religion offered up his prayers to God'.[55] Moryson, towards the end of his narrative, tenders this advice to those who would follow him to the holy city:

Let him daily commend himself to God's protection, and even in his journeyings, daily at morning and evening, not while he slumbers in his bed, but in private withdrawn from company, either kneeling as before his father or standing as before his Master and Lord, make his prayers, though never so short, to his almighty and most merciful God.[56]

Moryson dismissed as 'toys' the beads and crosses offered him in Jerusalem,[57] and Lithgow bathed where John baptized Jesus simply to wash and refresh his body,[58] but each in his own way was as devout as any of those who eagerly sought tokens or recalled their baptism as they swam the Jordan. This same balance between a restrained emotion wedded to an unquestionable devotion (but not one expressed in outward action) together with a deep interest in biblical history seems to have characterized all the Protestant 'travellers' of the post-Reformation era. George Sandys, seventh and youngest son of Edwin Archbishop of York is a case in point.

When, in 1610, Sandys and his party arrived at the door of the Holy Sepulchre, they were asked if they would like to have a conducted tour. Upon their agreeing, a further enquiry was made

> if devotion or curiosity had possessed us with that desire. So that for omitting *Pater nosters* and *Ave Marias* we lost many years indulgences, which every place doth plentifully afford to such as affect them, and contented ourselves with an historical relation.[59]

Indeed for Protestants the quest for indulgences was no more to be condoned in Jerusalem than it was in Rome. Henry Timberlake, who was there with his friend John Bunel in 1603, disagreed with their guide Father Tomasa on this issue. Apparently he was eager that they should visit as many places as possible and Timberlake's comment is:

> This is very Meritorious in the Roman church; and had we been of their Religion, it had been impossible to have missed Heaven; for we had received indulgences for all our Lives; which fancy I wist do not deceive too many.[60]

Timberlake and Sandys were sufficiently children of the Reformation to repudiate much of the mediaeval rationale of pilgrimage and the latter reported with some disfavour the kissing and kneeling that he witnessed as well as the rubbing with handkerchiefs of the place where the body of Jesus had been laid – handkerchiefs apparently to be taken home and used for burial purposes. Nevertheless upon reaching the actual tomb (Fig. 15), Sandys declared that there

> thousands of Christians perform their vows and offer their tears yearly, with all the expressions of sorrow, humility, and penitence. It is a frozen zeal that will not be warmed with the sight thereof. And O that I

Fig. 15 The Holy Sepulchre (from G. Sandys, *Relation of a Journey Begun An: Dom: 1610*, 3rd edn Allet 1632)

could retain the effects that it wrought, with an unfainting perseverance.

The verse that he was then inspired to dictate was later to provide hints to Milton for the seventh stanza of his 'Ode on the Passion' and it reveals Sandys' appreciation of the relationship between the past events of Christ's death and rising again (historical) to the present (moral) and to his own eventual destiny (eschatological).

> Saviour of mankind, Man Emmanuel:
> Who sinless died for sin, who vanquished hell:
> The first fruits of the grave. Whose life did give
> Light to our darkness: in whose death we live.
> O strengthen thou my faith, correct my will,
> That mine may thine obey: protect me still.
> So that the latter death may not devour
> My soul sealed with thy seal. So in the hour
> When thou, whose body sanctified this tomb,

Unjustly judged, a glorious judge shalt come
To judge the world with justice; by that sign
I may be known and entertained for thine.[61]

Sandys' unquestionable devotion was combined with scepticism about many of the claims of which he heard. So, for example, he refers to the fountain near Emmaus where Jesus was said to have had his feet washed by the two disciples on the first Easter Day, which water is said 'to retain a curable virtue against all diseases. But relations of that kind have credit only in places far distant.'[62]

Throughout the seventeenth century, and beyond, suspicion persisted about the pilgrimage concept and about practices thought to be superstitious, although this was combined with an attitude that can best be described as one of restrained devotion. In a letter from Jerusalem, penned in the year 1600, William Biddulph states that he and his company were

not moved as Pilgrims with any superstitious devotion to see Relics, or worship such places as they account holy; but as Travellers and Merchants, occasioned by Dearth and Sickness, Pestilence, and Famine in the City where we sojourn.

This, however, did not prevent his reporting joy on beholding Jerusalem nor describing how they sang psalms all the way to the city.[63] Indeed the first view of Zion scarcely ever failed to move believers of every denomination. According to Bunel:

Before Noon I had sight of the Holy City, and thereupon kneeling down and saying the Lord's Prayer, I gave God most hearty thanks for conducting me to behold with my eyes this Renowned Place . . . When I and my companions came within a furlong of the Gates, we went all along singing and praising God.[64]

Samuel Purchas, who included Biddulph's letter in his collection of pilgrim records, was himself in Jerusalem in 1625 and was severely critical of the motives of many going there. He quoted John 4.19ff.: 'The hour is coming when neither on this mountain nor in Jerusalem will you worship the Father . . . the true worshippers will worship the Father in spirit and truth.' His ensuing comment is as follows:

Although I deny not that a place dignified with holy actions or passions may be a place to the memory and affection exciting holiness, yet for Religion of place to leave or neglect our place and calling in Religion is superstitious; and to ascribe sanctity to the place is Jewish.[65]

Purchas railed against what he called 'Superstitious Pilgrimage' and naturally condemned the indulgences associated with them,[66] precisely as Fynes Moryson did before him. Moryson, when passing through Venice, had discovered that 'Papists think they must have the Pope's License to go on this journey . . . It may give some credulous men the hope of fuller indulgences or merit, surely it will serve them for no other use.'[67]

Old practices, however, died hard. When Sanderson was in peril of drowning in the Straits of Gibraltar, he had no scruple in making a vow that if he were preserved and arrived safely on the Algerian coast he would join with others in redeeming a captive.[68] He was prepared to inscribe his name on the wall of Lazarus' tomb at Bethany[69] as Bunel 'graved' his in the Church of the Nativity.[70] Many of them, while rejecting pilgrim badges, were ready to be tattooed as a sign of a completed pilgrimage.

Thomas Coryate, who passed through Jerusalem on his way to India in 1614, had the city arms on his left wrist and on his right a cross (Fig. 16) with the words *Via, Veritas, Vita* around it. Coryate was wont to display these signs with some pride and to quote Gal. 6.17: 'I bear on my body the marks of the Lord Jesus.'[71] The employees from Aleppo provide the additional information that a representation of the Sepulchre was also on offer[72] and Henry Maundrell (1697) refers to the 'usual ensigns of Jerusalem' and gives an interesting description of the process.

> The artists who undertake the operation do it in this manner. They have stamps in wood of any figure that you desire, which they first print off upon your arm with powder of charcoal; then, taking two very fine needles tied close together, and dipping them often, like a pen, in certain ink, compounded, as I was informed, of gunpowder and ox-gall, they make with them small punctures all along the lines of the figures which they have printed, and then, washing the part in wine, conclude the work. These punctures they made with great quickness and dexterity, and with scarce any smart, seldom piercing so deep as to draw blood.[73]

Devotional practices also had some continuity. Writing to his mother in 1614 Thomas Coryate told how 'before the Holy Sepulchre at Jerusalem, I have poured forth my ardent Orisons for you to the most sacrosanct Trinity, beseeching it with all humility of heart to bless and prefer you in a solid health'.[74] He even discloses to her that he 'visited and kissed three or four times' the sacred tomb.[75] But in general there is reticence about spiritual exercises which these Protestants clearly

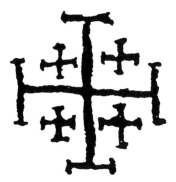

Fig. 16 The tattooed cross
(from J. Sanderson, *Travels
1584–1602*, f. 127a)

regarded as matters of private concern. Hence John Sanderson accepted the jibe at Bethlehem that he was no Christian because he would not sign himself before the icons nor make any reverences[76] and he seldom refers to his own acts of piety, although on the summit of the Mount of Olives he does acknowledge that 'I prostrately prayed, in which I yet am comforted. Let the eternal God be ever glorified in Jesus Christ, my Saviour and Redeemer'.[77] In Gethsemane he simply remarks: 'Here I prayed.'[78] The spiritual concern implied by these simple phrases is no whit less than that of the most devout Roman Catholic, but fear of appearing to be idolatrous or of condoning superstition or of seeking to win divine favour by good works – all these have combined to create a devotional practice that is very different from the norm of the Middle Ages.

According to Reformation piety the Word of God requires words, not outward acts, and words preferably uttered in seclusion – 'When you pray, you must not be like the hypocrites; for they love to stand and pray in the synagogues and at the street corners, that they may be seen by men . . . But when you pray, go into your room and shut the door and pray to your Father who is in secret' (Matt. 6.5f.).

However, the rediscovery of the Bible through vernacular translations had created a new and intense interest in the meaning of its various books. To go to Palestine was to have an opportunity to recover this biblical past, to enable it to come alive, which is what motivated Origen and so many others in the early days of Christian pilgrimage. Henry Maundrell, chaplain of the English factory at Aleppo, wrote an account of what he termed his *pilgrimage* to his patron the Bishop of Rochester at Easter 1697. On the 24 March, near Mount Gerizim, he sought out the chief priest of the Samaritans, as advised to do by a scholar in Frankfurt, and asked his help in relation to 'difficulties occurring in the Pentateuch'.[79] Or again, crossing the Brook Kishon and then encamping, 'we were sufficiently instructed by experience what the holy psalmist means by the dew of Hermon, our tents being as wet with it as if it had rained all night'.[80] But he too would have nothing to do with what he regarded as superstition and so he described with obvious disapproval what he had seen in a church at Bellulca:

> The whole room was hung with bags of silkworms' eggs, to the end that, by remaining in so holy a place, they might attract a benediction, and a virtue of increasing.[81]

Despite this and many another example that Protestants abhorred, Palestine did not cease to exercise a powerful attraction, whereas local shrines became, as it were, out of bounds. Indeed strictly speaking they had ceased to be shrines since they no longer housed sacred objects. Governments in Protestant countries kept a watchful eye to prevent any renewal of previous practices. Thus in 1632 the Privy Council in London acted to suppress pilgrimages to Lough Derg in Donegal, but in the second year of Queen Anne they had to be prohibited yet again and reference was made to 'the superstition of Popery . . . the pretended sanctity of places . . . All such meetings and assemblies shall be deemed and adjudged Riots and unlawful Assemblies'.[82]

However, continued Protestant condemnation was particularly aimed at the observance of Holy Years (Fig. 17). As far back as the one proclaimed by Clement VII for 1525 a set of satirical verses had had a wide circulation in Germany. The first stanza, which contrasts the papal Jubilee – costly and only obtainable at Rome – with Christ's Jubilee, or act of liberation, given freely everywhere to all who repent – is translated by Herbert Thurston as follows:

> This booklet tells, 'tis plain to see,
> How men keep twofold Jubilee;
> The one is that of Christ our Lord,
> The other what the popes accord.
> Who wisely reads this book at home
> Will not for pardon run to Rome.[83]

Fifty years later, at the Jubilee of 1575 under Gregory XIII, according to Zerola, 'very few Englishmen and hardly any Scotch, Saxons, Bohemians, Frenchmen and Germans came to Rome to profit by this time of spiritual gain'. He was writing in 1600 and went on to express the view that it was likely 'that there will be extremely few in the present year'.[84]

Fig. 17 Holy Year. The Jubilee Medal of Clement VIII. One side depicts the beginning of the celebration and the other the walling up of the Holy Door at the end

In 1675 broadsides attacking such Jubilees were circulating in England, one of which had the subtitle: *The Catholicks Encouragement for the Entertainment of Popery*. It contained 'an account of an eminent Mart or Fair, which is to be kept by his Holiness, where all sorts of Indulgences, Pardons, Remissions, Relicks, Trash and Trumperies are to be exposed to sale, and may be had for ready money at any time of the day; with the usual ceremonies thereunto appertaining'.[85] But none of this pamphlet skirmishing could deter the faithful.

The Continuity of Roman Catholic and Eastern Orthodox Pilgrimages

The Reformers could say and do what they liked about pilgrimages, but neither Roman Catholic nor Eastern Orthodox Christians could see any reason for discontinuing an age old devotional exercise. Hence while the story in Protestant countries is of a progressive decline in religious journeys, elsewhere there is little evidence of any break in the practice or of the ways in which it was understood.

(a) Roman Catholic Pilgrims

At the very time when Luther was mounting his attack, Ignatius Loyola, the founder of the Jesuits, was visiting the Holy Land. His intended departure from Spain in 1522 was delayed for nearly a year which he spent at Manresa and there completed the general structure of his *Spiritual Exercises*. The notes for these he took with him when eventually he sailed from Venice and his experiences undoubtedly influenced his final version which was completed in 1535. In his autobiography, where he refers to himself in the third person, he was reticent, e.g. 'On beholding Jerusalem, Ignatius was deeply affected, and the rest affirmed that they experienced a sort of heavenly joy.'[86] But the method he devised for meditation or contemplation rested upon an imaginative recreation through 'the five senses of the body' of the incidents recorded in the scriptures so that the one making the exercise feels that he or she is an actual participant in the scenes as they happened in Palestine.[87]

> The first point is to see the persons in my imagination, contemplating and meditating in detail the circumstances surrounding them . . . The second point is to hear what they are saying . . . The third point is to smell and taste in my imagination the infinite fragrance and sweetness of the Divinity . . . The fourth point is to use in imagination the sense of touch, for example, by embracing and kissing the place where the persons walk or sit, always endeavouring to draw some spiritual fruit from this.[88]

In the line of the Stations of the Cross, Loyola was seeking to help those who were unable to go on a pilgrimage to savour what it could be like and what spiritual benefit might be derived from it; at the same time he inevitably encouraged a desire to go in person rather than to spend time recreating the locations in the imagination.

Not that without such encouragement people would fail to take the staff. In 1532, in the midst of the furore initiated by Martin Luther, Denis Possot and his friends set off 'moved by good devotion to go and both to see and visit the Holy Sepulchre in Jerusalem and other holy places where our Saviour and Redeemer Jesus Christ suffered death and passion'.[89]

Seven years previously, pilgrimage to Rome had been fostered by one of the now regularly observed Holy Years or Jubilees. The attendance was impressive despite the pestilence raging in the city and the war that was in evidence almost everywhere in Europe.[90] This great opportunity to venerate the tombs of the apostles and at the same time to earn indulgences continued to draw pilgrims. In 1575, under Gregory XIII, the Venetian ambassador reported no fewer than 100,000 every day.[91] By 1600 contemporaries were estimating that 3 million came to Rome over the whole year, with never fewer than 200,000 on any single day,[92] while Evelyn the diarist was informed that during that year 444,000 men and 25,000 women were registered at the

Hospice of the Holy Trinity[93] – this had been founded in 1362 for English pilgrims, had diminished in importance after the Reformation and was reconstituted as the English College in 1579.[94]

Yet the Holy Land itself was not the destination for great numbers, despite the example of Ignatius Loyola. Notices of individuals, however, are not lacking; such a one was Deshayes whom Louis XIII sent there in 1621.[95] More influential was de Thévenot who arrived in Palestine in 1656 and recounted his travels in a work published in Paris nine years later, an English translation appearing in London in 1687.[96] De Thévenot deliberately affected a dry descriptive style, but he could not avoid vivid touches as when he reported that at their reception in the Convent of St Saviour they had their feet washed in warm water by the monks and that tattoo marks, to prove that they had visited the holy city, were made on their arms by wooden moulds with varying designs.[97] Much was as it had been in the Middle Ages; in the Holy Sepulchre each monk had a wax taper and a book containing 'proper prayers for each station' (i.e. Felix Fabri's processionals).[98] On Good Friday a very dramatic ceremony was enacted with two monks playing the roles of the women visiting the tomb. 'One carries a Box of Aromaticks, and the other a Bottle of odiferous Oyl.' They go to the stone of unction bearing a crucifix wrapped in a winding sheet; there the crucifix is taken out, placed on the slab and anointed before being borne to the sepulchre and laid to rest.[99]

Dramatic representations of this kind were not uncommon, one having been witnessed earlier in the century by two Protestant pilgrims, Henry Timberlake and John Bunel, who were present on Whitsunday, 1603, in the chapel on Mount Sion. When Acts 2 was read

> a Father on the terrace was appointed to throw down a white Pidgeon drest up with Ribbons in imitation of the Holy Ghost, but he met with some difficulty; for the Window was so fast shut that he could not open it a great while, so that we had like to have gone away without their Holy Ghost: but this difficulty overcome, he made the Dove descend among us.[100]

Towards the close of the Middle Ages, as previously noted, there had been a decline in Holy Land pilgrims, and this continued as a consequence both of the Reformation and the Wars of Religion. The Counter Reformation provided some fresh stimulus and by the eighteenth century the numbers were on the increase. Local shrines too were beginning to exercise their old attraction; Compostela, in particular, was one of these, although with the invasion of Spain by

Napoleon it almost ceased to function, only to be revived on a smaller scale in the present century.

, If Napoleon's Peninsula campaigns had an adverse effect, his expedition to the Middle East and especially to the Holy Land in 1799 revealed to French Catholics a possibility they had been in danger of forgetting. Seven years later Chateaubriand set out and his *Itinéraire de Paris à Jérusalem* became a best seller and awoke an echo in many hearts. In the preface to the 1827 edition, he remarked that after an anti-religious century even the memory of the birthplace of Christianity had been lost and so it had been his intention to open the way to the Holy Land; he was glad to report that since he had first published his itinerary many had followed in his tracks.[101] His account is a scholarly one, listing his predecessors, including de Thévenot, and discussing the genuineness of the sites, but he does not omit reference to contemporary devotional practices and to his own reactions.

At the Holy Sepulchre Chateaubriand remained kneeling for half an hour with his gaze riveted on the stone, while a monk lay prostrate with head on the marble. A second monk read passages from the gospels relating to the tomb and between the verses he recited a prayer:

> Lord Jesus Christ, who at the evening hour of day was taken down from the cross, and lay in the arms of your most sweet Mother, and at the last hour on this most holy monument your body *ex anime contulisti*, etc.

Chateaubriand does not complete the prayer but continues by describing his own feelings.

> All that I can with certainty recall is that when beholding this triumphant sepulchre I could feel nothing but my own weakness; and when my guide cries out with Paul: O death where is your victory? O death where is your sting? I listened as if death would reply that it was vanquished and chained within this monument.[102]

One of those who did follow Chateaubriand was Léon de Laborde who, in 1830, provided evidence of the continuation of another devotional practice in that pilgrims were still eagerly seeking tokens. He reported how bags of shells were imported from Suez and had engravings or low reliefs of the Sepulchre depicted upon them – these were then made into chaplets which were sold in great quantities.[103] An equal interest in relics was manifested by Alphonse de Lamartine who diligently collected pebbles along the bank of the Jordan and filled his pistol holsters with them.[104] Lamartine's mother had instilled into him from his earliest childhood a great love of the Bible and, as he himself says at the beginning of his narrative, 'from the love of the things themselves, to the desire of seeing the places where these things had occurred, there was but a step'.[105] Regarding his journey as a pilgrimage, he included in his account many references to prayers and meditations. Indeed he states: 'My journey became often one continual prayer.'[106] At the Sepulchre he describes how he prayed.

> With moistened eyes, a heaving breast, a prostrate forehead and lips glued in silence to the stone, for my father here below, for my mother in another world, for all those who live or are no more, but our invisible link with whom is never dissolved; the communion of love always exists; the names of all the beings I have known and loved, or by whom I have been beloved, passed my lips. I prayed last for myself, but ardently and devoutly.[107]

A like ardour is evident in the case of Isabel Burton, herself a Roman Catholic, who was there in 1871. Time and again, in *The Inner Life of Syria, Palestine, and the Holy Land*, she speaks of her tears, her prayers and her meditations.[108] She was determined 'to go over the Bible lands with the Bible'.[109] Her intention, she reports, is 'to follow my redeemer . . . to instruct myself, as well as I am able, at the fountainhead, with the Book in my hand, and to draw therefrom strength and grace . . . I ask for no vision or extraordinary thing, but I would realize in a sensible manner the invisible presence of my Saviour.'[110]

Her account, at times moving, echoes unconsciously that of Felix Fabri. As he did, she in her turn touches the holy places with numerous objects and, like him, she buys many contact-relics for her friends and relations, viz.

> glass necklaces, bracelets, bangles, and rings like old Venetian, mother-of-pearl mirrors, crosses, large crucifixes, trays, and shells representing holy subjects, and all sorts of objects carved out of olive wood from the Mount of Olives; large crosses, rosaries, crowns of thorns, and coffee cups of bitumen from the Jordan valley, and other things too numerous to mention. On Good Friday I carried them in trays, and had them laid upon the Sepulchre. I asked, and obtained, that a mass should be said over them, as they lay on the grave, and at *Ecce homo*, on the precious slabs of stone where our blessed Saviour's blood had fallen. At Calvary they were laid on the hill of the cross itself. They were blessed by the Latin Patriarch, Monsignor Valerga,

and by Père Maria Alphonse Ratisbonne, with all possible indulgences.[111]

Isabel Burton was not one of a large company of Roman Catholics; the many whom she mentions pouring in from all points of the compass were in the main Eastern Orthodox and Coptic, for although pilgrimages to the Holy Land were increasing among those in allegiance to Rome, it was the local shrines that exercised the most drawing power. Indeed while the Protestants had destroyed them, the Catholics were adding to their number, either by restoring the old or recognizing new ones. In 1858, for example, Bernadette Soubirous had visions of the Virgin and immediately Lourdes became a centre of attraction; its popularity might be attacked by an Emile Zola (1894) or by a J. K. Huysmans (1906) but the annual count of pilgrims was to reach two million. Pilgrimages to Walsingham by Roman Catholics restarted. They went to the Slipper Chapel where the mediaeval travellers had removed their shoes before proceeding barefoot to the principal church where the figure of the Madonna was to be venerated.[112]

In 1917 further Marial visions were experienced at Fatima in Portugal and more than a million were present when Pius XII chose that venue for the solemn closing of the Holy Year in 1951. Not that indulgences were restricted to Jubilees; nearly a hundred years previously a report in *The Guardian* of 5 September 1860, described the exhibition of relics in Rome throughout Lent and how indulgences for the traditional seven-year period were granted to those who visited the main basilicas.[113] Earlier still Lithgow observed the continuing pentitential aspect of pilgrimages when he met two gentlemen from Rome on the way to Loreto; they informed him they were going thither 'for devotion sake and for the penance enjoined to them by their father confessor'.[114]

This devotion has continued to be stimulated right up to the present day by a series of Marial visions, each location naturally becoming a pilgrimage centre. Amongst the many sightings is the one associated with the Three Fountains in Rome (1947), that in Nicaragua (1980) and from 1981 onwards at the mountain village of Medjugorje in Yugoslavia. The resulting increase in devotion to the Virgin recalls the mediaeval piety that was so strongly objected to by the Reformers.

Other motives, previously chronicled in connexion with the Middle Ages, continued and continue to operate. There is, for example, an annual pilgrimage on 6 August to Bom Jesus da Lapa in north-east Brazil. In general those who go there do so from a sense of obligation to fulfil a 'contract' made with the saint; they are making payment for an answered prayer. Consequently, as of old, they present offerings – ex-votos in the shape of wax effigies of parts of the body healed, crutches, even X-ray plates, and they buy pilgrims' tokens.[115] At Lourdes, on the other hand, the visit is not *post factum* but to seek healing and similarly at Fatima favours are sought exactly as in mediaeval times. Relics are still in eager demand; even new ones are being brought to light – in the course of the seventeenth century, for example, Cologne was proud to claim that it had discovered a piece of the cloak that Elijah threw down to his disciple as he went up into heaven in a fiery chariot.[116] Continuity, not excluding the repetition of some mediaeval practices that might be questioned, is undeniable, and the same can be said of Eastern Orthodox believers.

(b) *Eastern Orthodox Pilgrims*

From the earliest days of the introduction of Christianity into Russia, pilgrimages to local shrines were a normal feature of religious life, exactly as in western Europe, nor did they cease throughout the centuries until the 1918 Revolution, and at Kiev they only came to an end in 1922. It was, for example, the custom of the Muscovite Tsars to go twice a year to the monastery of the Trinity St Sergius; first, in the spring, in honour of the Godhead and then in the autumn to celebrate the saint's feast day on 25 September. This tradition was still being observed in the eighteenth century by the empresses Anna, Elizabeth and Catherine II, while the hostelry, which was built in 1892 to accommodate five thousand pilgrims at any one time, was always full. Possibly the most important centre, and the one that persisted the longest, was Kiev and the nearby monastery of Petchersk with its many relics, visited annually in the 1860s by some two hundred thousand people. At the same period the monastery of Solovki on the White Sea drew each summer between ten and fifteen thousand pilgrims, while that of Valaam on Lake Ladoga attracted five thousand visitors on the feast day of its founders Sergius and German. People from the East were accustomed to going to Sarov in honour of St Seraphim and several hundred thousand gathered there in 1903 when he was canonized.[117]

There were even perpetual pilgrims recalling those Irish monks who travelled with the express purpose of passing their lives in a condition of exile.[118] However, their Russian counterparts tended to engage in this for nine months in each year to collect gifts for the holy places in Palestine and then spent the remaining quarter going to and from the Holy Land.[119]

Pilgrimages then were by no means confined to local shrines. Beyond the borders of their country, Russian Orthodox Christians would go to Mount Athos, to Bari to venerate St Nicholas and even to Rome. Yet Jerusalem was their principal goal, with a prolonged stop at Constantinople on the way; Greeks as well as Russians, Armenians as well as Copts headed for the holy city. The numbers were remarkably constant. In the year 1600 William Biddulph recorded falling in with some four to five hundred Greeks and Armenians near Damascus[120] and in that year too Samuel Purchas encountered there a group of the same size.[121] Twelve years later Lithgow travelled from the same city with nine hundred of them.[122] When the several parties eventually joined up in Jerusalem itself, the crush was immense as Thomas Coryate witnessed during August 1614 in the Holy Sepulchre where he estimated there were two thousand present.[123] Later in the same century de Thévenot (1656) saw 'many' Armenians, Copts and Greeks by the river Jordan collecting mud, earth, sticks and water in bottles 'all to be kept as relics'.[124] Sinai, although less accessible, continued to receive pilgrims and when J. L. Burckhardt reached there in 1816 he was shown a document over a hundred years old which recorded the arrival on a single day of eight hundred Armenians from Jerusalem and another that referred to the coming of five hundred Copts from Cairo.[125]

Information concerning Palestine is consistent over the centuries, so in 1834 Robert Curzon estimated that seventeen thousand pilgrims, mainly though not exclusively Orthodox, were in Jerusalem for Easter Day.[126] In 1839 the painter David Roberts joined a party of four thousand 'Eastern Christians' who were leaving Jerusalem for Jericho and the Jordan.[127] In 1853 A. P. Stanley referred to 'huge masses' on Easter Eve,[128] while another outstanding water colourist, Edward Lear, taking the steamer from Alexandria to Jaffa five years later, found it crammed and Jerusalem itself so congested that, abhorring crowds, he stayed only one day intending to return at a less popular time of the year, only to find in 1867 the same great numbers.[129]

Shortly after the midpoint of the nineteenth century, in 1859, the Russian authorities decided to introduce some organization into their pilgrimages. The Grand Duke Constantine Nikolaevitch travelled to Jerusalem to assess the situation and induced the imperial treasury to make a grant for the purchase of land just outside the walls; there the new Trinity cathedral was opened in 1864 – gatherings of pilgrims up to two thousand at any one time now became the norm and by 1876 E. M. de Vogüé could report that annually three to four thousand Russians were visiting the holy places.[130] Hence in 1881 the Grand Duke Sergey Alexandrovitch paid a visit and the result of this was the establishment of the Imperial Orthodox Palestine Society which built a great hostelry to be opened in 1889.[131] When Stephen Graham travelled there in 1913 he was able to report that nine thousand Russians were participating in the Easter festivities.[132]

The journey, the dangers, the motives, the reception, the devotional practices – all these differed little from what had obtained a millennium before. En route the pilgrims took every opportunity to' visit shrines where relics could be venerated and ikons kissed. Hazards had repeatedly to be faced; in March 1893 nearly eight hundred Orothodox were returning from Nazareth to Jerusalem when they were trapped in a rain storm that continued for days and then turned to snow; many died and had to be buried where they expired.[133] Others caught in a tempest off Mersina near Tarsus did exactly as their mediaeval forcrunncrs, i.c. thcy vowed to present an ikon to St Nicholas the Wonderworker if he would preserve them, and a collection was immediately taken up for this purpose.[134] Motives for going on a pilgrimage included, as in former times, vows made before setting out e.g. by the young man whom Stephen Graham met: he had fallen ill and promised to visit the Holy Sepulchre should he be spared.[135] Greek Orthodox Christians, possibly influenced by the West, still offer their *tamata* (from *tasso*, I vow) both in anticipation of and in thanks for blessings, e.g. those with eye complaints present ex-votos depicting the affected parts (Pl. V). The arrival at one's destination was an opportunity for great thanksgiving as well as for learning firsthand more about each sacred site. In the twentieth century this information is imparted in Jerusalem not only by means of an address, as formerly delivered by the Father Guardian of Mount Sion, but also by the showing of lantern slides.[136]

The procuring of relics was a concern of all. Many regarded the pilgrimage as a means of preparing for death in the hope of resurrection. Wearing on their linen packs hand-embroidered crosses, like the mediaeval palmers, they had more crosses blessed in Jerusalem to wear around their necks when eventually they were laid

Plate V A modern Greek ex-voto

in their graves; they collected earth to be placed in their coffins; they had their arms tattooed with the word 'Jerusalem' in order that, so marked, they might rise at the last day. They cut out linen pieces in the shape of the stone of unction and placed these, together with the shrouds they had transported in their luggage, on the stone itself to secure a blessing, feeling that in so doing they were performing the same action as did Joseph of Arimathea for the body of Jesus.[137]

This idea of re-enactment through liturgical action, previously noted, was evident also when the pilgrims came to the place where the feeding of the five thousand was believed to have occurred. There they were told 'to sit down by companies' (Mark 6.39); next they scattered fragments of bread brought from Jerusalem, and after this 'they took up . . . broken pieces' (Mark 6.43). Similarly at Jordan, in the presence of fifteen thousand, an Orthodox priest consecrated the water, whereupon the faithful plunged in wearing their burial shrouds and singing: 'They baptized thee in Jordan, O Lord'.[138] These same pilgrims greeted one another daily with the words: 'Let us go and kiss the grave'[139] and, like their compatriot Abbot Daniel, who came there in 1106, they had brought with them their intercession lists.[140]

Before leaving, summarizes Pierre Pascal, the pilgrim has to fulfil his promises:

he purchases and lights candles, transacts the orders for commemoration for the living and the dead, brings blessed bread home, buys small crosses, painted or printed pictures, booklets, rosaries, everything he has been asked for. Finally he takes 'the blessing' of the monasteries which means a slice of bread for the road . . . On their return the pilgrims proceeded to distribute the blessed bread and souvenirs . . . Then the pilgrims spoke before an eager and admiring audience telling them wonderful stories about all they had seen and heard.[141]

The Attraction of the Holy Land to Protestants in the Nineteenth Century

Meantime, what of the Protestants? There were of course still those who from time to time undertook the journey to Palestine; one such was William G. Browne who published in 1799 his *Travels in Africa, Egypt, and Syria, from the year 1792 to 1798*.[142] He denied any intention of describing the holy places in view of the existence of previous accounts,[143] but he did observe that the Holy Sepulchre was in a sorry state with beams falling and snow cascading through the roof, and he sounded a disparaging note with a reference to the 'manufacture' of relics there.[144]

However the nineteenth century was to witness a considerable change in Protestant attitudes, influenced, in the first instance, by an Italian circus strong-man named Giovanni B. Belzoni. This colourful character penetrated to the Egyptian desert and there, by sheer chance, hit upon several lost tombs. The story of his discoveries was published in 1822 by John Murray of London and the public thrilled to his narrative. He fired people's imaginations to such an extent that by the 1830s the Near East was included in every well-to-do young man's grand tour and travelogues were becoming commonplace.[145] Indeed it has been estimated that between 1800 and 1875 some two thousand traveller-authors produced a minimum of one book or article each about the region.[146] Certainly one of the most readable of these was *Eothen* by Alexander Kinglake which was based on his tour in 1835, although the first edition did not appear for another nine years. The pilgrims he encountered, as was to be expected from the previous section of this chapter, were mainly Armenians and Greeks, and, in typically Protestant fashion and out of sympathy with their devotional practices, he commented that 'they seem to me to be not "working out" but *transacting* the great business of salvation'.[147] He was aware too that just as his co-religionists had questioned the authenticity of relics, now they were doubting the precise identification of the holy places.

> Many Protestants are wont to treat these traditions contemptuously, and those who distinguish themselves from their brethren by the appellation of 'Bible Christians' are almost fierce in their denunciation of these supposed errors.[148]

Whereas Kinglake took the view that the identifications were not unreasonable, others were not so sure. Dean Stanley, whose *Sinai and Palestine*, written four years after his first visit, was so popular that it went through four editions within twelve months of its publication (1856), was doubtful about the 'exact spots', but he did not think this a matter of concern because

> there is an absence of any allusion to local sanctity in the writings of the Evangelists and Apostles, who were too profoundly absorbed in the events themselves to think of their localities.[149]

Others again were frankly dissatisfied by what they saw. Herman Melville, the author of *Moby Dick*, came hoping to be impressed (1857), but went away disillusioned.[150] Another American writer, whose works were to become literary classics, Mark Twain, declared that 'no country will more quickly dissipate romantic expectation than Palestine – particularly Jerusalem. To some the disappointment is heart sickening.'[151] However, upon reflection, he was prepared to acknowledge that he was emotionally moved when he stood before Golgotha – 'one fully believes that he is looking upon the very spot where the Saviour gave his life'.[152] But the rivalry between the Christian denominations, each holding a part of the Church of the Holy Sepulchre and none in agreement to keep it in a state of overall repair, disgusted many.[153] William Hepworth Dixon was but one who went into considerable detail in his two-volume account and was very bitter about these feuds.[154]

The devotions both of the custodians and of the pilgrims did not meet with the approval of Western Protestants. Harriet Martineau (1847) dismissed what she saw at the Holy Sepulchre as 'mummeries done in the name of Christianity'.[155] She regarded the claim that Jesus had left the marks of his feet at his ascension as 'idolatrous nonsense'[156] and she asserted that

> in Italy I found the Christian mythology and superstitious observances very distressing to witness: but I could have had no idea how much more painful the spectacle is in Palestine.[157]

Following her nine years later, J. W. de Forest was equally scornful:

> There is such an air of absurdity about most of the sacred localities and traditions which abound in Jerusalem, that they excite unbelief and irreverence rather than faith and devotion.[158]

Yet the majority did come away impressed and their narratives encouraged more people to make the same journey. There were few who did not admit how upon their first view of Jerusalem they knelt or prostrated themselves or even wept.[159] Harriet Martineau herself wrote that

> at every step we found the scriptural imagery rising up before our eyes ... These places have been familiar to my mind's eye from my youth up: and now I looked at the ground they occupied, amidst scenery but little changed, with an emotion which none but those who have made the Bible the study of the best years of their life can conceive of.[160]

Moreover, however much she may have disparaged the devotions she witnessed, she was not above bathing in the Jordan nor of taking home some water from that river.[161]

It is, however, the description given by Robert Curzon of his behaviour, when, in 1834, he caught his initial glimpse of the holy city, that most clearly reveals the dilemma of the nineteenth-century Protestant, anxious not to appear superstitious, inhibited in displaying emotion through bodily gestures and yet deeply moved at the prospect.

> It is not easy to describe the sensations which fill the breast of a Christian when, after a long and toilsome journey, he first beholds this, the most interesting and venerated spot upon the whole surface of the globe. Every one was silent for a while, absorbed in the deepest contemplation. The object of our pilgrimage was accomplished, and I do not think that anything that we saw afterwards during our stay in Jerusalem made a more profound impression on our minds than this first distant view. It was curious to observe the different effect which our approach to Jerusalem had upon the various persons who composed our party. A Christian pilgrim, who had joined us on the road, fell down upon his knees and kissed the holy ground; two others embraced each other, and congratulated themselves that they had lived to see Jerusalem. As for us Franks, we sat bolt upright on our horses, and stared and said nothing; whilst around us the more natural children of the East wept for joy, and, as in the army of the Crusaders, the word Jerusalem! Jerusalem! was repeated from mouth to mouth;

but we, who consider ourselves civilized and superior beings, repressed our emotions; we were above showing that we participated in the feelings of our barbarous companions. As for myself, I would have got off my horse and walked bare-footed towards the gate, as some did, if I had dared; but I was in fear of being laughed at for my absurdity, and therefore sat fast in my saddle. At last I blew my nose, and, pressing the sharp edges of my Arab stirrups on the lank sides of my poor weary jade, I rode on slowly towards the Bethlehem gate.[162]

Harriet Martineau's reference to the Bible, cited above, is typical of the period under review and W. H. Dixon can be quoted as yet another of the many who echoed the same concern, a concern which is identical with that which promoted the very first pilgrims some seventeen hundred years before, such as Melito of Sardis and Origen.[163]

In reading my camp Bible at the very spots which it describes so well, I was surprised to find how much good history lies overlooked in that vast treasury of truth.[164]

This interest arose directly out of the contemporary situation. Throughout the nineteenth century supporters of traditional Christianity felt themselves under siege. The veracity of the Bible was being questioned from the side of science, on the one hand, especially in the light of Darwin's theory of evolution, and from historical criticism, on the other, with its doubts about the authorship of numerous books in the canon and about the accuracy of its contents. In this situation thoughts turned to Palestine. Would it not be possible 'to prove the Bible true' by seeking evidence in its support from the very country where it originated and where the events it details were enacted? Here was motive enough both for biblical scholars and archaeologists to head for the land of promise. The pioneer among the former was without question Edward Robinson.

Robinson was Professor of Biblical Literature at Union College, New York, and he was deeply interested in biblical topography. When he came to report on his first visit of 1838, he declared:

The object of my journey to Jerusalem . . . was the city itself, in its topographical and historical relations, its site, its hills, its dales, its remains of antiquity, the traces of its ancient population; in short, everything connected with it that could have a bearing upon the illustration of the Scriptures.[165]

Already the great missionary awakening had resulted in men going to Palestine – such people as William Jowett (1815–20) and the American Pliny Fisk (1823)[166] – and now biblical scholars followed in their wake. They were not as yet pilgrims in the proper sense of the term, but they were scholars with a religious intent. That this was their incentive is unmistakable and it was expressed with the utmost lucidity in the original 1865 prospectus of the Palestine Exploration Fund which was launched to support their endeavours.

> No country should be of so much interest to us as that in which the documents of our Faith were written and the momentous events they describe were enacted . . . Even to a casual traveller in the Holy Land the Bible becomes, in its form, and therefore to some extent in its substance, a new book.[167]

A second statement opens with the quotation of Isaiah 51.1: 'Look unto the rock whence ye are hewn, and to the hole of the pit whence ye are digged.' In this way the religious motive of the Fund is stressed from the outset. It continues:

> What we want to do – the reason for which we exist – is so to clear up our geographical and archaeological knowledge of the country as to make its history contained in the Bible intelligible to its readers . . . To know that country intimately, to be able to describe its peculiarities, and to illustrate by its present condition the narrative of the Old and New Testament is the aim of every earnest student of the Bible.[168]

This account of the Committee's work concludes with an impassioned plea for assistance.

> The words that move our hearts, the hopes that nerve our hands, the faith that heals our sorrows – these are all associated with those barren hills, those ruined heaps of stones and rubbish, those dry watercourses of the Holy Land. Take the Bible in your hand, and as you light upon some passage that is cleared up and illustrated by some of those who have gone before us in research, confess that the aims of the Association which only exists by reason of its love for the Bible, and of its general desire to do all it can for the illustration of God's word, are noble indeed. Help us, you who can. Wish us God speed, you who can do us no other service.[169]

Although somewhat sentimental and to that extent expressive of Victorian piety, the genuineness of the religious concern cannot be denied. Even its reference to research does not mean that the members of the Committee were wedded to the idea of research for research's sake nor were the pioneers of archaeology that was rapidly developing in the Near East during this period.

In the early years of the nineteenth century, stimulated by the travels of M. Seelzen (1805–9) who was employed by the Oriental Museum of Gotha to collect antiquities and natural objects, some British citizens formed themselves into the Palestine Exploration Society. Little is known of its activities and it did not long survive but it was a pointer on the way to an investigation of the Holy Land more co-ordinated and systematic than that which could be achieved on occasional short visits by individuals, however much their narratives might arouse interest. Planning became more of a possibility when in June 1865, under the presidency of the Archbishop of York, a meeting of Sir Charles Groves and his friends decided to establish the Palestine Exploration Fund, whose first prospectus has been quoted above. This incidentally was to be followed by similar societies in Germany (1877), France (1891) and America (1900). Expeditions to Jerusalem were soon set in train and financed by the Fund and amongst the first was the one headed by Charles Wilson, who had drawn up an ordinance survey of the city[170] and another by Charles Warren that began in 1867 and lasted for three years.[171]*

However the earliest archaeological observations were those of Edward Robinson whose book became the *vademecum* of all who came after him.[172]* But thorough digs were first undertaken in the region of ancient Assyria – even so the biblical connexion was paramount. This is placed beyond doubt by the report in *The Illustrated London News* of 26 June 1847 of the excavations at Nineveh. They have 'excited the curiosity not only of the antiquarian but also of all scriptural students, for the illustration they afford of passages of Holy Writ'.[173] On 21 December 1850, announcing the delivery to the British Museum of the Nimroud (sic) sculptures, it is pointed out how they illuminate the metaphor of the cup in Psalms 16.5 and 23.5, while an entry of 24 April 1869, headed 'The Underground Survey of Jerusalem', notes that while the work is in the interests of historical and scientific enquiry, it has also been undertaken 'with a view to biblical illustration'.[174] Still in the same magazine, an article of 3 April 1875, describing excavations at Ephesus, observes how 'antiquarian studies constitute the most undeniable witness to the modern world of faith in Jesus Christ'.[175]

When such was the interest, it is understandable why Prince Albert, planning the education of his son Edward (later Edward VII), should include a visit to the Holy Land. He sought Stanley's advice, as did later Queen Victoria when her husband died before the programme had been completed, and on 5 February 1862 the journey began, with the Dean of Westminster in the company as guide. The sermons that Stanley preached during this tour in the Near East were published in 1863 and they shed light on the way that the journey was being understood.

> To see that Holy City, even though the exact spots of his death and resurrection are unknown, is to give new force to the sound of the name whenever afterwards we hear it in church or read it in the Bible. I do not wish to exaggerate in this matter. It is, thank God, perfectly possible to be just, and holy, and good, without coming to Palestine. Pilgrimage is not really a Christian duty. Holy Places are not really holy in the sight of God, except for the feelings they produce. The Crusaders were in error, when they thought to save their souls by fighting to regain the Holy Land. It is not the earthly, but the heavenly Jerusalem, which is 'the mother of us all' – our mother in the widest and most endearing sense. But not the less are all these things helps to those who will use them rightly.[176]

Undoubtedly these sermons, together with the royal example, encouraged the emergence of a favourable view of pilgrimages among Protestants and there were other factors too leading to the same result. Back in 1847 Benjamin Disraeli, always acutely sensitive to contemporary currents of thought, had made a pilgrimage the background of *Tancred or The New Crusader*. His novels were popular, and his vivid description of Palestine, of the visit of Tancred to the monastery on Mount Sinai and of his devotions at the holy places must have influenced many to adopt once again a sympathetic attitude to setting out as a pilgrim. The land too was being made familiar by the water colours of David Roberts, Edward Lear and David Wilkie together with the works of Holman Hunt. Photography also, while still in its infancy, had a contribution to make with the prints of Francis Bedford and F. Frith.[177] An even greater impact was made by the publication of the accounts written by pilgrims in the past.

In 1848 T. Wright issued his *Early Travels in Palestine*;[178] even before this Titus Tobler, who visited the Middle East for the first time in 1838, had realized that these narratives, while of interest in themselves, contained also valuable topographical data to assist both biblical scholars and archaeologists seeking to identify the original locations.[179] It was his editing of many texts in their original languages, especially the new edition of 1879 under the auspices of the *Société de l'Orient Latin*, that led to the creation in England of the Palestine Pilgrims' Text Society of which Charles Wilson was the director and George Grove a council member. The discovery of the *Pilgrimage of Egeria* in 1884 kept interest alive and in a prospectus, issued in 1896, the Society announced that it had now completed its original task in twelve volumes (which included Egeria's account). This task had been to provide translations, with notes and where necessary plans and drawings, of pilgrim accounts from the fourth to the fifteenth century. As the public became familiar with these records, the Reformation condemnation of pilgrimages, already being forgotten, became a thing of the past. Nor were visits to Palestine any longer to be confined to a few experts and to those with only aristocratic connexions – this breakthrough was occasioned by a development in transport.

The Contribution of Thomas Cook

Already in the early 1850s the Austrian Lloyd and the French Messagines Maritimes had begun to call at ports along the coast of Palestine.[180] With the opening of the Suez Canal in 1869, a further impetus was given to travel in the Near East and that in fact was the very year that Thomas Cook led his first party to Jerusalem. Soon the visits he arranged to that part of the world 'generally included a tour of the Holy Land, a region that lay close to Thomas Cook's heart because of its religious connotations'.[181] For two decades he had played with the idea, as he himself recorded in the July 1872 number of *Cook's Excursionist and Tour Advertiser* which he had begun to issue in 1851.

> I make no pretension to the origination of Tours to the Holy Land, as I remember to have seen, more than twenty years ago, proposals advertised in Scottish periodicals, of a projected Tour to Palestine, at a cost of about £200 . . . I believe it is now twenty-three years since I met, in one of my Highland Tours, a distinguished English clergyman, who first led me to think of the matter seriously, and from that time, however silently the idea slept under the heavy load of other engagements, I had always anticipated that it must be done at some convenient season.[182]

In 1867 he made a preliminary sortie to the eastern Mediterranean but did not actually go as far as Jerusalem. The following year he planned a full scale organized tour to set out just before Christmas but then decided to postpone it in the hope that congregations might be encouraged to give their ministers extra large Christmas boxes to enable them to afford the journey. 'It would be a glorious thing for all ministers and students of divinity to visit the lands from which they draw so much of their pulpit inspirations.'[183]

Then in the Spring of 1869, fifty-two people formed his first party: sixteen ladies, thirty-three men, Cook himself and two assistants. They divided into two groups, one starting from Bayrouth and the other from Jaffa.[184] When it is recalled that by the turn of the century, only thirty-one years later, Thomas Cook and Son had enabled some twelve thousand people to visit the Holy Land,[185] then the firm's contribution to the re-emergence of Protestant pilgrimages cannot be overestimated. Yet among that number were not a few Roman Catholics, including the one thousand and four Fathers of the Assumption who travelled as pilgrims under their aegis from Paris in 1882. Cook's own comment was entirely justified – 'It need scarcely be added that this is the most gigantic undertaking of its kind that has ever been recorded since the days of the Crusaders.'[186]

Cook's own understanding of these enterprises and their results is presented in two numbers of the *Excursionist* for the year 1872.

There is one predominant feeling of interest that underlies all our visits to these lands and waters of biblical history, i.e. the abiding impression that we are travelling amongst and gazing on scenes with which we have been familiarized from our earliest recollections. Soon as our infant lips could speak or our perceptions could realize historical facts, we were taught to think and speak of Egypt and Canaan, of Joseph and Jesus, of Pharoah and Pilate, of Jerusalem and Jericho . . . It is a great event in one's life to be able to come and see these wonderful places and countries, and with the Bible in one hand and Murray in the other, to trace out sites and scenes immortalized by imperishable events . . . Like the Israelites of old, we came from the 'land watered with pools' to the 'Land of Promise'.[187]

The educational and social results of these four years of Eastern travel have been most encouraging. A new incentive to scriptural investigation has been created and fostered; 'The Land and the Book' have been brought into familiar juxtaposition, and their analogies have been better comprehended; and under the general influence of sacred scenes and repeated sites of Biblical events, enquiring and believing spirits have held sweet counsel with each other. Devoted ministers have gone to investigate scenes and objects of long study and practical illustration, and have returned richly laden with additional and corroborative facts to enrich their ministrations, while in general their physical health has been equally benefited. It is not in time that the full benefit of Travel in Bible lands can be fully realized: the information acquired, the facts studied, the aspirations engendered, reach beyond time and add to the obligations and hopes of futurity.[188]

Cook's reputation as an organizer of pilgrimages now stood so high that he was responsible for a visit by Prince Albert Victor and Prince George (later George V) in 1882[189] and four years later, at the request of the Governor-General of India, he drew up plans for the better treatment and subsequent travel of Muslim pilgrims to Jeddah and Yambo.[190] The arranging of the visit of Kaiser Wilhelm in 1898 was but one more of his successes – the German ruler came to Jerusalem for the consecration of the Lutheran Church of the Redeemer on 31 October which was the anniversary of the nailing of the Ninety-Five Theses to the door at Wittenberg in 1517![191] Efficiency and the example of such well-known public figures were winning their way, so that Isabel Burton's unkind and probably snobbish comment, when encountering Cook's third party in 1871, was no longer applicable, if indeed it ever had been: she referred to Cook's clients as 'a menagerie of curious human bipeds'.[192]

Of course the ascetic element, so marked a feature of the mediaeval scene, was scarcely present: Cook took great pains to ensure the comfort of his nineteenth-century pilgrims. What exactly was involved can be gleaned from the many details that abound in various numbers of the *Excursionist*. We are informed that one Alexander Howard is 'our chief Eastern dragoman',[193] that in the party of May 1872 there were to be found 'half a dozen Christian ministers of the Church of England, Scottish Presbyterian and Welsh Methodist, and American denominations united in the worship of God and all seemed animated by one spirit' – they had the help of forty saddle horses, sixty baggage mules, twenty-two donkeys and fifty dragomen, servants and muleteers.[194] The pilgrims were accommodated in tents (Pl. VI) 'with iron bedsteads, wool beds, carpeted floor, and an ample supply of excellent well cooked food',[195] the last including 'preserved meat, salmon, lobster, pickle and jams'.[196] The cost in the early 1870s was 125 guineas, decreasing with an increase in the number of takers,[197] but this sum did not include the price of an English saddle which was apparently more comfortable for West European posteriors than those used by the locals.[198] The devotional aspect was not neglected in the midst of the relative 'comfort' and there are

Plate VI A Thomas Cook tent in the Holy Land, 1880

several references to services conducted in the camps and to addresses delivered by different clerics.[199]

Although all was done to safeguard the well-being of the pilgrims, there were mishaps. One unfortunate gentleman was kicked by a horse near Solomon's Pools but was reported to have recovered quickly.[200] A rather more bizarre incident was confided to her diary, the manuscript being preserved in Thomas Cook's archives, by a Miss Riggs of Hampstead who was a member of the very first contingent. Under 18 February 1869, she recorded how a Mrs Samuels was taken ill and died at Ramlah. Since a corpse could not be moved without permission and since the widower wished to have his wife buried at Jerusalem, they pretended she was only indisposed and was carried thither in a covered palanquin.

> We all felt the solemnity of the event and I felt, and, I am sure others also, how God in his merciful goodness had conducted us safely and well through so much of this wonderful Land of Promise, so interesting to the spirit but so difficult to the infirmities and weaknesses of the flesh.[201]

The same diarist provides evidence of the unbroken continuity of pilgrim devotional practices in that when they reached the Jordan they 'rushed into the sacred river . . . and to make it more complete dipped seven times'. The reference is to the leper Naaman the Syrian who, to be healed of his leprosy, washed himself in the Jordan at Elisha's comand (II Kings 5). This is typical of her record throughout which she makes frequent allusions to biblical characters and events associated with the various places where they halted. However in addition to the usual bathing in the Jordan, sometimes baptism was administered; William Henry Leighton mentions two in his letters written during a Cook's tour of 1874.[202]

When, in 1891, there was published the first edition of *Cook's Tourist Handbook for Palestine and Syria*, although the word 'tourist' stands in the title, Cook's own contribution to the development of pilgrimage was further increased. The book itself was expressly printed very clearly in order to be read either on horseback or by the dim light of a tent and it contained the complete text of scriptural references so that travellers in the saddle did not have to juggle with more than one book. The biblical basis of the journey was in this way very much emphasized. Indeed Thomas Cook's pioneering work was acknowledged in an unexpected way by Sidney Heath in his *Pilgrim Life in the Middle Ages* (1911). After printing some extracts from a mediaeval guide book, described above,[203] including the suggestions about what food to take when going down from Jerusalem to Jericho, Heath adds the comment: 'The modern tourist to the Jordan no longer carries with him "harde eggys and chese", for Mr Cook is a more up-to-date organizer than were the patrons of the fifteenth century.'[204]

The extent to which pilgrimage had become a widely accepted concept and practice among Protestants can be gauged from the fact that a popular novelist could now use it as a title. Jerome K. Jerome's *Diary of a Pilgrim* was first published in 1891 and in it he describes his visit to Oberammergau for a performance of the passion play. Although his gift of humour was not to reveal itself fully until 1917 when *Three Men in a Boat* was issued, this one abounds in amusing touches until he comes to recount his reaction to the dramatic presentation itself; this reaches a crescendo in the final paragraph.

> Few believing Christians among the vast audience but must have passed out from that strange playhouse with their belief and love strengthened. The God of the Christians, for his sake, became a man, and lived and suffered and died as a man; and as a man, living,

suffering, dying among other men, he had that day seen him . . . The unbeliever, also, passes out into the village street full of food for thought. The rude sermon preached in this hillside temple has shown to him, clearer than he could have seen before, the secret wherein lies the strength of Christianity; the reason why, of all the faiths that Nature has taught to her children to help them in their need, to satisfy the hunger of their souls, this faith, born by the Sea of Galilee, has spread the farthest over the world, and struck its note the deepest into human life. Not by his doctrine, not even by his promises, has Christ laid hold upon the hearts of men, but by the story of his life.[205]

Jerome here, very poignantly, has put his finger on one aspect of pilgrimage to the Holy Land that has always had an appeal and which time has not diminished. The way, then, had been opened for the continued development of Protestant pilgrimages in the twentieth century, but before carrying this story forward an explanation is needed for the recovery of the other main type of pilgrimage, viz. that to local shrines.

The Re-emergence of Local Pilgrimages within Protestantism

With pilgrimage so much in the air, albeit involving travel overseas, the possibility of going to centres in one's own country, even if it was one that at the Reformation opted for Protestantism, was bound to arise. On Tuesday 27 June 1876, Parson Kilvert, whose diary provides such a vivid account of his times, made this entry: 'At noon I became a Canterbury pilgrim and went to Canterbury on pilgrimage, nine miles, but by train.'[206] In this note Kilvert provides the key to unlocking the problem of why local Protestant pilgrimages began again in the last quarter of the nineteenth century – in brief, they began because a new function was discovered for British cathedrals.

In the Middle Ages every cathedral, whether monastic or secular, was a great charity foundation whose *raison d'être* was to offer regular intercessions on behalf of its founders and benefactors.[207] So, comments Hamilton Thompson:

> the modern idea of a cathedral is that of a centre of diocesan activity. But the mediaeval conception, which long survived the Reformation, was somewhat different. The cathedral church, it is true, was the mother church of the diocese . . . but it was essentially the church of a closed corporation with individual interests quite detached from those of the diocese at large, and insisting, to an extent incredible today, upon its independence of episcopal interference.[208]

What Thompson calls 'the modern idea' was the product of the reaction of the Church of England to successive attempts to change the cathedral system during the Victorian era. In the 1830s reform was to the fore; no aspect of national life could expect to escape it. The cathedrals were particularly vulnerable because, in the words of Owen Chadwick, 'no one knew what they were for'.[209] Yet through the conservatism of the English Reformation, they and most of their finances had been preserved. In 1836 a Commission was set up to review them under Sir Robert Peel and the outcome was the Dean and Chapter Bill of 1840 which reduced the establishments and employed the money thus appropriated for other ecclesiastical concerns. This was not the end of the matter by any means. On 10 November 1852 a new set of Commissioners was appointed to 'inquire into the state and condition of the cathedral and collegiate churches in England and Wales'. This Commission produced its first report in 1854 and its second and third in 1855, but their recommendations did little to illuminate the role of the cathedral.

On 20 May 1869 a letter from the two Archbishops to all Deans asked them to review what changes could or should be made, and, in the opinion of the Dean of Norwich, they were saying in effect that

> as the Cathedrals are very commonly (I do not say justly) supposed to be the most vulnerable parts of the Church system, it should be suggested to cathedral authorities to set their house in order, and to reform for themselves their chief abuses, before reform is rudely thrust upon them from without.[210]

The debate that ensued generated a number of studies among which *Essays on Cathedrals*, edited by J. S. Howson in 1872, was perhaps the most significant. According to one of its contributors, the Dean of Cashel, 'the primitive Cathedral was the centre and focus of church work in the diocese, and the cathedral clergy were equally the working bees, not the drones, of the diocesan hive'.[211] This idea immediately received general support and the Bishop of Ely, Edward Harold Browne, writing to the Dean of Norwich, could say:

> The only hope of saving the Cathedral bodies is to make them once more part, and the highest and chief part, of the great machinery of the Church in each diocese.[212]

The bishop sought to put this idea into effect and in 1873, on the twelve hundredth anniversary of the foundation of his cathedral by St Etheldreda, services were held on five successive days for children, choirs, working folk and so on – in effect, if not in name, this was to make the cathedral a centre of diocesan pilgrimage.[213]

It was this stress upon the cathedral as the mother church of the diocese that was to be taken up by E. W. Benson who, in the words of Roger Lloyd, 'founded a new tradition of capitular devotion'.[214] In 1878 Benson published *The Cathedral. Its Necessary Place in the Life and Work of the Church*. In this he advocated the revivification of cathedrals by the restoration of the ancient close relationship between the chapter and the bishop. He rested this upon historical precedent referring to the *Regula Canonicorum* of 816 in which the chapter is described as 'the senate of the diocese' and its duty as aid to 'the bishop when the see is filled, to supply his place when it is vacant'.[215] Benson acknowledged that in time bishop and chapter had drawn apart, but he saw hope for the future in that naves were no longer empty; 'diocesan gatherings and city organizations also are beginning to require and replenish them at intervals'.[216]

When, the following year, yet another Royal Commission was appointed, there was a strong likelihood that this view would prevail. One of many who communicated with the Commission was the Bishop of Exeter whose diocesan conference of 1880 had discussed the issue and was strongly in favour of a closer association of cathedral and diocese. Together with his report on this meeting, Temple forwarded a memorandum of his own which began in the following manner:

> It seems to me that, in any alterations affecting the law which governs the cathedral, three aims ought to be kept in view:–
> To improve the services.
> To attach the diocese to the cathedral.
> To render such services to the diocese as the cathedral body can best render.[217]

Temple was also in favour of encouraging choir festivals in cathedrals, but in this he had been anticipated by a quarter of a century at Lichfield. In 1856 choirs from several parishes were invited to take part in a joint service. An anonymous report of the occasion was published in the *Churchman's Companion* and then reprinted as a small pamphlet under the title *A Day at Lichfield*. There were present some three thousand voices and the writer asserted that a cathedral is both the head and heart of a diocese and that 'such must our cathedrals again become, and their revenues will not be alienated, but they will be venerated and loved as the mother churches of the dioceses'.[218]

Not surprisingly the Royal Commission endorsed this view. In the opening paragraph of its final report it was stated that

> We have regarded the Cathedral and the members of the Cathedral body with reference not merely to the city in which they exist, nor, on the other hand, merely to the Church at large, but also and perhaps chiefly to the interests of the Diocese of which the Cathedral is the Mother Church and the Dean the leading Presbyter.[219]

Not everyone concurred. Prebendary Perry of Lincoln responded by declaring that 'the cathedral . . . is in no sense the mother church of the diocese. Rather it resembles an extraneous ornament or decorative addition to the diocesan edifice.'[220] To a certain extent this understanding had a sound historical basis, at least with regard to the previous millennium, but it was not to prevail. As yet, however, apart from Parson Kilvert's remark, the idea of pilgrimage had not been associated with contemporary visits to a cathedral, but it is easy to appreciate how such a link could be forged.

Pilgrimage, as the previous section has shown, was coming into vogue. Moreover the antiquarian interest of the late Victorians, to say nothing of their fascination with the period of High Gothic, resulted in the discovery of the extent to which mediaeval cathedrals had been centres of pilgrimage. In 1877 Stanford of London published E. R. James, *Notes on the Pilgrims' Way in West Sussex*. In 1889 a translation of J. J. Jusserand's study appeared with the title of *English Wayfaring Life in the Middle Ages*.[221] Julia Cartwright followed this in 1893 with *The Pilgrims' Way from Winchester to Canterbury*[222] and further interest in that particular route was fostered by Hilaire Belloc with his *The Old Road*.[223]* Encouragement was also forthcoming from A. T. Quiller-Couch with *The Pilgrim's Way. A Little Scrip of Good Counsel for Travellers*.[224] This consisted of poems, meditations and prayers, and in the preface he remarked that 'it is a disease of us English, and I think a reproach to that reformed religion that most of us profess, that we no longer go on pilgrimages'. He then proceeded to recommend to every reader to go at least once in a lifetime on a pilgrimage, 'for it proceeds from those impulses which, though he repress them by daily work, still intrudes and whispers that he was born for higher things'.[225]

The first direct bringing together of pilgrimage and diocese did not however relate to the cathedral but to the practice of bishops circumambulating the area under their oversight. It was Theodore Woods who, as Bishop of Peterborough, initiated in 1917 the custom of going on a pilgrimage throughout the rural parts of his diocese during the summer months. When he was translated to Winchester in 1924 he continued the practice, travelling on foot from parish to parish.[226] His example was followed in 1921 by Garbett who saw this as an admirable way of becoming more closely acquainted with the clergy of Southwark; he too went on to Winchester and set out on his first pilgrimage there in September 1932; this became for him an annual event which he did not discontinue when he became Archbishop of York, his first outing in that capacity beginning on 24 July 1942.[227]

What meanwhile of the cathedrals of Britain? Benson, it will be recalled, made them useful, but according to Roger Lloyd he did not make them lovable; for this there was required what Lloyd calls 'a second reforming movement' and of this the leader was F. S. M. Bennett.[228] It was he who above all stressed that the cathedral should be not only a focus for the diocese but also a pilgrimage centre. In 1925, five years after he had become Dean of Chester, Bennett published two books, the one entitled *Chester Cathedral* and the other *The Nature of a Cathedral*.[229] In these he closely followed Benson, fully endorsing the concept that a cathedral is to be regarded as the mother church of a diocese[230] and therefore as 'a home by the whole diocese, that in it every pilgrim from near or far may find him, whose house it is'.[231]

Bennett was convinced that a distinction must be drawn between visitors who are simply sightseers and 'pilgrims who come to listen and to talk to God'.[232] To encourage the latter, he first of all persuaded the chapter to abolish entrance fees – to be followed in quick succession by Bristol, Ely, Salisbury and Worcester. Next he restored the monks' refectory at Chester to its ancient use as an eating place and he reported that

> throughout the summer many parties of pilgrims from the diocese and elsewhere are fed. Thus if a parish or a branch of the Mothers' Union or a choir or any other body comes on pilgrimage to the Mother Church of the Diocese, their physical as well as their spiritual needs can be provided for, and their cathedral will seem a more real home to them in that they have had tea in the Refectory. In summer there are many pilgrimages every week.[233]

A further step was the reintroduction of pilgrimage tokens, and he had copies made of one from the shrine of St Werburgh in Chester preserved in the British Museum. This represented geese in a basket and recalled how the saint had admonished certain birds who were destroying the crops and how they had agreed to do no more damage. According to Bennett: 'Reproductions of this sign can be obtained from the Cathedral vergers (1/–); they carry with them for the modern pilgrim the obligation of saying a prayer in the cathedral.'[234] Such devotional practices were already being recommended at Canterbury and Bennett quoted with approval a notice there about Reginald Pole, who was Archbishop from 1556 to 1558 and the last to acknowledge the authority of the pope. The notice was followed by a summons to prayer –

> Pilgrim, here we ask you to pray for the reunion of the whole Church, and that to her may be granted such peace and unity as is agreeable to her Lord's will.[235]

Bennett's understanding of the role of a cathedral naturally led him to stress the devotional aspect of pilgrimage.

> The primary business is to help those who come to feel and to profit by the religious impress of the place . . . The heritage from the past should be made alive with religion for the needs and appreciativeness of today . . . Every historic monument can be made alive with present day religious suggestion.[236]

To promote this the Dean produced two booklets, one entitled *Handbook for Pilgrims* and the other *The Pilgrim's Way*. These, like the mediaeval Holy Land processionals, were devotional aids, taking each individual on a mini-pilgrimage around the building and its precincts. The introduction to the second work makes his intention quite plain:

> This booklet is not a guide book to the Cathedral, describing features of historical interest that can be seen by visitors. Instead, you will find two routes of pilgrimage that can be followed.[237]

The theme of the first route proposed is life in the church and of the second the needs of the world, the former reaching its climax in the Lady Chapel and the latter in the Chapel of St Erasmus where the sacrament is reserved. These peregrinations are set within the context of the whole of life understood as a continuous pilgrimage and this is given expression in a prayer to be said in the Chapel of St George:

> O eternal God, heavenly Father, who hast given us thy children an abiding citizenship in heaven, and, in the days of our pilgrimage, a

citizenship also on earth; give us thine aid, as we journey to the heavenly city, so faithfully to perform the duties which befall us in our way, that at the last we may be found worthy to enter into thy rest.

The cathedral, comments Bennett, 'is missing a gorgeous opportunity if it does not make the pilgrimage to itself the most delightful outing of all'.[238]

The story of the re-emergence of Protestant local pilgrimages now becomes the record of the implementation of Bennett's vision. In 1926 G. K. A. Bell, two years after becoming Dean of Canterbury and three years before being consecrated as Bishop of Chichester, inspired a great diocesan pilgrimage to the cathedral. Representatives of every parish, with banner and clergy at their head, went in procession around the building and its precincts to the singing of hymns and were greeted by the Archbishop and the chapter grouped around the marble chair in the corona.[239]

The following year, which was the thirteen hundredth anniversary of the founding of York Minster, saw ninety-five separate parish pilgrimages being made, with Cosmo Gordon Lang presiding over the festivities.[240] Yet the extent to which pilgrimage was now fully accepted within Protestant practice in England is perhaps best illustrated by what happened in 1934 when, as a consequence of the Depression, there were huge numbers out of work. Some social workers advanced the idea of mass pilgrimages to all British cathedrals, and this proposal was speedily welcomed by the Dean of Canterbury and then by all cathedral bodies as a means of demonstrating both the church's and the nation's concern for the privations and anxieties of the unemployed. Between 1 and 14 July great numbers attended, headed by the King and Queen who went to Westminster Abbey and wore pilgrims' badges. Indeed everyone was asked to go to at least one cathedral during the fortnight and to make some offering, however small, that would be used for the unemployed. Writing in the *Yorkshire Post* on 7 July, Harold Nicholson said

> The whole world is tired of impersonal travel, and this scheme provides the desired touch of romance, of individual sense of purpose. The pilgrim will have before him on every journey a sense of destination. He will enter the cathedral feeling that he has come from afar to perform this service.[241]

'The old tradition of pilgrimage,' commented Roger Lloyd, 'that a pilgrimage was an event charged with spiritual potency, had reasserted itself.'[242]

It is doubtful if the revival of pilgrimages to Walsingham had much direct effect on this development. This was entirely due to the efforts of A. H. Patten who was inducted as vicar in 1921. His ardent desire was to return to the Middle Ages and his policy, in the words of Henley Henson, was one of 'undermining the Reformation'.[243] To restore the shrine at Walsingham and to encourage pilgrimages were the natural consequences of such a position, no doubt stimulated by the fact that Roman Catholic visits had restarted in 1897; so in 1923 Patten organized his first pilgrimage with increasing success and greater numbers as the years passed.[244] Indeed thousands now visit 'England's Nazareth' annually, many in search of healing[245] – the scenes and atmosphere recalling the very practices which the Reformers abhorred. Others go to Crowland in the Lincolnshire fens to honour the seventh-century hermit St Guthlac[246] or to the cell of Lady Julian of Norwich.[247] Still more travel to Lindisfarne where St Aidan was consecrated as bishop and where St Cuthbert was first interred before being several times transferred until he was finally laid to rest at Durham.[248] Nor is the pull of the cradle of Scottish Christianity to be forgotten – Iona, whither St Columba came from Ireland in 563. It was there that, as early as 1938, George MacLeod founded the community he named after this Hebridean island. Thither modern pilgrims make their way and a mini-pilgrimage, with various stations to provide for their devotions, has been devised on the same principle as those that have been followed throughout the centuries at Jerusalem and elsewhere.[249] Indeed many old shrines are recovering their attraction – witness the Chapel of Moluag, Eoropie, near the Butt of Lewis. This is on the site of the earlier St Olaf's, one of the four leading centres on the Outer Hebrides for the cure of both insanity and sores.

There has been, too, a further development in relation to cathedrals or, more accurately, in relation to one English cathedral in particular. The cathedral, as the mother church of the diocese, had, as previously explained, become a centre for parish pilgrimages, but then came the recognition that Canterbury is the mother church of the Anglican Communion in that it was the church of St Augustine whose mission in 597 had brought the faith to many. From this followed the idea that, just as parishes take the road to their diocesan centre, entire dioceses should go in the steps of the Canterbury pilgrims. First among these was the diocese of Winchester, to be followed in 1983 by Portsmouth and in 1986 by Birmingham. Speaking of these last two, the Archbishop of Canterbury, Robert Runcie, referred to what was being undertaken as 'all part of the liveliness of movement – a recognition that the church is not just stuck in old ways . . . There is a sense of moving on towards God . . . A diocesan pilgrimage helps us to see that the church crosses parochial and even diocesan and provincial boundaries.' He continued

> Compared with many parts of the world, we, with our customs, tend to be rather static in our church life. In other parts of the Anglican Communion, pilgrimage with its provisional and unpredictable side, seems much more characteristic of church life. And that is no bad thing. A little unpredictability, and the readiness to take a risk, declare our confidence in the object of our striving, which is to understand God better and to follow the way of Christ more faithfully.[250]

There remains one last milestone to describe in this continuing re-emergence of Protestant pilgrimages and that is marked by the temporary displacement of the Taizé monks just after Christmas to a different European city each year. This community, founded by French Protestants, is devoted to the furtherance of ecumenism and one of the ways it has adopted to promote this is the organization of these pilgrimages. In 1986, for example, some twenty-two thousand folk came to England from overseas, chiefly from Italy, Spain and Germany, with a contingent from Yugoslavia, and they joined a further three thousand from Britain itself. Twice daily gatherings were held in St Paul's and in Westminster Abbey as well as in Southwark and Westminster Roman Catholic cathedrals, and they divided into smaller groups for meditation and to visit church and community projects. Reporting this in *The Times* of 30 December, the Religious Affairs' Correspondent headed his column 'Pilgrims Take Over Cathedrals' – the wheel had come full turn.

The Resurrection of Pilgrimages to the Holy Land among Protestants in the Twentieth Century

If, as described in the previous section, the wheel has more or less come full turn in terms of the re-emergence of local pilgrimages among Protestants, the same is equally true of travel to the Holy Land. The factors that favoured this amazing resurrection – amazing in view of the concentrated repudiation of the practice at the Reformation – were the success of the Palestine campaign in 1916–17 and its aftermath, together with the example set by many leading ecclesiastics, the experience of soldiers and chaplains in the Middle

East during World War II and the establishment of Inter-Church Travel by Arthur Payton in 1955. This cryptic listing demands some elaboration if the several items are to be rendered intelligible.

It was on 11 December 1917 that General Allenby arrived on horseback at the Jaffa Gate of Jerusalem. Unlike the Kaiser, who rode into the city on a white steed, Allenby dismounted and entered on foot. This simple action proved to have immense symbolic power. In the first place it demonstrated his respect and reverence for the holy city which had already influenced his decision to avoid any fighting in its vicinity.[251] In the second place it marked its liberation from the Turks after more than seven hundred years of occupation. As a consequence of the British Mandate that was soon to follow, large numbers of civil servants, administrators, police and military personnel flocked to Palestine where naturally they visited the sacred sites and at the same time ensured their protection by establishing a degree of stability in the area that was to endure up to the outbreak of World War II.

It was this relative calm, together with the greater ease of travel, that facilitated the visits of a steady stream of influential ecclesiastics amongst whom one of the first in the period after World War I was Charles Gore, successively Bishop of Worcester, Birmingham and Oxford. It was in 1925 that he reached Jerusalem and there noted: 'This is a supremely wonderful and interesting place: but I cannot get our Lord weeping over Jerusalem out of my mind.' Gore joined the Palm Sunday procession from Bethany down the Mount of Olives and participated fully in all the Holy Week services.[252] Three years later William Temple, while still Bishop of Manchester but on the eve of becoming Archbishop of York, attended the meeting of the International Missionary Council in Jerusalem, a gathering that was to reassess Christian mission at the place of its origin. He followed the Way of the Cross along the Via Dolorosa, but particularly valued praying in the quiet of Gethsemane until pilgrims, led by the Crown Prince of Italy, disturbed the peace.[253] It is perhaps not without significance that back in 1920 he had undertaken the editorship of a monthly magazine devoted to Christianity and politics and entitled *The Pilgrim*.[254]

Cosmo Gordon Lang had been Archbishop of Canterbury for four years when in 1932 he went to the Holy Land to be received with great acclaim. Of the Church of the Holy Sepulchre this was his impression:

> There was a real spirit of reverence. I say nothing about the historical authenticity of the sites: enough that they have been for centuries symbols of faith and reverence and devotion.[255]

Cyril Forster Garbett, who had played a part in the re-emergence of local pilgrimages, was Bishop of Winchester when in 1936 he paid his second visit to Jerusalem – he had first been there in 1913 when, at that time vicar of Portsea, he had had as his fellow pilgrim his life-long friend F. O. T. Hawkes who was to become Bishop of Kingston.[256] In Jerusalem Garbett conducted the round of Holy Week and Easter services.[257] In 1946, by then Archbishop of York, he was back again and, gazing across the countryside from the hills above Nazareth, he remarked that 'the whole Bible seemed to spread before us.'[258] In 1955 he noted: 'This is my fourth visit, and I was moved almost to tears when I saw again the city walls. If I should die here, *Nunc dimittis,*'[259] On Maunday Thursday he participated in the Feet Washing in the Armenian cathedral of St James and throughout his brief stay went regularly to Gethsemane and the Holy Sepulchre to pray. He was seriously ill at the time and it was later reported that he had expressed a wish to make this one additional pilgrimage before he died. His death occurred not many months after his return to England.

Moving forward fifteen years we encounter Geoffrey Fisher who visited the Holy Sepulchre on 25 November 1960 and recorded in a small diary what his feelings were: the passage is worth quoting in full.

It is really impossible to describe or even to remember the impressions of this day. Moving beyond belief; not merely or chiefly because of the historic scenes of Our Lord's Passion; but because of these events recalled on such hallowed ground in the midst of clergy and people of all sorts and all churches, and myself in their midst . . . I cannot describe the church. I hardly saw it. I remember the first place I knelt – a stone on which Our Lord's body was supposed to have rested after being taken down from the cross. Why can I not recall all of this with exactitude? Because throughout, in a strange way, I became mentally passive; feeling a kind of victim with Our Lord. From the moment I entered the church, I was engulfed in a great crowd of Orthodox monks and Franciscans and others, who surrounded me and, almost literally, carried me from place to place . . . At a place I would kneel and feel Our Lord looking at us in this strange mixture of past and present; then be borne on again, this way and that, and feeling lovingly at their mercy. And I felt that somehow like this Our Lord was pulled and hustled and felt at the mercy of his unloving guides. More than that I cannot recall. At intervals the bells would clang again. The whole thing was an

Plate VII Archbishop Geoffrey Fisher at the Jordan

astonishing outpouring of every kind of excited motion, all flowing round and over me, not me as a person, but as a kind of centre point of that triumphal showing forth of Christian fellowship.[260]

Two further pointers in the wind: in 1962, R. C. Mortimer, Bishop of Exeter, became a member of the Advisory Committee of Inter-Church Travel (see pp. 165f.), serving for eleven years, and in 1978 that Robin Woods, Bishop of Worcester, became chairman of the Ecumenical Institute at Tantur between Bethlehem and Jerusalem. In a sense this was the climax of many visits going back to 1933 when, as a young man in his late teens, he had had a stay of ten days of which he observed: 'It was then that the ministry and passion of Our Lord and all that they meant came home to me.'[261]

This roll call of twentieth-century 'palmers' need not be extended. Sufficient have been named to substantiate the thesis that pilgrimages to the Holy Land must have been revitalized by the example set by church leaders to the men and women in the pews. However it is now necessary to go back in time and to review the effect of World War II. Thousands of men and women had been introduced to the holy places while serving in Palestine under the British Mandate and more still, particularly those in the army and airforce, were to come to Jerusalem during the Second World War. The opportunities for teaching and for the development of spirituality that pilgrimages can afford were quickly grasped by the chaplains who included such men as Joe Fison, later to become Bishop of Salisbury and in that capacity to continue fostering travel to Palestine.

Special courses for ordinands were organized and a key figure in this respect was Ronald Brownrigg, himself a serving officer and a candidate for the ministry. He was invited by the chaplains' department to establish a centre in the Orthodox Convent on Mount Sion whence he planned and led pilgrimages in and around Jerusalem. His efforts were encouraged and supported by Eric Bishop of the Newman School of Missions, Constance Padwick, an Islamic expert, and among Jewish scholars there were Norman Bentwick and Rabbi Wilhelm. As long ago the Crusaders brought back the pointed arch from the Middle East, so in the present century troops returned home to share their love of the Holy Land. In the immediately post-war era, Brownrigg, two years after his ordination in 1949, returned to Jerusalem as Sub-Dean of St George's and made it his special task to welcome pilgrims.

It was at this time that one who was to become another leading figure in the promotion of modern pilgrimages went to Liverpool as vicar of St John's Toxeter. Arthur Payton found his parishioners to be a mixture of Irish Catholics and Orangemen together with blacks of West Indian and West African descent. It soon became apparent to him that what the area needed above all else was some sense of unity and that the only way to encourage this was to open channels of communication between those divided by culture and denominationalism. As a first step he organized a lunch club, meeting fortnightly, where statutory and social workers could discuss the problems which Toxeter shared in common. When he observed how this led to the breaking down of barriers, he took a further step inspired by the example of the leaders of the Victoria Boys' Club who had recently arranged for their football team a successful tour of Belgium. At the time there was still a lingering hostility on the part of Britons to that country because of its capitulation during the war before the onslaught of the Nazi Panzer divisions. When Payton saw how this visit resulted in the establishment of friendships with the regular passing of letters, he himself led thirty members of his youth club to Germany and then began to perceive how the gulf separating Christians of different ecclesiastical allegiances might be bridged if they were taken out of their habitual situations and induced to mingle away from their home surroundings. Pilgrimage as a means to foster ecumenism now seemed a viable option.

Meanwhile a friend of Payton, Lewis Edwards who was a Quaker, had established a Youth Travel Club which concentrated on exchanges between Britain and Europe with considerable success. It was under the umbrella of this organization that Payton explored the possible support that might be forthcoming for Inter-Church exchanges and to this end he approached Oliver Tomkins. Tomkins, who was later to become Bishop of Bristol, was at that time with the Youth Service of the World Council of Churches and he informed Payton of an existing widespread desire for youth exchanges and at the same time put him in touch with Old Catholics, Methodists and others in Europe. The first result of this was the arranging of a tour to cover Sweden, Germany, Austria and Holland – attention being drawn to it by putting the question: Are you interested in Christians meeting one another?

Payton's next move was to make approaches to the British Council of Churches and to the Archbishop of Canterbury, raising the same question, only to be told that everyone approved and was happy to give their blessing but no one had any money to support such a venture. Undeterred, with a capital of only a hundred pounds and with the assistance of friends in the Youth Travel Club, Payton launched Inter-Church Travel in 1955 with the specific purpose of advancing Christian unity by enabling fellow believers of different denominations to mix with one another as members of the same party on holiday, and with congregations in the places visited. Itineraries were at first restricted to Europe, looking, for example, at post-war churches in Germany and meeting Lutheran clergy.

Meanwhile in Rome a remarkable American lady named Barbara Simmonds was preparing her contribution. She had attended the inaugural meeting of the World Council of Churches in Amsterdam in 1948 and had then gone on to Rome with the intention of creating a centre where Roman Catholics and other Christians could meet. She also decided to map out a mini-pilgrimage in and around Rome itself, the sites to be visited in historical sequence, and in 1951 her first group (of women) took the trail. In 1953, with the help of Oliver Tomkins, she arranged a larger pilgrimage and two years later settled permanently in Rome. Next she sought the co-operation of Arthur Payton, who brought a party of clergy and then in 1958 took over from her.

Four years previously a very fruitful association had been established between Payton and Brownrigg, the latter, on his return from Jerusalem in the autumn of 1954, having phoned Payton and offered his help. From 1956 Brownrigg was involved in drawing up itineraries – he was also assisted by a Methodist colleague – and the planning included five successive Winchester diocesan pilgrimages, which were under the patronage and later the leadership of the Bishop of Southampton, and four for Southwark. Episcopal and even archiepiscopal interest was growing as evidenced by a letter from Fisher to Payton which posed the question: Can you create a Holy Land pilgrimage within the limits of a workingman's holiday and for as near a hundred pounds as possible? The resulting first visit to Jerusalem in fact cost a hundred and three pounds. By 1961 Inter-Church Travel was making great steps forward and a report in *Time and Tide* on 13 April was to the effect that that year a thousand people would make Holy Land visits against two hundred four years previously.

To bring this brief history up to date: it was in 1967 that a pioneer parish pilgrimage took place with thirty-six young people being commissioned by the Bishop of Southampton at the parish eucharist at Bletchingley. A detailed account of the journey, together with much other information both practical and devotional in that it provided scriptural passages related to each site visited, was published in 1968 expressly to stimulate further interest in pilgrimages: its author was Ronald Brownrigg and its title *Come and See*.[262] He followed this in 1985 with *Come, See the Place. A Pilgrim Guide to the Holy Land* which is a mine of indispensable information.[263] Under the auspices of Inter-Church Travel the furtherance of pilgrimages goes on with training sessions and conferences for parish and congregational leaders. Yet . . . all was not plain sailing.

Under-capitalized from the start and in difficulties following the sinking of one of the ships chartered for a cruise, in 1958 Inter-Church Travel became a subsidiary of Thomas Cook, but with a large measure of autonomy accorded to it. Its identity has not therefore been lost and it continues to pioneer the concept and practice of Christian pilgrimage under the aegis of a firm which, as recorded in the last chapter, had itself been Christian in its original inspiration and had been among the first to facilitate passage to the Holy Land in the final three decades of the nineteenth century.

From the streamlined accounts that form the bulk of this chapter there is one omission that cannot fail to have been noticed, and that is the lack of attention paid to the meaning of pilgrimage. If there was any concern in the late nineteenth and present century about the Reformation arguments against the practice of pilgrimage, it has not been made public. Whether or not the case has any abiding validity has not been given an airing. Certainly few senior chaplains or early leaders can have failed to ponder the issue of theological justification, but unfortunately what they learned through practice was not shared with a wider audience through print. Few Protestants would be prepared to tolerate the mediaeval interpretation in full, bound up as it is with indulgences and the search for effective intercessors with the God of the *Dies Irae*. Practice had tended, as is so often the case, to precede theory. However if, with Dean Bennett of Chester, sightseers visiting a cathedral are to be distinguished from true pilgrims and if a pilgrimage is something more than a package tour, then the differences between these categories of persons and between these activities have to be considered. Hence the need to undertake the task, to which the next chapter will be devoted, of formulating a theology of pilgrimage. What, after all, does it mean to be a pilgrim in today's world?

4

The Meaning of Pilgrimage Today

The understanding of pilgrimage is not something static: it changes from culture to culture and from age to age. Indeed 'journeying to shrines takes on different meanings and forms in different places at different times'.[1] So, for example, in the early Christian centuries pilgrimage was an allegorical journey, most suitably performed in Palestine, whereby the life of Christ was re-enacted and impinged upon the present, whereas by the late Middle Ages it tended to be a perfunctory rite undertaken for the automatic accumulation of thousands of years of indulgences.[2] Indeed the practice and the interpretation in every period go hand in hand with a culturally specific and socially constructed reality – but alter this and both form and significance cannot remain unaffected. Hence it is unlikely that what would be acceptable in the late twentieth century would be identical with previous ideas – judicial pilgrimages and the Crusades are scarcely relevant – but this is not to say that it is necessary to disregard or reject totally everything that has been believed about pilgrimage in the past. There were, however, some features of the mediaeval understanding and practice that were properly queried by the Reformers: to review these is one way to clear the ground for a more positive statement that may qualify as a contemporary theology of pilgrimage.

Hints from the Past

The main onslaught of the Reformers, as previously outlined, was concentrated upon local pilgrimages, the climax of such journeys being the cult of the saints and their relics. It was held that this resulted in the saints usurping the role of Christ as sole mediator and intercessor and even of the Father himself as the source of all gifts. It was further contended that the veneration of the images of saints as well as of their relics – or indeed of any relics – was equivalent to idolatry. An assessment of these charges must rest upon an answer to two questions: what is a saint? how should relics be treated? According to S. Wilson:

> Saints belong to and reflect the societies which produce and honour them and no one would expect late-twentieth-century believers or non-believers to have the same saints necessarily as the contemporaries of St Simeon Stylites or St Francis of Assisi, or to regard them in the same way.[3]

In other words, any definition is bound to be as culturally determined as is the concept of pilgrimage itself. In the period of the persecutions under the Roman emperors, it was the martyrs who were held in high esteem. The honour accorded to them was intense, since the faithful believed they were sharing in the suffering of Christ. Had they not been warned that they would be persecuted as he had been? (John 15.20). Was not death a gain since Christ was their life? (Phil. 1.23). Their recompense in heaven was declared to be great indeed (Matt. 5.10ff.).[4] No wonder they were respected. It is not surprising that, in an epoch when a false anti-materialist spirituality had not yet developed, this respect should manifest itself by kissing their bonds[5] nor that there was a tendency to think that God would refuse them nothing. Tertullian, however, reproached those who thought that they had an authority that belongs to God alone[6] and to that extent he was anticipating the Reformers.

The status of these athletes of God was a matter for constant vigilance on the part of the Church leaders and Augustine very clearly spelled out his concern.

> The martyrs are not gods, because we know only one God, who is the God both of us and of our martyrs . . . We Christians construct, in honour of our martyrs, not temples as if to gods but memorial shrines, as to men who are dead, but whose spirits are living with God. We do not in those shrines raise altars on which to sacrifice to the martyrs, but to the one God, who is the martyrs' God and ours; and at this sacrifice the martyrs are named, in their own place and in the appointed order, as men of God who have overcome the world in the confession of his name. They are not invoked by the priest who offers the sacrifice. For, of course, he is offering the sacrifice to God, not to the martyrs (although he offers it at their shrine), because he is God's priest not theirs. Indeed, the sacrifice is the Body of Christ, which is not offered to them, because they themselves are that Body.[7]

Augustine's reference to the martyrs as those 'who have overcome the world' points the way towards the next step in the development of the cult of the saints which began with the end of the persecutions. The lists of martyr-saints, i.e. of those who had borne witness by their deaths, was abruptly closed. Who then were to be the models for Christian living? A new concept was required and this was minted by assimilating asceticism to martyrdom – sanctity now became a property recognizable in monks and nuns.

By the late Middle Ages the role of these heroes and heroines of the faith was necessarily defined in categories derived from the feudal system that prevailed in Western Europe. Feudalism designates a form of society within which the principal bond is constituted by the relation between lord and subordinate, a relationship implying on the lord's part protection and on the subordinate's service with reverence. Saints were consequently regarded as seigneurs who could provide assistance in time of need. They were wire-pullers in the court of heaven, mediators or go-betweens, advocates pleading before a stern judge. Just as the tie between serf and master was regarded to be of the most sacred kind, with dependence very much the condition of the inferior, so individual Christians and saints were linked within a similar relationship. The fealty or homage rendered to the superior was paralleled by the veneration accorded to a St Thomas of Canterbury or to the Virgin Mary. Vows to the saints were then equivalent to oaths to land owners. Indeed oaths played an important part in the administration of law in feudal society, for the oath was binding because it involved an appeal to God – a person would not forswear himself, though he might tell a lie: between mere lying and a false oath there was a great gap. Trials were therefore not concerned with evidence, as conceived today, but with oaths, i.e. the means of proof were considered to lie in swearing to the truth of what a person had said or done. Consequently a vow to go on a pilgrimage, if a saint would vouchsafe a particular favour, imposed an obligation on the oath-taker to fulfil his undertaking as well as on the saint to accede to the petition and in this way the vow bound both parties.

Reflecting as they did the structure of the society which produced and honoured them, the saints and their role were bound to be envisaged differently if and when that society changed as was the case with the dawn of the Reformation. When the mould of the static feudal world began to crack, there emerged a more individualistic society within which the rights and duties implied in the feudal relationship were no longer recognized. Devotion to the saints did not commend itself to those who felt themselves freed from middlemen. The transactional form that the cult had taken was not acceptable to those who were convinced with St Paul that eternal life is a free gift from God in Christ Jesus (Rom. 6.23). The attempt in the mediaeval period to attain salvation through devout observances, the emphasis upon saints, relics and pilgrimages had tended to allow the personality and being of Jesus to recede from the centre of the picture. The constant representation of the horrors of hell and of the labours of purgatory had meant that simple folk felt more comfortable with the saints than with God and regarded the Virgin as a mediator who could placate the wrath of her Son when he came in judgment.[8] The Reformers would not endorse these beliefs about the saints and rejected the corresponding devotional practices, including pilgrimages – they could find no scriptural support for them.

At the present day, an understanding of pilgrimage that continues to see it as in some way associated with the saints must involve an acceptable redefinition of their role. This task can be left until later in the chapter since the principal object of this present section is to clear the ground and to do so by excluding whatever is not unquestionably legitimate. However this does not mean neglecting three other factors of the cult of the saints, viz. the miracles they were expected to perform and the images and relics connected with their shrines.

Whether miracles took place or not is not a question that has to be faced here: it was universally *believed* that they did happen. Yet the existence of this belief underscores one of the great weaknesses in the mediaeval understanding of the saints – at least as far as the present day is concerned – because it means that they were regarded primarily as sources of power, partly thaumaturgic. In the patristic period sainthood was not determined by an ability to perform wonders; it was based upon heroic virtue and ardent Christian discipleship.[9] Indeed many of the Fathers, now regarded as saints, never had miracles attributed to them: certainly not St Augustine nor St Basil and not even St John Chrysostom. In the mediaeval period, on the other hand, the miraculous was right to the fore and this exaggerated stress detracted from the uniqueness of each individual saint, with the consequence that they were 'lessened as persons and became more conduits for favours, miracles and interventions'.[10] Since the benefits were largely similar in kind, the real person became lost behind the type, each saint being represented as a wonder-worker, and the way each one incarnated the gospel in his or her day and age was obscured. However carefully theologians might phrase their statements to the effect that God alone is the source of all benefits and that whatever help is forthcoming derives ultimately from him, even though he may use saints as his agents, ordinary Christians, who outnumbered the schoolmen by millions to one, addressed themselves directly to their patrons in the various pilgrimage centres in the conviction that it was either from them immediately or through their effective intercession that blessings were to be obtained. Practice was prone to overthrow doctrinal verity. Moreover how to understand the intercessory activity of the saints is by no means simple.

The New Testament, with its emphasis upon doing the will of God here and now, is notoriously reticent, not to say at times apparently contradictory, about the condition of the departed. In the few places where intercession is specifically mentioned, it relates to the activity of the Holy Spirit and of Christ (Rom. 8.26f., 34; Heb. 7.25). But more important than what is or is not stated in holy writ is the understanding of the nature of God that is implied in the view that saints possess special powers of intercession. Can it really be believed that God is a being who has favourites and will grant their requests rather than those of others? It would seem more sensible and to detract less from the majesty and mercy of God to see intercession rather as a form of comfort and support to the one offering the prayer and an expression and experience of the real communion or fellowship of the saints and so of all believers in Christ. There was indeed a widespread belief in the early church that death does not interrupt the relationship previously enjoyed with those left behind. One epitaph among many can be quoted to illustrate this.

> Genantius, a believer, in peace, who lived 21 years, 8 months, 16 days, and in your prayers ask for us, because we know you are in Christ.[11]

This, be it noted, does not refer to petitions to a saint, the surviving relatives are asking their son to pray for them, as he did in life. In similar vein, Jerome, writing from Rome in 389 to Paula upon the death of her daughter Blesilla, remarks that 'for me too, I feel sure, she makes intercession and asks God to pardon my sins'.[12] Here the communion of saints, i.e. of all Christians, is very succinctly expressed, but it does not provide any basis for being a pilgrim with the primary intention of seeking help in need under the patronage of a particular saint. This is not to deny the devotional value of petitioning them – this has had too long a history and has proved itself viable in terms of the spiritual growth of individuals both within Roman

Catholicism and Eastern Orthodoxy for it to be discarded lightly – but this is insufficient to consider it a satisfactory key to the interpretation of pilgrimage today.

What then of images and relics? If the Reformation rejection of images may be said to have gone too far, the same could apply to mediaeval behaviour at local shrines. Here again a distinction has to be drawn between popular religion and what is regarded as permissible in the light of the careful pronouncements of the theologians. Gregory the Great condemned 'the adoration that has been improperly paid to pictures ... To adore a picture is one thing, but to learn through the story of a picture what is to be adored is another.'[13] This is eminently sensible but while the schoolmen could differentiate between *latria* to God and *dulia* to saints, it is obvious that this meant little to the average pilgrim.

It is also clear that respect for a statue does not necessarily mean that there is a confusion between the image and that which it represents – despite Thomas Cranmer's opposite opinion.[14] In general the adoration of images does not *simpliciter* involve idolatry, since in most religions the physical object, which may serve as a focus for devotion, is not identified with the divine. An image may foster a consciousness of the divine presence, but it is the presence that is or should be the object of the cult and not the statue or picture. It is true that the Decalogue does condemn images of God, but this is not to oppose the visible to the invisible nor the material to the spiritual. It is simply to affirm that Yahweh is unlike any other god – he cannot be localized; he is free in his activity. Thus the Reformed contention that the only true images of God are human beings is beside the point. Even so this does not of itself provide any sound basis for becoming a pilgrim – does the veneration of relics fill the gap?

Relics are left-overs, as the etymology indicates (from *relinquere*, to leave behind). In Latin usage they could be remains of any kind such as fragments of food – indeed *reliquias* in this sense is to be found in the Vulgate of Matt. 14.20 specifying 'that which remained over' after the five thousand had been fed. Equally the word could designate the ashes of a dead person burnt on a funeral pyre. In this sense a corpse is a relic or, if it has decomposed, the bones, teeth, etc. The personal effects of the deceased may be brought under the same heading, such as a piece of the cloak of St Martin of Tours or indeed anything that had been closely linked with the departed like the gridiron on which St Lawrence was roasted alive. It is this association with someone who has been loved and honoured that explains the respect with which relics were treated throughout the ancient world and eventually by Christians too.

Relics then are objects that have been in physical contact either with Christ (e.g. the wood of the true cross) or with his saints and consequently they constitute memorials of them, not by means of a simple representation like images but because they have an historical link either with the body of Jesus or with those of the saints. In time a kind of chain reaction was endorsed in that over and above those relics that were cherished because they were either what was left of a person or had been in direct touch with him, a further category was accepted, viz. contact-relics which had been brought into touch with the original remains. That the original remains should be treated with care is a natural human response, especially when this is associated with the beliefs that the bodies of the saints had been temples of the Holy Spirit and will be raised at the last day. This legitimate respect and reverence for relics is most movingly expressed in Christian literature for the first time in a letter (c. 156) from the congregation at Smyrna to their fellow believers at nearby Philomelium describing the martyrdom of their Bishop Polycarp. After declaring that the Son of God alone is to be adored, whereas martyrs are to be respected as 'disciples and imitators of the Lord', they go on to tell how

> we afterwards took up his bones which are more valuable than precious stones and finer than refined gold and laid them in a suitable place; where the Lord will permit us to gather ourselves together, as we are able, in gladness and joy, and to celebrate the birthday of his martyrdom for the commemoration of those that have already fought in the contest and for the training and preparation of those who shall do so hereafter.[15]

It is a far cry from this to the last quarter of the fourth century when such outstanding Fathers as Ambrose, Augustine and John Chrysostom leant their considerable authority to the view that relics can be remedies for almost every ill and protections against evil, with adoration, if not actual worship, replacing that reverence that had been so seemly in previous centuries.

To the Reformers, as previously noted, this was nothing but superstition and certainly the appeal to scripture by Roman Catholics, such as Thomas More and even by the Council of Trent,[16] cannot be regarded as well founded. The making whole of the woman with the issue of blood (Matt. 9.20f.), when she touched the hem of Jesus' garment, was not a healing miracle by means of a relic but by the virtue or power that emanated from Jesus himself. Further the cures effected by Peter's shadow (Acts 5.15) and by the 'handkerchiefs or aprons carried away from' the body of Paul (19.12) were anything but the outcome of contact with relics since both men were alive at the time. It is difficult to dispute the truth of Calvin's verdict on these passages:

> the papists are deceiving by the wrong use they make of this, not only to get support for false miracles, which they say take place at the tombs of martyrs, but to vaunt their relics to us.[17]

In fact the Acts 19 passage serves a twofold purpose in the text and it is certainly not to vindicate the use of relics for miraculous ends, let alone as the objectives of a pilgrimage. First, it is stated that 'God did extraordinary miracles by the hands of Paul', and these are recorded in conscious analogy with those ascribed to Peter in Acts 5 precisely to enhance the apostleship of Paul. Second, it is clear from the verses that follow, describing the vain efforts of the sons of Sceva to perform mighty works, that the intention here is to intimate that Christianity was not meant to be a magical art.[18] It is then not possible to support the cult of relics by an appeal to the New Testament and it cannot therefore supply a clue to the meaning of pilgrimage at the present day.

There were other aspects of mediaeval pilgrimage, in addition to the cult of saints, images and relics, to which the Reformers had objections and so, because these can also apply to going to the Holy Land, this preliminary review has to be extended. As previously reported in the chapter on the Reformation condemnation, one of the reasons advanced against travelling to a specific locality was the fact of the divine omnipresence: if God is everywhere, no one has to go to a particular country or town to meet him. It was further contended that the view that there are specially holy places is false: no one place is to be considered more holy than another. Also repudiated was the close link between pilgrimages and indulgences together with the belief that devotional journeys constitute good works by means of which salvation and forgiveness can be earned. Religion, it was argued, is to be internalized if true spiritual growth is to take place – the spiritual was in this way identified with inwardness. Taken all in all these together form a powerful case against accepting pilgrimage in anything like its mediaeval sense. However, when they are examined more closely it becomes apparent that some at least of these adverse criticisms miss the mark.

Opposition on the grounds of God's omnipresence was fully recognized by Evelyn Waugh in his short meditation on the holy places. 'The pilgrim's instinct,' he wrote, 'is deep set in the human heart. It is indeed an affair of the heart rather than of the head. Reason tells us that Christ is as fully present in one church as in another.'[19] But to believe that God fills and contains the universe is in fact not a valid argument against pilgrimage. Whatever grounds there may be for rejecting the practice, the divine omnipresence is not one of them. Those who advance this argument are in danger of affirming the non-presence of God everywhere. If to go to Rome or Jerusalem is not to have the possibility of encountering God, then to that extent his presence is limited. Yet it has always been a Christian belief that however transcendent God is, in the sense of being other than his creation, he is also immanent within his world – and not only in one or a few localities but everywhere. According to Kierkegaard,

> the meaning of God's omnipresence is not simply that he is present everywhere and at all times, but also that he is wholly present in his presence, absolutely present in every individual, wholly present in each and yet in all. He is not, as it were, broken up and partially present in each and wholly present to himself through a sort of succession; that is pantheism. He is wholly present in everyone in particular and yet in all things.[20]

Advocates of pilgrimage in former times were well aware of this. They knew that one did not have to go to Palestine to meet God, but this did not mean that if they chose to go there no encounter could take place. It is at this point that the biblical understanding of the divine presence needs to be taken into account together with a recognition of the extent to which it underwent a development.

The Israelites were slow to learn that Yahweh's presence cannot be limited in space. Like all other nations in the ancient Middle East they believed initially that God was not ubiquitous but localized. Consequently, to give one illustration, when Elkanah wished to perform his religious duties, he 'used to go up year by year from his city to worship and to sacrifice to the Lord of Hosts at Shiloh' (I Sam. 1.3). Such a journey often required penetrating into a strange territory where one was consequently a foreigner, a temporary visitor, a sojourner or pilgrim.

The longer the journey the more the tendency to regard it as an essential part of the religious exercise; it assumed a quasi-sacred character. But over the centuries recognition of the universal presence of God emerged and found classic expression in verses 7–10 of Psalm 139.

> Whither shall I go from thy Spirit?
> Or whither shall I flee from thy presence?
> If I ascend to heaven, thou art there!
> If I make my bed in Sheol, thou art there!
> If I take the wings of the morning
> and dwell in the uttermost parts of the sea,
> even there thy hand shall lead me,
> and thy right hand shall hold me.

Yahweh is here no longer conceived as a static baal restricted to a hill top sanctuary. He may be met in a locality but not localized. But then a reverse process of thought and practice took place. The high places were destroyed. Yahweh's presence, in reality universal, was deemed to be centred in the holy of holies of the Jerusalem Temple and henceforth pilgrims were to go to that sanctuary. It was now declared to be the divine will that all males should appear there before the Lord three times a year, for the feasts of Passover, Weeks and Booths (Deut. 16.16), and this injunction was read back into the Exodus period (Ex. 23.17; 34.23). While God's omnipresence was not denied by worshipping him in a particular place, no place was to be regarded as the exclusive focus of his presence.

> Thus says the Lord:
> 'Heaven is my throne
> and the earth is my footstool;
> what is the house that you would build for me,
> and what is the place of my rest?
> All these things my hand has made.'

These verses from Isaiah (66.1f.) are quoted in Stephen's speech immediately after the statement that 'the most High does not dwell in houses made with hands', (Acts 7.48). Yet this does not exclude the possibility of there being religious buildings nor pilgrimage centres, because, although infinite and outside space and time, the Christian God participates in a time-based world and in space; the eternal God does make himself accessible to limited human beings in space and time – it is the humans who are limited, not God. This after all is the message of the Incarnation which focuses without confining the divine presence. 'God was in Christ reconciling the world to himself,' (II Cor. 5.19) wrote Paul, but at the same time God did not cease his surveillance of that same world. Proclus, later to become Bishop of Constantinople, stressed this point in a sermon delivered on Lady Day, 429:

> He was in the Father's bosom and in the womb of his mother. He lay in a mother's arms, while he walked on the wings of the wind. He was adored by angels, while he sat at meat with publicans. The cherubim dare not behold him, while Pilate interrogated him. The servant smote him, and creation shuddered. He hung on the cross, but he was not absent from the throne of glory; and, while he lay in the tomb, he was spreading out the heavens like a curtain.[21]

These seemingly paradoxical statements may be illuminated by recourse to a modern analogy, viz. that of a radio set. We know that all about us wireless waves are present in the air, but they remain undetected unless they are focused in and by a receiver. The waves are virtually omnipresent but that does not mean that they cannot be concentrated coincidentally in one spot without detriment to their continued universal presence. So the omnipresence of God is not compromised by his being embodied in Jesus Christ. But like every analogy this one is not to be pressed too far; there is more to immanence and Incarnation than a matter of degree; in particular Incarnation is not simply presence but atoning action.[22]

In Proclus' statement incarnate presence and transcendence are nicely balanced; similarly immanence is to be understood as a correlative of transcendence; they are like the convexity and concavity of a single curve. Hence there is no contradiction between holding that God may be worshipped anywhere and worshipping him in a particular place. Jerome was certain that 'access to the courts of heaven is as easy from Britain as it is from Jerusalem',[23] but this did not prevent him being an ardent advocate of pilgrimages – indeed, despite the Reformers, there is here no proper basis for repudiating the practice.

However, what about the strongly held mediaeval belief that some places are holier than others? It was accepted that those places where there had been an intersection of the human and the divine, such as Bethlehem, were holy. Jerusalem was a case in point because there Jesus had completed his earthly ministry; Compostela was holy because there God had performed miracles through his saint. As former interaction points of heaven and earth, it was believed that such holy places could be the scene of renewed divine activity and so doors into eternity. They are centres of power and by visiting them pilgrims can acquire some of the holiness that inheres in them, not only by being there and by engaging in devotional exercises but also by simple physical contact. Pilgrimage was therefore meaningful in that it denoted a journey to a destination where holiness was present, could be encountered and acquired.

The weakness of this formulation is that it appears to be clear but in fact it is ambiguous in that holiness is being used with two different connotations: on the one hand it is applied to a relationship and on the other to a quality of being. A glance at the biblical understanding of holiness will make this plain. In both the Old and New Testaments the 'holy' is the divine. 'Holiness' is distinctive of God, that which constitutes his nature. To declare that God is holy is not, in the first instance, to assert anything about his character but to affirm his supreme Godhead. As an adjective, then, 'holy' stresses the uniqueness of God, who is not to be confused with the deities worshipped by anyone else – 'There is none holy like the Lord' (I Sam. 2.2). Holiness refers to the inner essence of the divine being. So the statement that 'the Lord has sworn by his holiness' means exactly the same as 'the Lord God has sworn by himself' (Amos 4.2//6.8). Indeed the only appropriate way to give glory to him is to sing, with the four living creatures in the Apocalypse, 'holy, holy, holy' (Rev. 4.8), hymning him for being himself. Holiness is not then an attribute of God; it does not refer to a quality of being; rather it expresses what is characteristic of God and corresponds to his deity. Holiness is synonymous with divinity; holy with divine. It follows from this that these two words can only be applied to persons or places in a derivative or secondary sense. Since God alone is holy, nothing and nowhere can be holy in themselves; they are only holy when placed in relation to the divine being. Holy and holiness in this connection do not refer to a quality but to a relationship: in other words, places can only be called holy or have holiness ascribed to them in virtue of their relationship to God.[24] This view is identical with that of many Islamic pilgrims as represented by Ahmal Kamal.

> Today we venerate Mecca, the Ka'bah, the Black Stone, the well Zamzam and its water, the Place of Ibrahim – the holy places – for their history and association, but *not* for themselves. God and God alone is the object of our worship.[25]

However, while the mediaeval divines were truly biblical in

regarding those places where there had been an intersection of the human and the divine as holy, they were not in accordance with the New Testament in going on to hold that this relationship meant that such places had a quality of being inherent in them that could be communicated. A useful analogy in this context is that of 'a healthy seaside resort'. Obviously such a place is not healthy in itself, nor is healthiness a quality that can be ascribed to it. The phrase only has meaning if it refers to the people who go there. Healthy may be applied to a place when it denotes a relation between the place and the health of those who stay or live in it. Similarly, holy can be applied to a place when it refers to a relation between the place and God – Mount Tabor is then properly called holy because it was the scene of Jesus' transfiguration, but Newcastle has had no such revelation and could not legitimately claim the adjective with any meaning. It is consequently not acceptable to rest the interpretation of pilgrimage upon the idea of going to a 'holy place' to acquire the holiness present in it – to that extent the Reformers were right. There is, however, no reason why one should not regard, say, Rome, where God inspired the witness of the apostles Peter and Paul, as a holy place and visit it to see where their witness was consummated by martyrdom. Yet, it must be added, this will not ensure a renewal of divine activity; that would be to assume that God can be manipulated and a pilgrimage then becomes an attempt to achieve one's ends by magical means. It may be that God will vouchsafe himself, but the fact that he has acted in a certain place in the past does not tie him to do anything in the same place ever again.

To complete this process of sifting the mediaeval ideas and the corresponding Reformation objections in the hope of discovering hints from the past for the formulation of a modern understanding of pilgrimage consideration has to be given to three final items, viz. internalization, indulgences and good works.

The view that pilgrimage is totally unnecessary because it is an affair of the 'heart' began to develop, as noted previously, in the twelfth century with its emphasis upon the internalization of religion and this was fully endorsed at the Reformation. Luther was one of many who held that the true and indeed sole legitimate pilgrimage is the reading of the scriptures and that instead of walking about holy places the faithful should engage in introspection.[26] It is true that a distinction between the inner and the outer, with some prior emphasis being given to the former, may appear to receive support from certain passages in the letters of Paul (e.g. II Cor. 4.16), but the apostle was no dualist and he did not think that the inner and the outer are totally distinct and without effect the one upon the other. Indeed it is notoriously difficult to draw a hard and fast line between the two. Suppose, for example, that it were to be argued that the outer is that which occupies time and space, it could nevertheless be contended that human thoughts, which are usually regarded as inward, do at least occupy time and if they are related to chemical activities in the brain then they are spatial too – this way of differentiating them then falls to the ground.[27]

Nor, in view of Christian sacramental theology, can the inner, however defined, be equated with the spiritual and the outer with the material, the two then being regarded as antithetical. To accept the practice of celebrating the sacraments is to acknowledge that matter is to be regarded as qualitatively spiritual through and through; spirit, in other words, is something materially given. Indeed Christianity endorses a kind of religious materialism and this involves the recognition of the importance of actions and indeed of physical actions. After all, the material world, including the humans who inhabit it, is the creation of a spiritual being. As C. S. Lewis once remarked: 'God likes matter; he created it.' But this means that the universe is a sacramental kind of place in which the material elements and bodily actions can speak of God. This was recognized long ago by John Chrysostom, even if his terminology smacks a little of dualism:

> If you had been incorporeal, Christ would have given you likewise gifts incorporeal; but because your soul has been joined to your body, he gives you spiritual things in material things.[28]

To the same effect Thomas Aquinas was to observe much later that people forget they are human when they think that bodily acts can be dispensed with in either private or public worship.[29] If matter has a spiritual dimension then the possibility cannot be ruled out that physical actions, such as going on a pilgrimage, may be related to the world of the spirit and if stress on interiorization were held to deny this, then the stress must be regarded as misplaced. God relates to us through our bodiliness; consequently space-time, matter, sacraments, bodily actions – all may be interpreted as possible means of furthering communion with him who is the maker of heaven and earth and took flesh on our behalf. There is then no basis in Christian thought for undervaluing the going on a journey for religious purposes, on the spurious grounds that outward acts are not needed.

In fact few religions, Christianity included, could persist without some material representations of their central tenets nor without some movements that expressed devotion. Every culture in the past has had its archetypal quest and this search was embodied in journeys to places that enshrined religious values. It still remains to consider what this amounts to at the present day, but certainly there is nothing in the concept of internalization to rule out *a priori* the possibility of pilgrimages. Some of the Reformers may have hankered after an unmediated devotion, but human nature is such that the desire is vain – the role of pilgrimage within such mediation remains to be reviewed.

It would not appear to be a sensible pursuit to consider in any detail the second of the remaining mediaeval ideas, viz. indulgences. Their history has been bedevilled by controversy and by imprecision and by incompleteness of definition that render analysis far from easy. More to the point, however, is the extent to which they have taken very much a back seat in Roman Catholic thought and devotions at the present day, despite the issuing by the Vatican in 1986 of a revised Latin list of them. According to Karl Rahner:

> Interest in indulgences is largely diminishing in the Church, even in circles where religion is devoutly practised. The genuine religious concerns of Catholics have profoundly changed in form, being transferred to the celebration of the eucharist, personal prayer and a truly Christian steadfastness in face of the tragic hardships of ordinary existence . . . The various degrees of partial indulgences seem to have lost all religious significance today . . . If indulgences are to be retained, the efforts in this direction should be prudently restricted, since otherwise too much pastoral time and energy would be consumed which should today be devoted to other objects.[30]

When the situation is such, it would certainly be a waste of time to resurrect the issue here and it could easily result in obscurity rather than clarity. Nevertheless in relation to sin and forgiveness the mediaeval concern was not solely to seek indulgences, with their underlying idea of a deferred payment; it was also to engage in a penitential exercise to obtain immediate gain, i.e. a pilgrimage could be an extension of the sacrament of penance interpreted according to a transactional or bargaining model which was basic to feudal society. This understanding is common to a number of world religions. Hinduism, for example, regards visits to the Ganges as having a purifying effect and leading to the 'disappearance of sins'.[31]

Ahmal, a pilgrim from Mauretania to Mecca *c.* 1830 expressed a similar belief:

> We praise God for the obligation of the pilgrimage. It is enjoined on true believers so that they may go around his holy house on the chief day of the pilgrimage, and so that he may pardon the sins of those who turn in repentance to him and who seek his pardon and forgiveness.[32]

Undoubtedly this penitential note derived in part from the arduous nature of the journey and the present-day ease of travel, particularly by air, has devalued the *hajj* to such an extent that there is an increasing tendency to regard pilgrimage on foot as conferring superior spiritual benefits simply because it demands more effort.[33] This reversion to a previous more difficult mode of travel indicates the extent to which pilgrimage interpreted in this way can be categorized as a 'good work' in the sense condemned by Martin Luther – no more in fact need be said, although something remains to be added on the subject of good works themselves.

It may well be asked what is wrong with good works? If a work is described as good, how can it be condemned as reprehensible? This apparent nonsense can be soon dispelled by recalling that it was not altruistic or charitable actions that Martin Luther in particular opposed: he was condemning the belief that salvation is obtainable by performing them. The idea that a human being can secure an entitlement to divine forgiveness by means of an autonomous action on his or her part compromised, in Luther's opinion, the sovereignty and unconditional freedom of God. It is not by our own striving that we make ourselves acceptable to him – salvation is his free gift. Works then cannot be the cause of justification, however important they may be as its fruit or consequence.

It is difficult to see how pilgrimage cannot be rejected as implying salvation by works as long as it is closely associated with indulgences. These rest upon a belief in the merit of Christ and his saints which can be tapped to the individual's advantage. The effort of travelling to Rome or Jerusalem and thereby to earn so many years of indulgences was to most people to execute a good work that would entitle them to a reward. This without question was rightly repudiated at the Reformation and would be a fallacious ground on which to try and build a modern understanding of pilgrimage. However, whether or not a pilgrimage may properly be interpreted as a spiritual exercise, rather than a good work deserving grace, and therefore as such constituting a feature in the ongoing process of sanctification, which springs from justification, is a different matter entirely and has to be considered next.

Pilgrimage as a Spiritual Exercise

A spiritual exercise is an activity that helps one to reach out towards God, to deepen one's relationship with him and so to enter into a closer union. It is a means to promote spiritual development and to fulfil the commandment to love God and one's neighbour. It may serve to inculcate a right attitude towards the deity – respect, self-surrender, dedication. It fixes the mind upon him. Spiritual exercises, then, include a whole host of devotional activities that have been tried and proved over the centuries within the Christian tradition of self-discipline: prayer, Bible reading, meditation, intercession, going on retreats. These are all spiritual exercises, undertaken not to please God nor to curry his favour but out of a desire to be at one with the ground of all being. They are therefore not 'good works' in the pejorative sense but so many means of spiritual growth.

The idea of growth is present in numerous passages of the New Testament. Paul is thankful that the faith of the Thessalonians is growing abundantly (II Thess. 1.3.). Christians are 'to grow up in every way into him who is the head, into Christ' (Eph. 4.15). The church 'grows with a growth that is from God' (Col. 2.19). In I Peter the exhortation is that the faithful 'may grow up to salvation' (2.2) and in II Peter: 'Grow in the grace and knowledge of our Lord and Saviour Jesus Christ' (3.18). This growth is a process of conformation to the image of the Son of God (Rom. 8.29) and it can be called sanctification (I Thess. 4.3). 'Follow after (Greek *diokete*, i.e. pursue, chase or hunt) peace with all men, and the sanctification without which no man shall see the Lord' (Heb. 12.14). Here Quietism is rejected, i.e. the belief is repudiated that Christians have to attain complete passivity, with the consequent minimizing of all human endeavour and responsibility. On the contrary, according to Paul, 'work out your own salvation with fear and trembling; for God is at work in you' (Phil. 2.12.f.) It is within this ambit of ideas that spiritual exercises become intelligible and acceptable.

But what does it mean to say that a pilgrimage is or can be a means of growth and so a spiritual exercise? There is one simple way of approaching this question and that is by comparing a pilgrimage with the Stations of the Cross. The Stations are a spiritual exercise which consists of pausing for prayer and meditation before each of fourteen representations of incidents on Jesus' way to Golgotha. This devotion probably derived from the practice of fourth-century pilgrims in Jerusalem following the street from Pilate's house to Calvary. Wishing to re-enact it when they returned home, they set up a series of pictures or carvings and those who were unable to make the journey overseas could participate with them in an act of piety. When the Franciscans were given custody of the holy places in the fourteenth century, they promoted this particular spiritual exercise in the churches under their control and it then spread into the parish churches. A pilgrimage is equally a way of the cross and, of course, if the destination be Jerusalem the actual route to Golgotha is followed: in fact the journey as a whole, the mini-pilgrimage upon arrival and the Stations of the Cross are to be understood as so many forms of response to the words: 'he who does not take his cross and follow me is not worthy of me' (Matt. 10.38). This does not mean that a pilgrimage is necessarily more beneficial than an observance of the Stations in one's home church or chapel, but clearly it will not be *less* beneficial.

A pilgrimage is also to be included within the category of spiritual exercises because the intention behind it is, or should be, identical with that of every other devotional practice viz., to concentrate one's mind upon God. It can be – to use a Hindu term applied to pilgrimage – a ford (*tirtha*) or bridge to the divine. There is of course a difference between the normal practice of religion at home and what goes on at a pilgrimage centre. This difference is largely a matter of degree; there is often an intensity of devotion greater than in one's habitual surroundings and this is induced by being present at places, such as Jerusalem or Philippi, which are full of meaning for Christian believers, being so intimately associated with the foundation of their religion. The pilgrimage experience is thus a peak one, a distillation of that which is part of religious observance in one's own locality. This is especially so when the pilgrimage is at the time of a major festival, e.g. on Christmas day at Bethlehem. Indeed to go to Bethlehem is to visit a place where heaven and earth have intersected. There is nothing to rule out such an intersection occurring today in the middle of Piccadilly Circus, Times Square or the Place de la Concorde, but in such surroundings the reality of the encounter is less easy to appreciate. In the Church of the Nativity, on the other hand, trust and hope can be encouraged. God ceases to be so mysterious and far off in a place where it is believed he has acted.

It is not that one cannot have a celebration of Christ's birth in one's parish church or regular place of worship, but it is without question intensified by being present in Bethlehem itself. Similarly, to walk in the footsteps of St Paul is to pursue with eagerness the traces of the Holy Spirit, for that is how the Acts of the Apostles interprets the apostle's missionary journeys, i.e. they are part and parcel of the Acts of the Holy Spirit.

A direct insight into the nature of this heightening of fervour, by someone in the process of experiencing it, is contained in the fourth sermon that Dean Stanley delivered before Edward, Prince of Wales, during their visit to the Holy Land. A little florid in expression, this passage nevertheless conveys the human reality very clearly.

> We should not be Christians – we should not be Englishmen – we should not, I had almost said, be reasonable beings, if, believing what we do about the events that took place here, we could see Jerusalem and the Holy Land as we could see any other town or any other country. Even if it were only for the thought of the interest which thousands in former ages have taken in what we shall see – if only for the thought that we shall now be seeing what thousands have longed to see and not seen – if only for the thought of the feeling which our visit to these spots awakens in the hearts of thousands far away in our own dear homes in England; – we cannot but gather up some good feelings, some more than merely passing pleasure, from these sacred scenes; and can we forbear to add, that there is, besides and above all this, the thought that we may possibly be thus brought more nearly into communion with that Divine Friend and Saviour, whose blessed feet, eighteen hundred years ago, walked this land, through whose words and acts in this country every one of us, at some time of his life or other, has been consoled and instructed, and hopes at last to be saved?[34]

To concentrate on the essentials of one's faith is rendered the more easy when freed from the distractions of everyday life and this freedom can be found when travelling as a pilgrim. In a sense it is a form of retreat, i.e. a withdrawal from the world of work and domesticity, undertaken out of love for God in the hope that that love may be increased. This suggestion of temporary disengagement from the workaday routine immediately focuses attention on the original connotation of the biblical terms that were first translated into English as strangers and pilgrims but in later versions were rendered differently. In the Septuagint and the New Testament there are two nouns, with their corresponding verbs, that are of primary interest in this respect, viz. *paroikos* and *parepidemos*. So Genesis 47.9, where the verb *paroikein* is employed, stands in the Authorized Version as 'the years of my pilgrimage', but became more accurately in the Revised Standard Version 'the years of my sojourning'. While 'pilgrims' for *parepidemoi* in the AV of Hebrews 11.13 is changed to 'exiles' in the RSV. The modern renderings are true to the etymology of the words which relates them to aliens or exiles. *Oikein* means to dwell, but put the preposition *para* in front of it and it denotes living alongside someone who is himself at home, i.e. the *paroikos* is a temporary resident in a foreign land. The same is true of *parepidemos* and of the slightly archaic English 'sojourner'. This last word derives via French (*séjourner*) from the popular Latin *subdiurnare* to spend a day, i.e. to make a short stay in a place. The use of *peregrinus* in the Vulgate brings that word too within the same range of meaning since it comes from *peregre*, itself from *per* and *ager* meaning 'in a foreign country'. An apt illustration of all this is provided by Psalm 39.12, where both *paroikos* and *parepidemos* appear in the Septuagint and *peregrinus* in the Vulgate, and the RSV translates accurately:

> For I am thy passing guest,
> a sojourner, like all my fathers.

The reference then is twofold: to the transitoriness of earthly life and to the fact that this world is not our true home. This tension between the present age and the age to come that has already broken in with the advent of Jesus is charmingly expressed in the late second-century *Epistle to Diognetus*.

> For Christians are distinguished from the rest of men neither by country nor by language nor by customs . . . They live in fatherlands of their own, but as aliens. They share all things as citizens, and suffer all things as strangers. Every foreign land is their fatherland, and every fatherland is a foreign land. They marry, like all others; they breed children, but they do not cast out their offspring . . . They are 'in the flesh', but they do not 'live after the flesh'. They pass their days on earth, but they have their citizenship in heaven. They obey the appointed laws, yet in their own lives they excel the laws. They love all men, and are persecuted by all. They are unknown, and yet they are condemned; they are put to death, yet they are made alive.[35]

It was this understanding that lay behind the exilic pilgrimages of the Middle Ages, described previously,[36] when homelessness became an ascetic ideal and wandering monks were not unusual. So while the biblical terms did not originally refer specifically to a physical movement, they were eventually applied to certain journeyings that dramatized the verse in the Epistle to the Hebrews: 'Here we have no lasting city, but we seek the city that is to come' (13.14). Later, however, there was a transition from *peregrinatio a patria* to *peregrinatio ad loca sancta*, and this was facilitated by the fact that in Latin *peregrinari* means not only dwelling in a foreign country but also travelling to distant parts to accomplish a definite project.[37]

The interpretation of the Christian way of life as either a procession to the heavenly sanctuary or a pilgrimage towards the divine rest is central to the Epistle to the Hebrews. The believer is to have faith and to practise hope (trust) that God will be with him or her to the end of the pilgrimage because 'faith is the assurance of things hoped for' (11.1). The Christian indeed can be properly described as a displaced person 'seeking a homeland . . . that is, a heavenly one' (11.14, 16). The identical view is present in I Peter 2.11: 'We are aliens and exiles.' Earthly life is therefore to be seen as an exodus, a constant migration in faith, of which Abraham is the representative figure (Heb. 11.8f.). The Exodus from Egypt was itself a form of discipline and Christians must submit to the same: 'It is for discipline that you have to endure' (12.7). Yet the goal is not Mount Sinai (12.18ff.) but the heavenly Jerusalem (12.22): the way is not that of the desert but 'by the new and living way' opened up by Jesus (10.20). Believers therefore must not 'drift away' (2.1), nor be led away (13.9) from the true path. This application of the Exodus image to the present of Christian pilgrimage is further emphasized by the quotation of Psalm 95.7–11 in Hebrews 3.7–11. These verses recall the pilgrimage in the wilderness as a type of contemporary discipleship. But while it has to be recognized that the central concept is not so much related to travelling through space as to passing through time, it is certainly applicable to pilgrimage today, which can then be interpreted as an embodied parable or effective sign of advancing on the way towards the heavenly Jerusalem, and as a discipline or spiritual exercise that takes the form of a retreat on the move.[38]

'The way' was of course a designation applied to Christianity from its earliest days, (e.g. Acts 24.14) and Christ too is so called in the Fourth Gospel (John 14.6). This usage explains the motto around the cross tattooed on the forearms of pilgrims in Jerusalem – something that Prince Edward himself underwent – *Via, Vita, Veritas*.[39] To be a Christian is to be on the way, pressing forward, asking new questions, seeking new truths and new life. To be a pilgrim is to have an opportunity to reorder one's priorities, rediscover perspectives and look to the future. It is a venture in faith like that of Abraham who at the command of God left Haran for an unknown destination and with uncertain blessings awaiting him (Gen. 12.1–3). To be a pilgrim is to set time apart to renew faith and obedience by recalling how God has revealed himself to particular men and women in particular places. We open ourselves to the possibility that he will renew our lives. The bodily movement that a journey requires is an effective symbol of the intention to make a personal approach to God which is at the heart of every spiritual exercise.

Pilgrimage as an Imitation of Christ and his Saints

There is one aspect of pilgrimage as a spiritual exercise that is so central that it demands a section to itself and that is the interpretation of it as an imitation of Christ. 'Imitation' is certainly not a new-fangled idea: unambiguous evidence of its importance in the past is supplied by the title of Thomas à Kempis' classic. Of course, it goes back ultimately to Paul; 'be imitators of me, as I am of Christ' (I Cor. 11.1). This is but one of numerous passages in which the apostle presented this theme and he connected it with the setting of an example. We 'give you in our conduct an example to imitate' (II Thess. 3.9). To similar effect is I Peter 2.21: 'Christ also suffered for you, leaving you an example, that you should follow in his steps.' In order to comprehend this theme completely, it is necessary to consider its roots in the Old Testament.

The Hebrew word *derek* (LXX *hodos*) signifies a road or a way, and then, by extension, it is used of a way of life (e.g. Ex. 18.20). In Deuteronomy there is a constant oscillation between *derek* denoting the actual historical way that Israel traversed from Egypt to the Promised Land, and *derek* meaning the way of life to which the people were summoned as a consequence of the covenant relationship established on Mount Sinai. The original 'way' had constantly to be made Israel's own and experienced anew as a present reality. This is made very plain by the opening verses of Deuteronomy 8 with their assertion that the necessity for the Jews to be humble and to obey the commandments rested upon the humbling of their forefathers in the wilderness when God disciplined them 'as a man disciplines his son'. So obedience to God 'takes the dynamic form of conforming one's conduct to what he has shown himself to be during the journey to the Promised Land'[40] – so E. J. Tinsley. Hence the *imitatio Dei* according to the Old Testament involves walking in the way of the Lord, and the historical journey must, in some sense, be lived again if the divine way for Israel is to be truly appropriated. It can in fact be followed, known and imitated through scripture reading, meditation, prayer and liturgy. So, for example, the Passover, which became a pilgrimage feast, was related to the Exodus, and according to the tractate on the subject contained in the *Mishnah*: 'In every generation a man must so regard himself as if he came forth himself out of Egypt.'[41] In effect, this means that the historical Exodus provides the pattern for Hebrew existence today; similarly it is the historical life of Jesus, who is the way, that has to be appropriated by his followers in the present, this appropriation being furthered by the work of the Holy Spirit. To quote Dr Tinsley again:

> The life of the Christian disciple as *imitator Christi* is not any kind of yoga of self-endeavour. It is not a process that is initiated and sustained by the Christian believer, as if the *imitatio Christi* were some kind of literal mimicry. It is a process initiated and sustained by the Spirit as Paraclete, and in it he conforms the pattern of the life of the believer to that of the Lord.[42]

This is the background to Paul's thought on the issue and it explains the method that he frequently adopted of drawing a parallel, and of even affirming a causal relation, between what the life of the Christian should be and what the life of Jesus had been. Christians are not to please themselves precisely because 'Christ did not please himself' (Rom. 15.1f.). They are to serve others because Christ undertook the task of a servant (Rom. 15.8 – *diakonos*). They are to be generous in giving because Jesus, 'though he was rich, yet for your sake he became poor, so that by his poverty you may become rich' (II Cor. 8.9). They are to be humble and obedient because 'he humbled himself and became obedient unto death' (Phil. 2.8). 'Therefore,' in the words of Ephesians, 'be imitators of God, as beloved children. And walk in love, as Christ loved us and gave himself for us' (5.1f.).

This re-calling of the life and example of Jesus corresponds to the re-calling of the Exodus in the Passover. To this Jewish liturgical practice there is a Christian counterpart in the form of the communion service, and so Paul saw the manna and the drink supplied in the wilderness as types of the eucharistic bread and wine. Within the same nexus of ideas, he regarded the passage through the Red Sea as a type of baptism (I Cor. 10.1–5). Jesus himself is regarded as having re-enacted the journey of the Israelites in that it had begun with the passing over of the angel of death while he himself was the paschal lamb (I Cor. 5.7). The sequence of his death, resurrection and ascension could then be summed up in a single word, viz. exodus (Luke 9.31: RSV departure; Greek *exodos*).

This theme of imitation has had its critics and Luther in particular considered that it could be a temptation to seek to acquire merit. He granted that Jesus was both example and gift, but he laid much stress on the latter and so emphasized the 'following' rather than the 'imitation' of Jesus. In so doing he was close to the terminology of the gospels where 'following' is indeed the normal word denoting the attachment of the disciples to Jesus, but then their historical situation differed from that of Paul and his correspondents. The disciples lived with Jesus, sharing his company throughout his ministry, but their successors did not. Consequently 'imitation' was the preferred term for them rather than 'following'. Yet even in the gospels 'following' has an imitatory aspect: 'Be merciful, even as your Father is merciful' (Luke 6.36). 'A new commandment I give to you, that you love one another; even as I have loved you, that you also love one another' (John 13.34). Moreover Paul does not imply that he is seeking to imitate some external model but someone who lives in him (Gal. 2.20). So imitation is not simply a matter of looking into the past to the historical Jesus; rather it is a sign of his presence and of his continuing activity in the world through the Holy Spirit.

When, in the Middle Ages, imitation was related to pilgrimage it often took the form of literal copying. So when Henry II went as a pilgrim to Canterbury in penance for the death of Thomas à Becket, he was scourged as was Jesus after his condemnation by Pilate (Mark 15.15). Many pilgrims to the Holy Land behaved in like fashion, as previously described,[43] lying on couches at Cana, plunging into the river Jordan or carrying crosses along the *Via Dolorosa*; their entire journey then became one long imitation of Christ. To a certain extent this may appear to be an antiquarian or romantic attempt to reproduce the historical past,[44] but this of course is not how mediaeval pilgrims understood their actions. Why, in the course of the Passover meal, do Jews eat unleavened bread and bitter herbs? '"Unleavened bread" – because our fathers were redeemed from Egypt; "bitter herbs" – because the Egyptians embittered the lives of our fathers.'[45] But in doing this the Jews have not been engaged in an historical reconstruction because they are not concerned merely to evoke a distant event. It is necessary, every year, for the event to become a present reality for each generation.[46] Why do Christians eat bread and drink wine? 'Bread' – because Jesus broke a loaf on the night before he was betrayed; 'wine' – because he took a cup prior to his 'exodus'. They are not re-staging the Last Supper – they are participating in the saving action of Christ which in the eucharist becomes a present reality. The mediaeval pilgrims were concerned likewise with the spiritual or mystical meaning of what they were doing.

At this juncture it is necessary to recall that in the Middle Ages scripture was considered to require a fourfold interpretation. Without repeating all that has been said already about this,[47] it is important to be aware that the pilgrims were not satisfied with the historical dimension alone and that they deemed every passage to have multiple meanings. Their pilgrimage was not a pageant recreating bygone days but a going to meet the Jesus whom they believed to be their contemporary. Their ardent desire was that Christ should take shape in their lives as they engaged in their devotions in Capernaum or Nazareth. The Holy Land processionals, with their prayers at each station, make this very plain: the past event is recalled at the place where it is believed to have occurred and its significance for the present and the future is drawn out in meditational form. The pilgrims were not indulging in reminiscences; it was the relevance to their present existence of what had happened and its capacity to nourish their spiritual progress that were all important. Imitation was and still can be understood today as a medium for the Holy Spirit's activity 'until Christ be formed in you' (Gal. 4.19). This formation, according to Dietrich Bonhoeffer,

> comes only as formation in his likeness, as *conformation* with the unique form of him who was made man, was crucified, and rose again. This is not achieved by dint of efforts 'to become like Jesus', which is the way in which we usually interpret it. It is achieved only when the form of Jesus Christ itself works upon us in such a manner that it moulds our form in its own likeness (Gal. 4.19).[48]

Bonhoeffer's words do not contradict the thesis that through a pilgrimage Jesus, in the power of the Spirit, may forward this process of conformation, although, admittedly, the process is not to be restricted to any one place. Nevertheless there is nothing here to support a denial that going to the Holy Land can provide an occasion for it.

Amongst the various elements within this process, Paul speaks of having the mind of Christ (Gal. 4.19). This aspect of imitation was commented upon by Dean Stanley in another of his sermons before Prince Edward and related by him to their journey through Palestine.

The *Mind*, the *Character* of Christ, that which he was and is . . . To have this in any degree is what makes a man a Christian; not to have it is to make all other Christian institutions and opinions almost worse than useless. To enter into the recesses of this Divine Character, more holy than the most revered of earthly shrines; to impress this Mind upon ourselves; to carry away some portion of it home for our daily use, more sacred than the most sacred relics – this ought to be the object of all that we see as we traverse the scenes of his earthly life.[49]

Victorian rhetoric? Yes – but the substance is perfectly acceptable. In the light of this, it would perhaps be not too difficult to agree that a Holy Land pilgrimage may be regarded legitimately as a spiritual exercise and one through which it may be possible to practise the imitation of Christ – but what of going to the shrines of the saints? The fact that Paul himself was prepared to tell his correspondents that they should imitate him as he imitated Christ (I Cor. 11.1) suggests that the imitation theme can also be applied to a pilgrimage in his steps or, for that matter, in those of any other saint. Before endorsing this, it is imperative to analyse what the imitation of the saints really means and especially how their function within the Body of Christ is to be defined.

The usurpation by the saints of some of the functions of Christ had earned the wrath of the Reformers; they objected to pilgrimages in their honour to seek help, gifts, intercession and mediation, all of which belong, according to the New Testament, within the domain or sovereignty of Christ. The role ascribed to the saints in many early Roman mass prefaces is however one to which the Protestants of the sixteenth century could scarcely have objected. According to these, the martyrs are to be revered because their witness has enabled later generations to confess 'that name in which alone salvation is determined for us'. Through their testimony, so it is stated, God continues to strengthen our weak faith as they extend over the forces of evil the victory already won by Christ.[50] Yet the stress on the miraculous powers of the saints, as indicated in the opening pages of this chapter, resulted in the undermining of their individuality; the person paled into insignificance behind the capacity to work wonders. Each one was held to be a locus of power and the intrinsic value of his or her life was passed over so that their exemplary role was neglected.[51] The real saints are the ones who provide models for others to follow – this is where imitation is relevant: they show what it means to be Christians in a given historical period and so they constitute examples to be followed by their fellow members in the

Body of Christ, 'The saint,' according to L. Cunningham, 'enfleshes Christian ideals in concrete historical situations'[52] and so assists believers to discern different ways of living out or incarnating the implications of the gospel. This certainly was how such an authoritative figure as John of Damascus (d. c. 749) envisaged them:

> The saints must be honoured as the friends of Christ . . . they have kept undebased the likeness of the divine image in which they were made . . . Let us set up monuments to them, and visible images, and let us ourselves by *imitation* of their virtues become their living monuments and images . . . Let us carefully observe the manner of life of all these and let us emulate their faith, charity, hope, zeal, life, patience under suffering, and perseverance unto death, so that we may also share their crowns of glory.[53]

The same view is expressed in more modern terms by Karl Rahner:

> Saints are the initiators and the creative models of the holiness which happens to be right for, and is the task of, their particular age. They create a new style; they prove that a certain form of life and activity is a really genuine possibility; they make such a type of person believable as a Christian type. Their significance therefore begins not merely after they are dead. Their death is rather the seal put upon their task of being creative models.[54]

With this both Protestants and Catholics can agree, as witnessed by *The Common Catechism* produced by representatives of the two traditions. This contains the following statement:

> The main intention of the veneration of the saints is to glorify God's grace in real men and women as they exist in historical time. Veneration of the saints is not adoration of the saints, but celebration of them as witnesses to the triumphant grace of God and as models for Christian life.[55]

Their sanctity, we may say, is for others, and if today we fail to be ignited by the holiness or God-relatedness of a Paul, we are to that extent not benefiting from the gifts that God bestowed upon him. His example tells against any fatalistic stance or form of Quietism. One has only to think of his immense labours for the gospel or recall again his exhortation to the Philippians: 'Work out your own salvation with fear and trembling; for God is at work in you' (2.12f.). But if the example of Paul is to be effective, he must be recalled as a real person and not as a symbol – this limits of course the number of New Testament saints to be imitated because so little is recorded about them. Who knows anything for certain about Matthias, the substitute for Judas Iscariot? or about Judas the son of James? From the second century onwards gifted story tellers rushed in to supply information in the form of apocryphal acts, but few of these contain accurate accounts. But of Paul much is known: the Acts record his missionary journeys and his letters provide autobiographical details and give an insight into his character and ideas. In fact Paul can provide a norm by which to measure the seriousness of our discipleship, although no slavish copying is to be attempted, any more than was the case with the apostle himself. Paul did not seek to repeat Jesus' gestures, his carpentry skills, his dress and so on. Instead he sought to open himself so that his Lord might live in him; his aim was to be integrated into the life of Christ.

It is here that pilgrimage can make its own particular contribution. Whoever has walked through the orchards and reached St Peter's Cave at Antioch (the present day Antakya) is vividly reminded of the confrontation between the two apostles on the subject of table fellowship with the Gentiles, as recorded in Galatians 2.11–21. What stands out in that account is Paul's directness – he does not beat about the bush but goes straight to the heart of the matter. Whoever has stood in the theatre at Ephesus (Pl. VIII) and heard the account of the immense crowd of silver smiths and other workers gathered there under Demetrius, of their rage at the way Paul, by his preaching, was affecting their trade in souvenirs of the goddess Diana, and how the apostle was restrained with difficulty from going there to face them (Acts 19.23–41), can appreciate, admire and be inspired to emulate his courage. Whoever has entered on foot into the silted-up mouth of the port at Miletus and has looked in the faces of the two stone guardian lions (Pl. IX) that looked into the face of Paul as he sailed into the harbour, begins to understand his kindness (listed among the fruit of the Spirit in Gal. 5.22) which expressed itself on that very quayside in his concern for others, viz. for the leaders of the infant Ephesian church summoned to meet him so that he might encourage and strengthen them for the future (Acts 20.15–38). If the speech attributed to him echoes what he actually said – and this is quite possible since it was delivered in the presence of the author of the we-document which is generally regarded as one of the sources of Acts – then his words reveal, as do many passages in his letters, that he was a man of hope who looked forward with confidence in the God of the future. To see the prison at Philippi in which Paul and his companions were held, with their feet in stocks, after being beaten

Plate VIII In the steps of St Paul. Modern pilgrims in the theatre at Ephesus (Acts 19.23–41)

with rods (Acts 16, 16–24), is to accept that witness may lead to suffering, although, as he reported to the Philippians when in prison elsewhere, this suffering is inseparable from joy because 'it has really served to advance the gospel' (Phil. 1.12–18). But suffering can be mental as well as physical: this is what Paul seems to have undergone at Athens when, like many a twentieth-century pilgrim, he stood on the Areopagus, and there was mocked for speaking of the resurrection (Acts 17.22–33).

Going south to Corinth and standing on the very spot occupied by Paul before the bema or tribunal of Gallio (Acts 18.12–17) (Pl. X) is to have brought home to one the intensity of that love which the apostle was to hymn in his letter to the Christians of that very same city: he was there because 'love bears all things' (I Cor. 13.7). Yet this was also a moment of anguish for him because, according to Acts, those who arraigned him were his fellow countrymen on whose behalf he was ready to be 'accursed and cut off from Christ' if only they would come to accept Jesus as the Messiah (Rom. 9.3).

A Christian saint is one whose life turns upon the centrality of God in Christ. As Paulinus expressed it long ago, 'it is surely true that the one Christ is present in each and every saint'.[56] Consequently the true saint is one who enables others to have glimpses of their redeemer. A pilgrimage can help towards this and at the same time it can be a means of imitation. What distinguishes the saint from the merely religious person is the extent to which his or her life is of value to others. To follow in the footsteps of St Paul is to be confronted constantly with a creative model, showing experimentally how to be a Christian. There is a newness too about saints: they exemplify what it means to be a disciple in consciously fresh ways; they often therefore occasion surprise – Paul and his companions were once referred to as those 'who have turned the world upside down' (Acts 17.6). Apart from those among one's contemporaries, each one belongs to a specific bygone age, and so no saint can provide a perfect blue-print to be imitated in every particular; that would be to treat them as if they were ahistorical, so the task of today's pilgrim is to devise an appropriate life-style that is inspired by, but does not mimic, what the saints were and did. If this is what directness, courage, kindness, hope, suffering and love meant in concrete terms to Paul – what should they mean to each of us? Christian values, Christian conduct – these are not abstract entities; they have been enfleshed in the saints; they have also to be incarnated in the late twentieth century not always in ways that

Plate IX One of the lions guarding the entrance to the harbour at Miletus
(Acts 20.15)

would have occurred to or even appealed to believers in previous centuries.

Of all this Dean Stanley was fully aware. In one of his sermons in Palestine he says of Paul: 'Let us ask, what are the practical lessons we may learn from his life?' Speaking of John the beloved disciple, whose burial place is shown at Ephesus, the Dean said: 'Let us ask ourselves what are the lessons he has left us? What are the truths which, without him, we should not have known as clearly as we do now?'[57]

Pilgrimage, in fact, can impel one to relate to the character of a saint and to grapple with his teaching. The places visited can often contribute to a fuller understanding of the culture which necessarily moulded the expression of his ideas. Indeed to be a pilgrim in western Turkey, on mainland Greece or in Italy, where so many traces survive of the civilization to which Paul belonged, is to be assisted to penetrate more deeply into his thought world. On every side there are remains that light up the images he took from contemporary culture as vehicles for his ideas. At Laodicea, to which he wrote a letter no longer extant (Col. 4.16), the outlines of the stadium are still to be seen. This and many another course for races and games provided the metaphor that Paul employed not infrequently for the Christian way of life (Phil. 2.16; 3.12ff.) and as a means of stressing the need for individual effort (I Cor. 9.24–27). At Rome the Colosseum bears mute testimony to what it meant to fight with beasts (I Cor. 15.32) and in the same city numerous triumphal arches shed light on the imagery he used to proclaim the victory of Christ over the forces of evil (II Cor. 2.14; Col. 2.15). At Salonika, whither he sent what is possibly his very first extant letter, viz. I Thessalonians, on the arch of Galerius, the emperor is depicted emptying a liquid offering on to the flames of the altar; this is a vivid illustration of Paul's statement: 'I am to be poured out as a libation upon the sacrificial offering of your faith' (Phil. 2.17). Saints, writes L. Cunningham, encourage us

> to be more self-giving, more loving, less inclined to hate, more compelled to love . . . Their lives judge the mediocrity of most lives while providing models to be emulated, either 'all the way' or in proportion to the actual potentialities of a person's individual circumstances.[58]

A pilgrimage, then, can be a spiritual exercise assisting the participants to explore their own potentialities as they seek to imitate the saint who is the ideal set before them in the course of a particular itinerary. The issue of relics is not raised by this because

Plate X   Pilgrims before the tribunal of Gallio at Corinth (Acts 18.12)

travelling the same routes as Paul, for example, there are no personal remains of any kind to view. Relics are not of the essence of pilgrimage. Nor does pilgrimage to a shrine where relics are preserved necessarily lead to their being the object of a questionable cult. There is nothing reprehensible in honouring the mortal remains of heroes and heroines of the faith. If thousands may visit the grave of Winston Churchill or the Lincoln memorial without anyone thinking such a practice to be wrong, no valid criticism can be levelled at those who go to Rome out of respect for Peter and Paul.

But what of such a centre as Compostela, where the legend that the body of St James was discovered there in the year 813 is scarcely credible? What indeed of any shrine where the genuineness of the relics may be called in question? If saints may be honoured as fellow and exemplary members of the Body of Christ, this legitimate *dulia* does not have to be tied to the presence of physical remains. Compostela, for example, is a place where for over eleven hundred years the apostle James has been revered – there is nothing superstitious in that nor any sound reason for terminating such a pious practice. If asked: why go to Santiago? a perfectly satisfactory reply is to say: because that is where the apostle has been and still is honoured. Or if the question is: why go to Walsingham? who can object to the answer: we do not go there because that is where a miraculous image of our Lady, destroyed at the Reformation, used to attract pilgrims; we go because that is a place where the Virgin has been venerated for centuries.

To sum up: a journey to the Holy Land is to be regarded as an *imitatio Christi* and one in the steps or to the shrine of a saint can be an *imitatio sancti*. If the goal of Christian endeavour is to become more and more Christlike, then to follow him who on the Emmaus road was himself fulfilling the role of a pilgrim (Luke 24.18; Vulgate *peregrinus*) is to enter upon a process of spiritual development. Moreover each and every saint is but a refraction of the glory of Christ, each an example to instruct how to imitate him. In this respect, the words of John Chrysostom in his homilies on Philemon, commenting on the benefit of visiting sites associated with the apostles, are as relevant today, after some fifteen hundred and fifty years, as they were when first uttered:

> Only seeing those places where they sat or where they were imprisoned, mere lifeless spots, we often transport our minds thither, and imagine their virtues, and are excited by it, and become more zealous.[59]

Equally today's pilgrims can be stirred to faith and inspired by the contemplation of their witness.

Pilgrimage, Identity and Unity

In the two preceding sections of this chapter the meaning of pilgrimage has been investigated in relation to the individual and with special reference to the practice of spiritual exercises and to the imitation of both Christ and his saints. A pilgrimage can in fact contribute to self-identity. The conscious decision to go to Jerusalem or Canterbury is one way of acknowledging and accepting responsibility which is an essential part of being human. But the notion of responsibility in turn implies a sense of obligation, and this is translated into action when anyone determines to set out on a pilgrimage as a way of expressing duty towards God. Further, to be responsible is to accept the task of actualizing values, and a pilgrimage can be an opportunity to review principles and make plans to embody them more fully in every day life; in this respect there is a close parallel between going on a pilgrimage and on a retreat, since the latter is frequently an occasion for devising or refurbishing one's rule of life. This is the intentional side of any spiritual exercise and it often results in framing a resolution or series of resolutions about future conduct.

Nevertheless, while the decision to become a pilgrim is individual, its implementation will bring one into association with others; pilgrimage nowadays is seldom a private venture but a sharing in a common undertaking which can promote a sense of fellowship. 'Where two or three are gathered in my name, there am I in the midst of them' (Matt. 18.20). The comfort, ease and speed of modern travel have largely displaced the penitential aspect and brought greater emphasis to the interaction of the participants. Hence Stephen Graham, travelling with a Russian contingent to Israel, observed: 'We were in a marvellous way equalled and made a family by the fact that we had come to Jerusalem together.'[60]

This sense of unity with others can soon extend beyond the limits of a particular group. So Philo of Alexandria, describing the pilgrimages made by 'countless numbers' of his fellow Jews to Jerusalem in the middle of the first century AD, remarked that

> friendships are formed between those who hitherto knew not each other, and the sacrifice and libations are the occasion of reciprocity of feeling and constitute the surest pledge that all are of one mind.[61]

Similarly the *hajj* binds Muslims together when, all wearing white robes and joining in common acts of devotion, they converge from every part of the globe on the prophet's birthplace. This was what particularly impressed Malcolm X who, when he was asked what was most noticeable about his journey to Mecca, replied:

> The *brotherhood*! The people of all races, colours, from all over the world coming together as *one*! It has proved to me the power of the one God.[62]

In the same way, when Christians visit those sites where the founder of their religion or some of his outstanding followers were active, they realize the world-wide character of the church, a factor that much impressed Chateaubriand at the beginning of the nineteenth century:

> I defy anyone with the least religious imagination not to be moved by meeting so many nationalities at the tomb of Jesus Christ and by hearing their prayers uttered in a hundred different languages.[63]

In this way a pilgrimage can be an exercise in experiencing the catholicity of the church, leading to a heightened awareness of belonging to a larger whole. As members of congregations enfolded in a denominational cocoon, pilgrims away from their home setting encounter representatives of the wider community of the universal church, both backwards in time to include the saints and at the present day to embrace every Christian no matter what his or her race, colour or denomination. To go to Rome, for example, is to deny daily routine,[64*] to leave known structures and to discover how divisions can be broken down and a sense of wholeness encouraged. Major pilgrimages do have an integrating effect and, at the same time, lead to a more profound comprehension of Christian identity.

Certainly the identity of French Protestants is confirmed by the pilgrimage every September of some ten thousand of them to the *Musée du désert* in the Cevennes. They come together for commemorative addresses, a celebration of the Lord's Supper and a picnic lunch in order to honour the Camisards. The Camisards, so-called because they wore a shirt (*camiso*) over their clothes, took up arms in 1685 in defence of religious liberty after the revocation of the Edict of Nantes which had previously guaranteed toleration to Protestants; many were killed in the ensuing struggle with the forces of the king. By this annual devotion today's members of the Eglise Reformée renew their contact with the past and, in so doing, realize afresh their identity as a people. They are returning to their roots.

For all Christians to go to Palestine is also to return to their roots because that is where redemption was wrought and the liberation of humankind set in motion. Such a journey fosters insight into what it means to be sons and daughters of a heavenly Father through whose Son they have died and risen in baptism when they became sharers in the Holy Spirit. Indeed a pilgrimage is to be understood as a special kind of spiritual exercise that increases attachment to one's religion – a Jew at the Wailing Wall, a Hindu on the banks of the Ganges, a Christian by the Sea of Galilee, each and everyone is placed within a tradition, experiences historical continuity and the possibility of contemporary responses. Faith may be rekindled in the joy of being in the proximity of a place full of meaning, such as the tomb of a martyr or the scene of Jesus' crucifixion.[65] At the same time a pilgrimage can be an act of witness, and, especially when the destination is Jerusalem, it is to be seen as an opportunity to renew the sense of mission at the original centre of mission. It is further a form of rededication. But witness, mission, rededication, these have each to be related to today's world: so to go to Israel with no knowledge of the present situation in the Middle East could be to treat the pilgrimage as a journey backwards in time and irrelevant to the contemporary scene. This is not what Christianity or pilgrimage is about.

It follows that a pilgrimage is not simply about places but about people; it is not only looking at stones and hills and valleys but encountering others and interacting with them. But, one must hasten to add, these 'others' are not to be confined to the fellow members of one's group; there must be an equal concern for the Christians of the land. A pilgrimage in fact may be – indeed should be – a practical manifestation of the communion of saints and an activity forging links between different Christian communities. The possibility of coming together with those who belong to denominations other than one's own and also with believers in the locality visited has played an important role in the re-emergence of Protestant pilgrimages and was very much a key factor in the establishment of Inter-Church Travel as previously explained.[66] The importance of meeting can be underscored by reference to the words of a Galilean believer:

> People normally come for holy shrines and holy places. For us local

Christians these are just sand and stone that are meaningless without a Christian community which witnesses to the presence of the Lord here today.[67]

Holy sites can become museums unless there are local people to maintain a living tradition of worship, community and service. To ignore indigenous Christians is to fail in love and support; it is to deny them the opportunity of extending that hospitality to strangers which is a way of encountering Christ (Matt. 25.35). The communion of saints excludes no one: it does embrace the many who have borne witness and died in a place, the many who have travelled the same road previously, those who dwell there now as well as those generations to come with whom Christians of today anticipate solidarity in the kingdom. In this way it is possible to experience the peace of God.

'Peace' is the usual translation of the Hebrew *shalom* and it is important to note that this is a social concept, being neither an inward feeling nor an individual possession. *Shalom* applies to the in-between of persons; it includes unity, solidarity, the exercise of mutual responsibility and confidence; it denotes all forms of well-being and happiness as these stem from community with others. So it involves neighbourliness, reconciliation, responsible faith and hope. Since a pilgrimage can comprehend all these, this section could well have been entitled 'Pilgrimage and *Shalom*', but, granted all this, it is important to recognize that it is possible to be so solemn about the subject that one important aspect can be entirely forgotten – that aspect is the exercise of humour.

Laughter usually functions within a communicative relation; it has to be shared and so it can promote interchange between persons because it possesses this element of reciprocity.[68] To laugh or to provoke laughter is to invite those present to come close. Laughter and humour are indeed like an invitation to start a conversation: they aim to decrease social distance.[69] Laughter therefore is ideally suited to a pilgrimage which is concerned to promote fellowship and indeed there are few incidents on such expeditions that cannot provide material for experiencing joy together in the form of laughter.

According to N. Hurley: 'Chaplin is the patron saint of the road . . . The eternal pilgrim, Chaplin's journey down the open road is a call to utopian thinking, to letting fall things we cherish and mistakenly think we cannot do without.'[70] Chaplin's little tramp discloses a way of life that overcomes evil by humour. Whether today's pilgrims think of themselves as tramps in the mould of Chaplin or as *joculatores* – God's merry folk – as St Francis dubbed his followers, this is all part of growing together in Christ to which a pilgrimage has a contribution to make.

Pilgrimage and the Bible

Left until last in this investigation into the meaning of pilgrimage today is that aspect which, as far as the surviving documents are concerned, was the first in time to motivate believers to travel to the Holy Land. It can be summed up under the heading 'Christian Education', i.e. it relates to visiting the holy places in order to understand the Bible more fully. This is a constant theme throughout the entire history of Christian pilgrimage and it is therefore unnecessary to produce a plethora of quotations to illustrate the point: a representative trio will suffice, two from the late fourth century (Jerome and Egeria) and one almost at the other end of the time span from the nineteenth century (A. P. Stanley).

'The man who has seen Judaea with his own eyes and who knows the sites of ancient cities and their names, whether the same or changed, will gaze more clearly on holy Scripture' – so Jerome.[71]

Egeria considered that the detailed description that she wrote out for her sister nuns in Galicia would enable them 'the better to picture what happened in these places'.[72]

According to Dean Stanley, who reached Jerusalem on Easter Eve 1853, and made numerous sorties from there to the Dead Sea and elsewhere, what is presented to every pilgrim 'is the passing of the parables before your eyes'.[73]

However, both Jerome and Stanley took the view, which has been shared by many, that such a visit serves to establish the 'truth' of the Bible. 'What previously I had heard by report,' said Jerome, 'I verified by the evidence of my own eyes.'[74] While Stanley held that a pilgrimage frequently confirms 'the authenticity of the Evangelical narrative'.[75] In saying this the Dean was taking his stand within a tradition that goes back to Cyril or John of Jerusalem and even earlier. In one of the lectures to candidates for baptism, delivered in the Martyrium adjacent to the area where it was believed that Jesus had been executed, the statement was made that 'Christ was truly crucified *for our sins*. Even supposing you were disposed to contest this, your surroundings rise up before your eyes to refute you, this sacred Golgotha where we now come together because of him who was crucified here.'[76] Yet, assuming the correctness of the identification of the site, it is only when, to use Jerome's words, 'the spiritual meaning'[77] is discerned that the italicized words become true. It is only then that one can say, not only that Jesus met his death there but that his death effected reconciliation. To die is the common lot of human beings, but for a death to bring about the expiation of the sins of all is only possible in the case of him who is confessed to be the redeemer of the world. Or again, the simple fact that there is a tomb close by where Jesus could have been laid to rest does not establish the truth of the resurrection. Even though the nineteenth-century visitors to Palestine, as seen in the last chapter, were motivated in part to rebuff biblical criticism by an appeal to geography and topography, none of this in the last analysis establishes the fundamental truth of the Bible. This said, no modern pilgrim who has been there would question the constant claim by their forerunners that understanding can be deepened both of the text itself and of Christian beliefs in general.

Piety may take the form of seeking to gain a more profound insight into the central doctrines of Christianity as one meditates on the Incarnation at Bethlehem, on the meaning of baptism by the Jordan or of death and resurrection in Jerusalem: in other words, it is important to realize that there are proper intellectual as well as emotional motives for pilgrimage. A main centre functions as a magnified focus of what is consciously accepted in the religion of the pilgrim; it is a distillation of the truths and experiences which are basic to his or her beliefs. This can lead, therefore, to an intensified appreciation of symbols, e.g. the cross with which one is familiar in the home church takes on an added significance when the place being visited is Golgotha. Of course none of this applies directly to pilgrimages to places other than the Holy Land. What if the destination is Philippi or Rome, how does the Bible relate in such cases? What is required to answer this question is a look at both those biblical personages who are presented as pilgrims and the meaning with which the Bible has invested the practice of pilgrimage itself.

Foremost among individual biblical pilgrims are to be numbered Abraham in the Old Testament and Jesus and Paul in the New. Of Abraham the main thing to note is how his departure from Ur of the Chaldees was perceived as an act of complete trust in God with the result that eventually he was regarded as the ideal of the man of faith (e.g. Heb. 11.8). In the light of his example it is obviously legitimate to include in any understanding of pilgrimage the fact that it may constitute a venture of faith in the God who calls us into ever closer union with himself. This note of trust is sounded very clearly in a 'Song of Ascents' chanted by Jewish pilgrims as they went up to Jerusalem.

> I lift up my eyes to the hills.
> From whence does my help come?
> My help comes from the Lord,
>   who made heaven and earth (Ps. 121.1f.).

In the case of Jesus, it will be recalled how the disciples on the way to Emmaus addressed him as a *peregrinus* who had come to celebrate the Passover (Luke 24.18), exactly as had his parents when they took him with them on a pilgrimage to Jerusalem for the same feast, a journey that they apparently made annually (Luke 2.41).

Paul, towards the end of his final missionary journey, was 'hastening to be at Jerusalem, if possible, on the day of Pentecost' (Acts 20.16); he was therefore a pilgrim on the way to join in the Feast of Weeks (Ex. 34.22f.).

Christians are bidden to be imitators of both Jesus and Paul, and if imitation were simply mimicry then their precedent would provide ample justification for our becoming pilgrims too, but imitation is more than that and it is necessary to understand why Jesus and Paul did what they did. What were these pilgrimage celebrations laid down in the Old Testament in which they engaged? Whatever their origins, and they were probably agricultural and possibly Canaanite, the three great historic feasts enjoined by the Mosaic law became liturgical re-callings of the Exodus. The Passover commemorated the destroyer 'passing over' the houses of the Hebrews in Egypt and so sparing them on the eve of their liberation (Ex. 12.12ff.). The Feast of Weeks was eventually interpreted as the occasion for commemorating the giving of the law on Mount Sinai. The Feast of Booths involved a re-enactment in that the Jews had to move out of their houses into leafy tents 'that your generations may know that I made the people of Israel dwell in booths when I brought them out of the land of Egypt' (Lev. 23.43; Neh. 8.13–18). All these were landmarks of the faith of Israel, anniversaries of their salvation and, after the centralization of worship in the seventh century BC, they were to be observed in Jerusalem: 'Three times a year all your males shall appear before the

Lord your God at the place which he will choose' (Deut. 16.16). All participants had to take to the road; they were in effect 'pilgrims', although the term is not actually used. The legitimacy of designating them in this way rests on the fact that a pilgrimage is by definition a journey undertaken for religious purpose usually to a destination associated with a divine being. This applies to what the Jews, Jesus and Paul included, were doing.

These pilgrims came in vast numbers from within Israel itself but also from the Diaspora,[78] and even after the destruction of the Temple they did not cease, although lamentation then replaced the joy of former times. All this combined to strengthen the national consciousness and to increase social solidarity.

Although Jewish pilgrims were not confined to the three great festivals, nor even to the land of Palestine itself – they went, for example, to the tomb of Mordecai and Esther at Hamadan in Iran – it was the Exodus that dominated their acts of devotion. The Exodus was not simply an escape from slavery but a pilgrimage (Ex. 3.18; 5.1) and one that was in two parts. The first part was a trek that culminated at Mount Sinai where God entered into a covenant with his people; the second part is usually called the wandering in the wilderness and that eventually reached its climax with the entry into and occupation of the Promised Land to which Abraham, in his turn, had been led in the course of his pilgrimage from Ur (Gen. 11.31–123). No wonder that the march from Egypt became a paradigm inspiring hope that from Babylon there would be a similar return and one that was also to be understood as a pilgrimage.

> I will bring your offspring from the east,
> and from the west I will gather you.
>   .   .   .   .
> For your sake I will send to Babylon
>   and break down all the bars,
>   and the shouting of the Chaldeans
>   will be turned to lamentations.
> Thus says the Lord,
>   who makes a way in the sea,
>   a path in the mighty waters,
>   who brings forth chariot and horse,
>   army and warrior;
>   they lie down, they cannot rise,
>   they are extinguished, quenched, like a wick.
>
>   .   .   .   .

I will make a way in the wilderness
and rivers in the desert (Isa. 43.5, 14–17, 19b).

The Exodus pilgrimage was also a process of education: the Jews learned about God; they were taught that he was always with them (Ex. 13.17–22), that he sustained them (Ex. 16) and that, though he was demanding, he was also patient (Ex. 20.1–20).

When the pilgrims flocked to Jerusalem to hold the Exodus festivals, their devotion was nourished by the songs they poured forth on the way. 'You shall have a song as in the night when a holy feast is kept; and gladness of heart, as when one sets out to the sound of the flute to go to the mountain of the Lord, to the Rock of Israel' (Isa. 30.29). Many of the Psalms have in fact been identified as pilgrim hymns.

Fifteen psalms have each been given the ambiguous title of 'A Song of Ascents'. Of these Psalm 122 is unquestionably a pilgrim song; there is less certainty about the others. In this psalm there are three keynotes:

1. Joy – 'I was glad when they said to me, "Let us go to the house of the Lord"' (verse 1).

2. Gratitude 'Give thanks to the name of the Lord' (verse 4).

3. Peace – 'Peace be within you' (verse 8).

In Psalm 84, also a pilgrim song, there is similarly an expression of joy ('My heart and flesh sing for joy to the living God' (verse 2), leading to the giving of praise (verse 4). It was C. S. Lewis who, in his *Reflections on the Psalms*, pointed out how enjoyment spontaneously overflows into praise and how praise not merely expresses but completes the enjoyment.[79] Jewish pilgrimages, according to the Bible, were indeed acts of praise and thanksgiving and the same should be true of Christian pilgrimages today when they culminate in that peace or *shalom* discussed in the preceding section.

These are the pilgrimages that Jesus and his apostle joined. They took part in them to celebrate the acts of God who had chosen Israel to be his people and had made a covenant with them; praise and thanksgiving was on their lips. When Christians go on pilgrimages, they are continuing the same tradition, re-calling the divine advent and affirming their re-engagement in the new covenant.

Yet there is a fundamental difference between Jesus as a pilgrim and his followers today. He was 'tempted as we are, yet without sin' (Heb. 4.15), whereas we are numbered among those of whom it is written 'all have sinned and fall short of the glory of God' (Rom.

3.23). This consciousness of sin was present in many Jewish pilgrims and was voiced in another 'Song of Ascent', viz. Psalm 130, usually known as the *De profundis*, often found in funeral services. It sounds a note of alienation together with a plea for redemption. The condition out of which the author speaks is neatly summarized in Isaiah 59.2:

> Your iniquities have made a separation
> between you and your God,
> and your sins have hid his face from you.

This the psalmist, in turn, also acknowledges:

> If you, O Lord, should mark iniquities,
> Lord, who could stand?
> But there is forgiveness with you,
> that you may be feared.

Pilgrimage, it is hoped, may help to overcome this separation – the application of this to the present raises no difficulty. The point has already been made that, as a spiritual exercise, a pilgrimage may contribute to closer union with God: this is its positive side. But to draw near to him is to reduce the alienation that is the effect of sin. Hence while there are few sound grounds, if any, for linking pilgrimages in the twentieth century with all the penitential aspects of the Middle Ages, there is no reason why a repentant sinner should not take the road with the same hope and intention as those who wrote the psalms so many centuries ago. The Bible in fact does provide examples and interpretations that are directly relevant to a contemporary theology of pilgrimage. This does not require the adoption of mediaeval literalism as when the pilgrims of that epoch adopted the very garb of the Israelites on the night of the first Passover: 'In this manner you shall eat it; your loins girded, your sandals on your feet, and your staff in your hand' (Ex. 12.11). This is not of the essence of pilgrimage, but if the biblical teaching is taken seriously it is not to be forgotten that the image combines two aspects. The first aspect of pilgrimage is one mentioned just above, i.e. the sense of alienation but felt as a distance from one's true country; the second aspect is a sense of belonging, belonging to heaven which is one's true homeland. These dimensions of Christian discipleship find expression in the imagery of a journey from earth to heaven and in the practical exercise of travelling through space from here to there. In this way, as F. C. Gardiner has

Plate XI The Pilgrim Way from Neapolis: the Via Egnatia (Acts 16.11f.)

pointed out, there emerges an emotional landscape that provides us with a framework of ultimate destiny so that pilgrims are stimulated to hope and to seek for the transcendent promised at the end of their journey.[80]

5

Devotions for Today's Pilgrims

Lest the title of this chapter should mislead, it is perhaps necessary to stress that it is not concerned with practical instructions in devotional techniques. Rather it consists of suggestions about appropriate forms that may assist present-day pilgrims to benefit from a journey that is intended to be a spiritual exercise. It is the *approach* to the Bible that is important, not the exegesis of particular passages. It is the *contents* of a meditation that require to be indicated, not how to engage in recollection. Consideration needs to be given to the themes that should be constantly to the forefront of attention. The possible value of re-enacting biblical episodes as well as of such features as pilgrim tokens has to be assessed. The meaning of the two gospel sacraments has to be explored in direct relation to the pilgrimage experience, since worship en route will often centre in the celebration of the eucharist, while the renewal of baptismal vows is by no means unusual.

All these devotional practices constitute that 'extra' that can differentiate a pilgrimage from a tour. Indeed were it not possible to distinguish a visit to Israel from a pilgrimage to the Holy Land or a holiday along the west coast of Asiatic Turkey from a religious journey in the steps of St Paul, there would have been little point in extending this study up to the present day. Pilgrimage, properly so-called, would be a thing of the past and the package tour the only current option. Of course, a pilgrimage does involve a tour and can be a real holiday, but obviously, from a Christian point of view, it has to be something more. This 'something more' has already been in part defined in the previous chapter which set out a modern interpretation of pilgrimage, seeking to demonstrate that pilgrimage and tour are not identical because the nature and intent of the journey in each case are not the same – in particular it was stressed how a pilgrimage is to be regarded as a spiritual exercise – so also, it may be added to sharpen the contrast, is churchgoing, which is by no means the same as church visiting. A pilgrimage also has a distinct character because of the inclusion within it of a series of devotions whose purpose is to promote closer communion with God. These practices are to be related not solely to pilgrims as individuals: there is a corporate aspect to pilgrimage that will be readily apparent when the first liturgical act that may be deemed appropriate is passed in review.

At the Point of Departure

In today's western world with its excessive individualism, it is all too easy to forget that when Christians depart for Rome or Jerusalem they are not embarking on a purely private venture. They go as members of the Body of Christ. Although it is not always the case, most will belong to local congregations from which they set out and to which they will eventually return. Their pilgrimage, then, should be a matter of concern to their home communities. In the past this concern took the form of commissioning the pilgrims before they left, praying for them while away and welcoming them back on the completion of their self-appointed task. If the corporate nature of each worshipping body is to mean anything, then this proper concern on the part of a congregation as a whole for those who are temporarily absent from it should be expressed and in this way a close link between the worshipping body and the absent pilgrims can be forged.

In the Middle Ages, it will be recalled,[1] not only did the parishioners intercede regularly for those members who had gone overseas but a special order of service was devised to commission them before they departed. This included a confession and absolution together with some prayers, and it reached its climax with the presentation to each one of a wallet and staff as tokens of the new role with which they were being invested. One of these orders is readily accessible in the *Sarum Missal*[2] and can be adapted with ease for modern use. However the scrip and staff no longer have much significance because neither of these originally utilitarian objects is needed for contemporary travelling. These tokens did have a symbolic value in that they operated not simply as physical aids but as signs of Christian fellowship. A substitute therefore has to be found to continue this useful function, and it may be suggested that a simple cross – of wood or metal – would be suitable. The cross itself featured in the mediaeval rite of commissioning those who were joining a crusade and so it would be particularly relevant to a journey to the Holy Land as well as being fitting for other destinations where a renewal of baptismal vows is in prospect because in baptism itself the candidates are signed with the sign of the cross.

The order that follows is then based upon the Sarum service with some slight alterations and additions.

A Service for the Commissioning of Pilgrims

The choir and clergy enter to the singing of
'He who would valiant be'

Priest For you Lord have commanded us:
    to persevere in all your precepts.
If only my ways were unerring:
    towards the keeping of your statutes (Ps. 119.4f.).[3]

So that you may set out on your pilgrimage at peace with God and with your fellows, let us join together in confessing our sins.

All Almighty God, our heavenly Father,
we have sinned against you and against our fellow
human beings,
in thought and word and deed,
in the evil we have done
and in the good we have not done,
through our own deliberate fault.
We are truly sorry
and repent of all our sins.
For the sake of your Son Jesus Christ, who died for us,
forgive us all that is past;
and grant that we may walk before you in newness of life
to the glory of your name. Amen.[4]

Priest Almighty God,
who forgives all who truly repent,
have mercy upon you,
pardon and deliver you from all your sins,
confirm and strengthen you in all goodness,
and keep you in life eternal;
through Jesus Christ our Lord. Amen.

The peace of the Lord be always with you

All and also with you.

*All present exchange the Peace by shaking hands as
they repeat the formula*

Psalm 25: In you O Lord my God have I put my hope[5]

Old Testament Lesson: Genesis 12.1–7 (Abraham's
pilgrimage to Canaan)[6]

Priest   These all died in faith, not having received the promises, but
having seen them afar off, and were persuaded of them, and
embraced them, and confessed that they were strangers and
pilgrims on the earth (Heb. 11.13 AV).

New Testament Lesson: John 14.1–4 (Jesus goes in front)

Lord have mercy
Christ have mercy
Lord have mercy

      Our Father

Versicle . . . and lead us not into temptation,
Response. . . but deliver us from evil.

V.   I said, Lord, be merciful unto me;[7]
R.   Heal my soul, for I have sinned against you.
V.   The Lord show you his ways;
R.   And teach you his paths.
V.   The Lord direct your steps according to his word;
R.   That no unrighteousness have dominion over you.
V.   O that your ways were made so direct;
R.   That you might keep the statutes of the Lord.
V.   The Lord uphold your goings in his paths;
R.   That your footsteps slip not.
V.   Blessed be the Lord God daily;
R.   The God of our salvation prosper your way before you.
V.   The good angel of the Lord accompany you;
R.   And dispose your way and your actions aright, that you
          may return again to your own place with joy.
V.   Blessed are those that are undefiled in the way;
R.   And walk in the law of the Lord.
V.   Let the enemy have no advantage against you;
R.   And let not the son of wickedness approach to hurt you.
V.   O Lord, arise, help us,
R.   And deliver us for your name's sake.
V.   Turn us again, O Lord God of hosts;
R.   And show the light of your countenance upon us,
          and we shall be whole.

V.   Lord, hear our prayer;
R.   And let our cry come unto you.
V.   The Lord be with you,
R.   and also with you.

Priest   Let us pray

Assist us, O Lord, in these our supplications, and dispose the way of your servants towards the attainment of your salvation, that among all the changes and chances of the journey through life, they may ever be defended by your help. Through etc.

Let us pray

O God, who leads to life, and guards with your fatherly protection those that trust in you, we beseech you that you would grant unto these your servants here present, going forth as pilgrims from this place, the support of your presence; that they, being protected by your aid, may be shaken by no fear of evil, nor be depressed by any lingering adversity, nor be troubled by any enemy lying in wait to assail them; but that having prosperously accomplished the course of their appointed journey to . . .[8], they may return unto their own homes; and, having been received back in safety, may pay due thanks unto your name. Through etc.

Let us pray

O God, who always bestows your pity on those who love you, and who are in no place far distant from those who serve you, direct the way of your servants according to your will, that you being their protector and guide, they may walk without stumbling in the paths of righteousness. Through etc.

Hymn

Sermon

Here the pilgrims shall stand
The Lord be with you
and also with you.

Priest   Let us pray

O Lord Jesus Christ, who of your unspeakable mercy, and at the bidding of the Father, and with the co-operation of the Holy Spirit, were willing to come down from heaven, and to seek the sheep that was lost, and to bear it back on your own shoulders to the flock of the heavenly company, and did command the sons and daughters of mother church by prayer to ask, by holy living to seek and by knocking to persevere, that they may be able to find more quickly the reward of saving life: we humbly beseech you that you would vouchsafe to sanctify and bl + ess these pilgrimage tokens; that whosoever for love of you shall desire to wear the same, like the armour of humility, at their side, or to hang it from their neck, or to carry it in their hands, and so on their pilgrimage to seek your divine aid, with the accompaniment of humble devotion, may be found worthy, through the protecting defence of your right hand, to attain unto the joys of everlasting vision, through you, O Saviour of the world. Who lives etc.[9]

Come forward in the name of our Lord Jesus Christ to receive these crosses as the badges of your pilgrimage to . . . May they recall to you your baptism wherein you died with Christ, receiving the sign of the cross, and rose again to walk in newness of life. May you be found worthy to reach whither you desire to go, and, when your pilgrimage is finished, may you return here in safety. Through etc.

The pilgrims come forward to receive their badges at the hands of the clergy who shall say to each in turn

Receive the cross of Christ as the badge of your pilgrimage.

Each pilgrim shall reply

Amen.

When all have returned to their places and are kneeling, the minister shall say

May the almighty and everlasting God, who is the way, the truth and the life, dispose your journey according to his pleasure. May he renew you in his divine mission; may he foster in you a greater sense of the unity and catholicity of his church; may he enable you to live in accordance with your baptismal vows, advancing towards spiritual maturity and continuing to be steadfast in your faithfulness throughout the journey of your life, and may the blessing of God Almighty, Father, Son and Holy Spirit, be with you always.[10]

The mediaeval service reached its climax with a 'Mass for Travellers',[11] which included an offertory prayer, a post-communion and a collect, all of such simplicity and clarity that they are eminently worth reproducing.

Secret Be favourable, we beseech you, O Lord, to our supplication, and graciously receive these offerings which we present unto you on behalf of your servants; that you would direct their way by your preventing grace, and accompany and follow them, so that they may rejoice in the safe performance of their journey by your merciful protection. Through etc.

Post communion We beseech you, O Lord, that the reception of the sacrament of the heavenly mystery may further the good success of your servants' journey, and bring them all things profitable to their salvation. Through etc.

Collect O God of infinite mercy and boundless majesty, whom neither space nor time separates from those whom you defend, be present with your servants who everywhere put their trust in you, and vouchsafe to be their leader and companion in every way which they shall go: let no adversity harm them, no difficulty hinder them; let all things be healthful, and all things be prosperous for them; that whatsoever they shall rightly ask, they may speedily and effectually obtain by the aid of your right hand. Through etc.

As has been suggested at the beginning of this section, the use of this office or something like it can create a link between the local Christian community and the members of it who are going out on a pilgrimage, and that caring association can be extended by praying for the travellers while they are away. There is no need to include a specimen intercession here because the one that featured in the 'Bidding of the Bedes' and has been quoted previously is entirely suitable.[12]

Since the actual day of departure is unlikely to coincide with the commissioning, a form of devotion for use shortly before or after the start of the journey will help to concentrate the minds of the pilgrims on the purpose of what they are doing. Here is a suggested outline that can be said either privately by individuals or, preferably, can be a corporate act when a group is together in a coach or railway compartment.

Form of Prayer for the Outward Journey

Leader In the name of the Father and of the Son and of the Holy Spirit

All   Amen.

Leader O God make speed to save us

All   O Lord make haste to help us.

Leader   Glory be to the Father and to the Son and to the Holy Spirit

All   As it was in the beginning, is now and ever shall be, world without end. Amen.

Leader   Blessed is every one who fears the Lord,

All   Who walks in his ways (Ps. 128.1).

Leader   It is now . . . days since we were commissioned as pilgrims; as we set off on the first stage of our journey, let us repeat together one of the prayers that was used at that service.

All   O God, who leads to life, and guards with your fatherly protection those that trust in you, we beseech you that you would grant unto us your servants, going forth as pilgrims, the support of your presence; that we, being protected by your aid, may be shaken by no fear of evil, nor be depressed by any lingering adversity, nor be troubled by an enemy lying in wait to assail us; but that having prosperously accomplished the course of our appointed journey to . . . we may return unto our own homes; and having been received back in safety, may pay due thanks unto your name. Through etc.

Reader   Deuteronomy 30.15–20 (The pilgrimage to the Promised Land).

All   *Benedictus*

Leader   Almighty God, you have built your church upon the foundation of the apostles and prophets with Jesus Christ as the chief corner-stone. So join us together in unity of spirit by their doctrine, that we may be made a holy temple acceptable to you.

All   Amen.

The grace of our Lord Jesus Christ etc.

The Use of the Bible

Both the commissioning service and the prayers on departure rest heavily on the Bible, incorporating psalms, canticles and readings from the Old and New Testaments. Indeed it is difficult to conceive of a modern pilgrim without a Bible in hand, and this is especially so if the destination is Jerusalem. But careful thought has to be given to the appropriate use of the Bible in such circumstances, i.e. to its use in the course of a pilgrimage.

Pains have been taken throughout this study to maintain the view that a pilgrimage is not a mere tour – not even a tour with religious frills. Equally it now has to be stressed that it is not an excursion into past history like a visit to the battlefields of Flanders by a person interested in military campaigns. An enthusiast for the history of warfare can spend many an interesting hour on the field of Waterloo reconstructing the fortunes of the struggle between Wellington and Napoleon, or one can compare the records of Agincourt or Malplaquet with the lie of the land as it is today. Similarly a visitor to Israel can follow the campaigns of Joshua with the help of the book that bears his name, as Allenby did in 1917,[13] but this return to the past, quite legitimate in itself, is without any religious interest or concern to relate that past to the present. It is to regard the Bible primarily as an historical record – the question would still remain what it has to do with Christian discipleship in the twentieth century. Indeed from the perspective of pilgrimage the Bible is neither a guide book nor a history book to be related to particular sites and locations; rather it should be a tool to deepen the believer's relationship with God. Yet, according to historical criticism, which after some hundred and fifty years has achieved the position of being the scholarly orthodoxy presently in vogue, the Bible is essentially a source book for history. However, few Christians are trained historians and if this is the only way to approach the Bible, then it must be cut off from the majority of the faithful.

To many contemporary scholars, history is a succession of events that is irreversible, unforeseeable, unrepeatable and possessed of autonomous value. These events, so it is believed, can have no direct relation to the present, and consequently they can have no religious significance, especially as the current historical method does not allow for the presence of divinity. Yet to dismiss something as unhistorical because it does not fit the canons of modern research is not to recognize the relativity of those canons. Further, it scarcely needs pointing out that such a stance is at odds with the biblical understanding of history as the epiphany of God. Historical 'facts' are presented as 'situations' of human beings responding to God and precisely for that reason they have a religious import.[14] Not that the revelation of God takes place in mythic time; it confronts human beings within historical duration and each moment of revelation therefore remains a limited moment, precisely situated within the temporal sequence – but it is in this way that time itself can be given meaning. Both Judaism and Christianity broke with all other archaic religions in insisting on this, with the ironic outcome that the contemporary conception of history, which developed on a Judaeo-Christian basis, has turned against its progenitors by declaring that history is history, i.e. duration without any religious meaning at all and so it devalues the Bible as a witness to God. It will evidently not benefit the pilgrim to adopt this approach to the scriptures.

This approach can also result in relegating the Old Testament to the status of a non-Christian book. To the writers of the New Testament and to the Early Church Fathers, the Old Testament bore witness to Christ, but viewed solely as a history book it has little or nothing directly to do with him and so ceases to have interest for Christians, except possibly as background material to the New Testament. If the Old Testament cannot be interpreted as having anything to do with Christ, there seems no point in taking it into account on a Christian pilgrimage. But for Christians those writings have taken on a new meaning in the light of Easter – the Old Testament is then understood as a book of God's promises, and the New proclaims their fulfilment. This does not mean that the historical record is of no interest to believers; they hold that a pattern of promise and fulfilment has been disclosed in the historical process itself[15] but they also hold that historical reconstruction is insufficient to relate the Bible to the world of today.

In case the subject of this section appears lost in the sands of abstract argument, let us remind ourselves of its principal concern. In effect the quest is for an answer to the question: how is the world of biblical narrative to be related to present experience and, in particular, to the experience of being a pilgrim to the Holy Land or in the steps of St Paul? That the biblical narratives do have a realistic character is undeniable; they possess a history-likeness, but this is not to affirm their historical likelihood.[16] Simply because a story is like an historical account, it does not follow that it refers to an actual occurrence. Charles Dickens was but one of many who wrote realistic narratives, but in general his characters and their doings had no existence outside his own imagining. Yet even if the factual accuracy of a biblical passage is in question, there remains the task of perceiving the religious truth of the fact-like description.[17] To achieve this the reader has to adopt a personal or life stance towards the depicted reality. In other words the Bible has to be read hermeneutically and not historically, and an interpretation has to be sought which embraces what it means for the reader now. The question then is: how far does my understanding of the text correspond with, illuminate, extend and transform my experience? This is not historical enquiry but experiential.

The relevance of all this to the use of the Bible for devotional purposes can be illustrated by taking a particular passage and approaching it in the way just outlined. In II Samuel 11 and 12 there is the story of David's disposal of Uriah the Hittite in order to take his wife Bathsheba. Then, the narrative continues, 'the Lord sent Nathan to David'. The prophet tells a parable about two men, the one rich and the other poor, and how the former takes the latter's only possession – one ewe lamb. When the king condemns the rich man, Nathan retorts: 'You are the man.' David then recognizes that the story applies to himself, and in this way he shares in the narrative and becomes aware that in judging the rich man he is judging himself, and he is then able to perceive the judgment of God.[18] In this way he himself becomes part of the depicted reality and takes a stance towards it. Since the use of the Bible on a pilgrimage is primarily to foster union with Christ, and not to act as a source book for historical reconstruction, it is precisely this approach that is needed.

The meaning derived from a text can of course differ according to the use that is being made of it. It can be given a political reading; it can be given a Marxist interpretation; it can also be read as an aid to spiritual progress. Let the scholars pursue their scholarly tasks, while pilgrims seek to open themselves to the activity of the Spirit who is the continuing historical presence of God: it is he who links the biblical 'past' to today. It is he who enables pilgrims to declare: 'Today this scripture has been fulfilled in our hearing' (Luke 4.21). The urgency of this declaration in the synagogue at Nazareth by Jesus breaks through any attitude which a detached observer may claim to adopt.[19]

A modern insight into this process of understanding is provided by a passage in the autobiography of H. A. Williams. Speaking of the effect upon him of joining in the life of prayer at Mirfield, he writes: 'The gospel seemed more and more to be about realities which were present and inward, not about alleged incidents which were past and external.'[20] He goes on to state that Jesus' baptism, his temptation in the wilderness, his death and resurrection, all became 'living contemporary realities'. This is in line with the teaching and practice of many of the great mediaeval mystics, who saw in the historical life of

Jesus an epitome of the entire spiritual life. Hence his birth, for example, was a matter of immediate experience. 'If it does not take place in me, what avails it?' asks Meister Eckhart, who died c. 1327, 'Everything lies in this, that it should take place in me.'[21] It is not difficult to comprehend how a pilgrimage can be a means whereby the biblical stories become likewise contemporary realities. However, it is to be noted that Williams is not much concerned about whether or not the events actually happened as recorded; for him it is the realities they represent and externalize that is all important and he does not think that they rest on the historicity of the New Testament. Mediaeval pilgrims did not share this view – nor is this the place to discuss it – but if Jesus did not die on the cross and is not a living person, it is difficult to take the gospel seriously since its message is to the effect that through his advent the human condition has been transformed; something has happened and something new has emerged.

Relating the narratives to the present was a feature of the devotions drawn up for use in the Holy Land by the Franciscans and incorporated in the processionals[22] and thence into some guide books. In these, verses from scripture recall the story, while prayers and hymns spell out the contemporary reference and the eschatological dimension in a meditative fashion – the Bible in this way is made constantly living and immediate. Here, by way of illustration, is a station translated from a fifteenth-century guide book.

Where Christ washed the Disciples' feet

Antiphon	You call me Teacher and Lord; and you are right, for so I am. If I, then, your Lord and Teacher have washed your feet, you ought also to wash one another's feet.
Versicle	For I have given you an example
Response	That you also should do as I have done to you.
Collect	O King of kings, almighty and of infinite goodness, Our Lord Jesus Christ, who in this holy place of Mount Sion of your great humility did gird yourself with a towel and on bended knee deign to wash, dry and cleanse the feet of your disciples with your holy hands, graciously grant that we, who are unclean and full of the products and blemishes of sin, may be purified by the overflowing water of your compassion and grace. Vouchsafe to wash us and cover over our wrong-doings, that, following your humility without offence unto death, we may be deemed worthy to receive recompense and be exalted with your elect in glory. Who lives etc.[23]

The scriptural passage which is the subject of this station is John 13.1-11ff. and this tells the story of the pedilavium in the Upper Room at the start of the Last Supper. This is presented as an act of humility on the part of Jesus who is the model pilgrims are to imitate. The water is not explicitly associated with baptism – although it is certainly implicit – but instead it is interpreted in terms of overflowing mercy and grace. Applying the past to the present and beyond, the prayer reaches its climax with an eschatological note in a request that at the last day believers, who have persevered in humility, may be rewarded for their faithfulness by being received into glory.

It is interesting to set this devotion side by side with that described by Felix Fabri at the same place.

> We walked in procession further on towards the right hand part of the choir, singing the hymns appointed for the day of the Last Supper, and came to the holy place where the Lord Jesus washed the feet of his disciples. Here is a fair altar, before which we bowed ourselves to the earth and kissed the ground, and received indulgences. I beg of you, beloved pilgrim, leave not this place, any more than the other, without previous meditation. See and reflect upon the importance of what was done here. The Son of God, mighty by reason of his eternal Godhead, and mighty with the beauty of the mind of the Father, he who laid the foundations of the world, and made it pleasant to sight, he to whom the heavens and all the stars in their courses do homage, he who, as Job says, shakes the earth out of her place, and the pillars thereof do tremble, did so bow down and abase his divine majesty in this place as with his own hands to wash the foul, filthy, muddy feet of his disciples, low-born fishermen, sinners, and traitors as they were, that he might thereby give us a most wholesome example of humility.[24]

Fabri's meditation takes up the same theme as the prayer in the guide book but stresses the great contrast between the divine majesty and the menial task, which was normally that of a slave, but undertaken by the Son of God to give his followers a model to imitate, thus spurring them to behave in a similar fashion.

In ways such as this the Bible may become relevant and immediate and it has naturally been taken into account in those devotional handbooks that Inter-Church Travel realized, soon after its establishment, were necessary for those whose pilgrimages they were arranging. In 1959 the firm published *A Pilgrim's Handbook for the Holy Land;* this gives scriptural references and prayers to accompany the readings.[25] Ronald Brownrigg's excellent *Come, See the Place* (1985) is in the same vein but more comprehensive.[26]

Meditation

The importance of meditation for spiritual development scarcely needs stressing. In the words of Dom John Chapman: 'If our faith is to be made vivid, it must be by meditation . . . Meditation is meant to make our faith real to us, so that we shall realize in our lives what we know and believe.'[27] The principal basis for meditation has always been the Bible which is a book about the acts of God directed towards liberation in (and not from) history. Through meditation this unfolding and continuing story can be experienced as reality in the context of the commitment to which the story itself is a summons.[28] Such a summons may require a re-examination of one's rule of life or possibly the drawing up of one for the first time; in this way meditation can affect the future of a pilgrim even after the journey's end.

When meditation rests upon the Bible, attention is stimulated and sustained by the text, and the text itself can be illuminated during a pilgrimage by the different locations, by the scenery and even by the atmosphere. The imagination and the senses, on which Loyola based his method of meditation,[29] are aided by the surroundings. Having selected a passage, depending upon where he or she has reached, the pilgrim, adopting the advice of Evelyn Underhill, then 'broods on it in God's presence till it leads you into acts of penitence, love, worship, as the case may be'.[30] In her view 'meditation is a half-way house between thinking and contemplating; and as a discipline it derives its chief value from its transitional character'.[31] Moreover, 'the object of meditation is to arrive at loving'[32] and so to enter into a closer union with God and this is also the primary goal of any pilgrimage. Such meditation requires effort, concentration and the use of the mind, all of which can be focused most sharply when in the Holy Land or at some main pilgrimage centre.

However, what of the authenticity of the locations? Is there not some doubt about the identification of certain sites where the biblical 'events' are said to have happened? Will this doubt not affect the impact that the places might otherwise have had? Obviously, if it is possible to meditate on the subject of the Transfiguration in Birmingham or Brisbane, it is equally feasible to meditate on the top of Mount Tabor, even though it was not until the fourth century that Cyril of Jerusalem first declared it to be the high mountain to which Jesus took Peter, James and John and where 'the appearance of his countenance was altered, and his raiment became dazzling white'

(Luke 9.29). Yet anyone who has stood on the summit of Tabor and looked out towards Nazareth cannot but acknowledge the extent to which she or he is drawn into the story so that its impact upon them can be felt.

In the nature of the case, absolute certainty about any site is impossible. To many archaeologists, for example, it is highly probable that the Holy Sepulchre is close to, if not actually over, the place where Jesus was laid to rest, but 'likelihood' is not certitude, yet this need not effect the reality of a meditation there. A somewhat similar situation obtains in relation to the dating of Jesus' life. When his birthday was is entirely unknown; the choice of 25 December to commemorate it was almost certainly due to the church's wish to Christianize a pagan festival of the sun. Yet there is a 'fact' that Christians hold to be undeniable; Jesus was born. Christmas Day celebrates this, even if it actually occurred at some other period of the year. If we turn back from dates to places, the *Via Dolorosa* recalls Jesus' way to the cross, even if his precise course to Golgotha may be questioned. In other words, a degree of scepticism can co-exist with a fruitful meditation which in itself may be rendered more profound by the contours of a countryside, the configuration of certain buildings and by the very fact of being in Jerusalem itself or on Mount Tabor.

The Bible is full of themes for meditation, but other sources are not to be neglected. It can be of much assistance when following in the footsteps of St Paul but it does not contain much information about other saints of the apostolic period and certainly nothing about those later in time. But the gap can often be supplied by the lives of the saints – other than the spurious ones. At Smyrna, the modern Izmir, both the letters of its bishop Polycarp and the account of his martyrdom can provide material for reflection. In the same place and in a number of adjacent cities, the epistles of Ignatius are relevant. It depends where a pilgrim decides to go. To Tours? St Athanasius wrote a life of St Martin. To Assisi? Writings about St Francis are plentiful. To Canterbury? Details of the life and death of St Thomas are by no means lacking. Meditation on these followers of Jesus can further the process of imitation as they are taken for examples from whom to learn something for living in today's world. Yet in the final analysis, the purpose of meditation is to lead on naturally to prayer.

Prayers, Hymns and Psalms

In the days of the Early Church, 'to go on a pilgrimage' was often rendered by 'to go to a place on account of prayer' – so Egeria, to cite one example, went to the land of Uz to visit the memorial of Job *gratia orationis*.[33] Prayer indeed is the distinctive activity of pilgrimage: not an account has survived that does not refer time and again to this activity. The Lord's Prayer in particular was constantly on the lips of everyone, including, to take a couple at random, Denis Possot and Charles-Philippe de Champarnoy in the year 1532: when Bethlehem hove in sight, they knelt by the roadside and said together the *Pater noster*.[34]

Although intercession for others should certainly be practised, prayer, especially in the context of pilgrimage, is not simply petitionary as if, to use a vivid image employed by Evelyn Underhill, each time one prays one comes to God clutching a supernatural shopping list. Rather prayer, in its fullest sense, is communion with God, being still in his presence, contemplating him, adoring him, thanking him and frequently praising him.

Praise can take a person out of her or himself into the enjoyment of God and should be a keynote of any pilgrimage. It is often best expressed in the shape of hymns, in accordance with Augustine's definition:

> Do you know what a hymn is? It is a song with praise to God. If you praise God and do not sing, you utter no hymn. If you sing and do not praise God, you utter no hymn. A hymn then contains three things: song and praise and that of God.[35]

As with prayer, so with hymns. The pilgrim narratives abound in references to them and in declarations about both their suitability and their appropriateness to particular locations. Favourites from the past have not all lost their appeal, and so here, to give but a few suggestions for modern pilgrims, is a selection from a fifteenth-century processional. First, the rubric is quoted to indicate where the hymn was sung; then the first line in Latin followed by the date and author when known; then the opening words of the English version and, for ease of reference to the full text, the number of the hymn in the *English Hymnal*

At Bethlehem at the altar of the Magi
   Hostis Herodes impie by C. Sedulius *c.* 450
      Why, impious Herod, shouldst thou fear   EH 38
Then there is a descent to the holy chapel singing
   Christe Redemptor omnium 6th century
      Jesu, the Father's only Son   EH 17

Where blessed John the Baptist was born
   Ut queant laxis by John the deacon 8th century
      Let thine example, holy John, remind us   EH 223

Where Jesus gave a meal to his disciples there is sung
   Pange lingua gloriosi by Venantius Fortunatus 530–609
      Sing, my tongue, the glorious battle   EH 95

Afterwards the procession goes to the column where he was crowned with thorns, singing the hymn
   O crux ave, spes unica – a verse added to *Vexilla Regis* in the 10th century   EH 94 verse 6

The ascent is made to the hill of Calvary singing the hymn
   Vexilla Regis prodeunt by Venantius Fortunatus
      The royal banners forward go   EH 94

Finally the procession goes to the Holy Sepulchre singing the hymn
   Ad cenam Agni providi 7th century, sometimes ascribed to Ambrose 340–97
      The Lamb's high banquet we await   EH 125

Where Jesus entered in to his disciples, the doors being shut
   Exultet caelum laudibus 10th century
      Let the round world with songs rejoice   EH 176

Where Christ ascended into heaven
   Jesu nostra redemptio c. 8th century
      O Christ, our hope, our heart's desire   EH 144

At the tomb of Lazarus
   Iste Confessor 8th century
      He whose confession God of old accepted   EH 188

In the house of Mark
   Jesu, Corona Virginum by Ambrose of Milan
      Jesu, the Virgin's crown, do thou   EH 192[36]

Other popular hymns included *Veni Creator* (EH 154) and the Canticles were also in use – the *Te Deum* repeatedly, the *Gloria in excelsis* most appropriately in the Shepherd's Field on the outskirts of Bethlehem but also elsewhere, the *Magnificat* at the place where Mary and Elizabeth were believed to have met. It need hardly be said that these hymns and canticles, together with many of the psalms, numerous notices of which have been made previously,[37] expressing a whole range of responses to God, can also provide admirable material for meditation.

Stations of the Cross, Processions, Re-enactment and Movement-Prayers

It would be a severe limitation if pilgrim devotions were to be confined to either verbalization or mental recollection. According to St Theodore, who became head of the monastery of Studios in Constantinople in 799:

> If merely mental contemplation were sufficient, it would have been sufficient for him to come to us in a merely mental way.[38]

However, according to Christian belief, God was enfleshed precisely because the human condition is physical/spiritual in character. Response to God, if it is to be total, must therefore be embodied because human beings are not discarnate spirits nor angels. Hence the vital importance of physical actions, movements, gestures, etc., if pilgrims are to offer themselves in their entirety. One devotion that does take the human condition into account and gives it form is 'The Stations of the Cross', since in essence it is a procession, involving therefore physical movement, along the *Via Dolorosa*, either in Jerusalem itself or at home following a sequence of pictures. It was an appreciation of the importance of providing for the personality as a whole that induced Inter-Church Travel to publish *The Jerusalem Way of the Cross* in 1966 by Tita Madden, to be followed a year later by her *The Jerusalem Maundy Thursday Walk*. These two booklets pick out the relevant scriptural passages and sketch the routes to be followed. The second one is a recalling of the Last Supper and of the ensuing walk to Gethsemane, presented in eight stations that culminate with the Agony in the Garden. The continuity with mediaeval devotions of proven value is evident from the fact that versicle and response in all versions of 'The Stations of the Cross' stand in the fourteenth-century processional preserved in the Colombina Library.

Versicle We adore you, O Christ, and we bless you
Response Because by your cross you have redeemed the world.[39]

Going from station to station is a means of education by the processional method, because at each pause instruction is conveyed about what has happened or is believed to have happened there. The pilgrims are then encouraged to offer relevant prayers. In this way they are not simply spectators but active participants in a round of continuous spiritual exercises. Marching together reinforces the sense of belonging and of being united with Christ who is the way. This identification can also be reinforced by engaging in re-enactments which were customary in the Middle Ages. Indeed from the earliest days of Christian pilgrimage, it was normal to seek to follow literally in the footsteps of Jesus, as when Egeria preceded the bishop from the summit of the Mount of Olives down to the city and so into the Church of the Resurrection, and everyone was carrying either palm or olive branches and singing psalms and antiphons.[40] At Cana pilgrims lay down on couches as at a wedding feast, plunged into the river Jordan as if being baptized, even, as did Russian pilgrims, staging the feeding of the five thousand. At first hearing, this may sound like indulging in childish games, but in fact it is no more than role-playing, and role-playing is today widely accepted as an educational method designed to promote learning by experiencing. It can be a means of entering into a biblical situation, to feel what it is like to have been there, to react with the other characters and so deepen understanding whereby devotion can be increased. All this is of a piece with the approach to the Bible advocated earlier in this chapter – it too has to be experiential. Suppose, like Jerome's friend Paula, you wish to meditate on the parable of the Good Samaritan on the way down to Jericho. The parable has to be interpreted in relation to yourself; indeed it is incomplete until that interpretation has been effected – in other words, the parable-event is not over until an answer has been given to the challenge it presents and you have perceived some of its meaning in terms of your own existence.[41]

This involvement with a text can also be achieved dramatically by acting out a parable or an incident with the pilgrims taking the parts of the different characters, exploring the meaning of the story as they do so. So, suggests Ronald Brownrigg, when visiting the garden tomb in Jerusalem, it would be beneficial to have two members of a group playing the roles of Peter and John as described in the opening verses of John 20.[42] Representational dance, if there are sufficient numbers with the gift, can achieve the same effect.[43] Multi-part reading can also warm devotion, e.g. of the trial of Paul at Caesarea (Acts 25, 26). Active engagement can also take the form of renewing baptismal vows at the Jordan or at Philippi or, even further afield, before the cathedra of St Augustine in his *basilica pacis* at Hippo in Algeria, where he completed the initiation of so many North African Christians by confirming them. At Rome, the Lateran baptistery, whose foundation goes back to the emperor Constantine, is a suitable place for this reaffirmation.

Both the Jordan location and that at Philippi provide the opportunity for swimming or paddling in a river. Indeed Christians in the past, as has been chronicled in the first chapter, were remarkable for the range of their physical actions by which they expressed and, at the same time, intensified their devotion. They would prostrate themselves, kiss the ground and otherwise manifest their piety by movements and gestures. Fabri records how, at the first sight of Jerusalem, he and his companions dismounted from their asses, bowed their faces to the earth and greeted 'her King, the Lord God, with the sign of the cross'.[44] The importance attached to this sign, which was habitual for Christians at least from the second century, is evident from a prayer included by Giacomo de Verona in his *Liber peregrinationis*:

> Protect + save + bless + sanctify + your people + and by the sign of the cross avert all ills of body and soul. + Against this sign + no danger can prevail, O Lord. Be present to our supplications, dispose our lives in prosperity by your salvation, so that amid all the changes and chances of life we may be protected by your help, through Christ our Lord. In the name of God the Father + Almighty + and of the Son + and of the Holy Spirit. Amen + [45]

In effect this sign is a movement-prayer, i.e. the movement is the prayer and vice versa. It is within Eastern Orthodoxy that this sign has received the richest interpretation. Believers join at their tips the thumb and first two fingers of the right hand to represent the Three in One of the Trinity; the third and little fingers are pressed together and meet in the palm of the hand to signify the One Person of Christ in Two Natures. To touch the forehead with the fingers in this pattern is to confess faith in God the Father who is head over all; descent to the chest praises Christ who came down for our salvation, and passing the hand from shoulder to shoulder honours the Holy Spirit who is the bond of love between Father and Son – no verbalization is needed.[46]

This, and similar actions, should not be, as once they were, badges of a particular kind of churchmanship. They are the natural embodiment of the Christian belief that 'the body is not meant for immorality, but for the Lord' (I Cor. 6.13). While a movement-prayer can replace vocalization, as is the case with the sign of the cross, the same designation applies to an action which accompanies words and embodies their meaning, i.e. it incarnates the words. To exchange the kiss of peace with the usual formula is both to express loving concern by deed and by word and also to foster it. The prayer at the 'inclination' in the Armenian liturgy is founded upon this understanding. When the people bow in adoration, the priest is directed to pray that the Holy Spirit may 'keep them entire and stamp upon their hearts the posture of their bodies'.[47] In similar vein Ronald Brownrigg has suggested that after kneeling in the Cave of the Nativity, one should rise and touch the low ceiling 'in the spirit of the child who looked up from his manger'.[48]

Pilgrimage and the Gospel Sacraments

Those who pioneered the pilgrim trails in days gone by were accustomed to take communion as frequently as opportunity offered. Indeed there is a close relationship to be examined between both gospel sacraments and pilgrimage.

The appropriateness of renewing baptismal vows has already been mentioned; it is in fact a form of rededication that should be among the motives for setting out in the first instance. It is, however, the association of meaning between baptism and the eucharist on the one hand and pilgrimage itself on the other that is likely to provide the greatest illumination. But the two sacraments have to be considered in tandem because, as Daniel Waterland once phrased it: 'I know of no surer or shorter way of coming at a just and clear apprehension of what concerns the one, than by comparing and duly weighing the circumstances of both. '[49] Indeed baptism is not an end in itself because it is one of two poles that mark Christian life as a whole. That life is a process of becoming what we are. In baptism the entire life of the believer is summed up in one moment to be realized in all that follows, and this actualization is to be achieved primarily by means of the second pole which is the eucharist. By way of illustration, and at the same time to link these two with pilgrimage, one aspect of baptismal theology may be reviewed.

According to Paul, 'By one Spirit we were all baptized into one body (I Cor. 12.13) . . . As many of you as were baptized into Christ have put on Christ . . . for you are all one in Christ Jesus' (Gal. 3.27f.). According to these statements the individual is brought by baptism out of isolation into unity; he or she is admitted into the oneness of Christ's Body. But it is precisely that unity that is manifested and intensified by the eucharist which continues to actualize that participation in the Body previously made available through baptism.[50] 'We, who are many, are one loaf, one body; for we all partake of the one loaf' (I Cor. 10.27, RV margin). This theme was succinctly summed up by Augustine: 'The spiritual benefit which is here understood is unity, that being joined to his Body and made his members we may be what we receive.'[51] This growth in unity is also one of the features in the understanding of pilgrimage outlined in the previous chapter. There it was suggested that a pilgrimage can be a means of experiencing the catholicity of the church and may lead to a heightened awareness of belonging to a greater whole. It can be an occasion for entering into that *shalom* which is embodied in the liturgical *pax* or peace. Here then the complementary meaning of sacraments and pilgrimage becomes evident and, from this aspect, the importance of celebrating the Lord's Supper as pilgrims, not only within a group but especially with local Christians, can be readily appreciated.

Moreover, the eucharist is itself most properly to be understood as a pilgrimage. It is a journey, as Alexander Schmemann has expressed it, into the dimension of the Kingdom.[52] It is a passage from the old to the new. It is a bridge between the present and the age to come.

> A sacrament is always a *passage*, a *transformation*. Yet it is not a 'passage' into 'supernature', but into the Kingdom of God, the world to come, into the very reality of this world and its life as redeemed and restored by Christ. It is the transformation not of 'nature' into 'supernature', but of the *old* into the *new*.[53]

The eucharist re-calls the coming of Christ in Palestine; it looks forward to and anticipates his coming again in glory and it celebrates in the present the meeting of that past and that future. In this way it has a threefold reference to time – to time past, future and present – exactly like a pilgrimage and like the multiple interpretation of the Bible practised by the Church Fathers.

The apostle Paul, as noted previously, also connected the two sacraments with the archetypal Jewish pilgrimage, i.e. with the Exodus. He understood baptism in the light of the crossing of the Red Sea and the eucharist he related to the food and drink provided by God through the agency of Moses in the wilderness (I Cor. 10.1–4). When 'the sea returned to its wonted flow' (Ex. 14.27), the forces of evil and oppression were overthrown and the Israelites were severed from their past life of bondage. Similarly when baptism is administered, sin is overcome and the candidates die to all that has gone before. The eucharist is their iron rations for their continuing pilgrimage and through communion their baptismal remission is renewed as they

Plate XII The renewal of baptismal vows at Philippi (Acts 16.13–15)

receive the benefits of Christ's passion.[54] All this, in Paul's view, involves a baptismal co-death and co-resurrection with Christ. 'We were buried therefore with him by baptism into death, so that as Christ was raised from the dead by the glory of the Father, we too might walk in newness of life' (Rom. 6.4). Equally to feed upon the sacramental body and blood is to have a share in the death of Christ who is himself present among his followers as their risen Lord.

The Exodus story also presents the theme of death. When the Israelites hankered after the fleshpots of Egypt and thereby revealed their lack of trust in God, they were sentenced to die in the wilderness; only their children would live to enter the Promised Land (Num. 14.26–32). This sequence of life through death is central to the gospel story. 'Unless a grain of wheat falls into the earth and dies, it remains alone; but if it dies, it bears much fruit' (John 12.24). This is the paschal pattern, i.e. the succession of life to death and this is exemplified by a Holy Land pilgrimage – at Calvary the accent is on dying with Christ, at the Sepulchre on rising again with him. Nor are these foci missing from pilgrimages to other centres. To go to the tomb of a martyr – of Peter at Rome, of Martin at Tours – is to be confronted with the same paschal pattern – a pattern so entitled because it became discernible as the first Holy Week reached its climax during the feast of the Passover and Jesus was nailed to the cross and rose from the tomb.

This paschal pattern is not one that belongs solely to the confined world of religious observances; it is a 'law' of existence in general that life is secured through death. Scientific advance, for example, is only possible through the giving up of old certainties and the confession of ignorance in the hope of discovering new truths. Political and economic progress cannot be achieved unless people overcome their desire to retain what they have, to conserve the past instead of allowing it to die. Human maturity cannot be attained unless childhood and its ways pass away. Time itself illustrates the same structure, for tomorrow only comes through the ending of today. Human happiness is realized largely through the death of self-love. This same reality underlies the narrative of Jesus' ministry in Palestine[55] and it is therefore the central theme in any pilgrimage. Further, when a pilgrimage is interpreted in terms of the imitation of Christ and his saints, this same reality is again evident for imitation of the kind required should follow the death-life process. Here again the sacraments are relevant in so far as they are means of conformation to the image of God, defaced by sin but restored in baptism and progressively renewed through the eucharist. Jesus indeed was the one whose death, resurrection and ascension, as previously noted, were understood to comprise his own 'exodus' (Luke 9.30).

It is not to be forgotten that the Exodus reached its initial climax with the establishment of the covenant on Mount Sinai and its second with the entry into the Promised Land. Similarly baptism, which is spiritual circumcision (Col. 2.11), is the seal of the new covenant. The eucharist in turn derives from the Last Supper when Jesus took a cup of wine, saying: 'This is my blood of the new covenant' (Mark 14.24). The Lord's Supper thus corresponds to the Passover when the people of God re-engage themselves within the covenant relationship.[56] Today the recalling of baptism and the celebration of the communion service are key devotional acts that constitute so many high points during the course of a pilgrimage and point forward to the consummation in the age to come when the messianic banquet will be held as a feast of triumphant joy.

Yet the gospel sacraments are not to be separated from the proclamation of the word. This means that in acknowledging that the eucharist is not a mere pious remembering but a reactualization of the saving deeds of the Word incarnate, the equally important truth is not to be neglected that a pilgrimage can involve a reactualization of the Word of God contained in the Bible. It has been repeatedly stressed throughout this study that the deeds of Christ are not just happenings in past history; the Christ event impinges on the present through word and sacrament. During a pilgrimage the regular celebration of the Lord's Supper relates the past to the present in anticipation of the future, and similarly the reading and exposition of the Bible relate what is narrated to the present in anticipation of the future. Here are themes in plenty to nourish the devotions of pilgrims.

The Return Home

Just as the three apostles had to descend from the Mount of Transfiguration and return to the work-a-day world, despite Peter's desire to remain there permanently in booths (Mark 9.5), so today's pilgrims have to take their leave and make the journey back home. Many, before departure, obtain souvenirs which correspond to the mediaeval tokens providing evidence of a task completed.

The return journey differs in character from the outward one, in the same way that going up to the altar at the Lord's Supper differs from the reverse movement after communion. To approach the Lord's table is to advance with anticipation, to leave it is to be full of gratitude. In like manner to travel homeward from the Holy Land or Rome or wherever should be an act of thanksgiving for the fulfilment of what ideally has been a spiritual exercise leading to a closer union with God. It is appropriate therefore that the form of prayer used at the start of the outward journey should be counterbalanced by a similar brief office as the pilgrimage draws to its close.

Form of Prayer to be Used on the Return Journey

Leader It is good to give thanks to the Lord,

All To sing praises to your name, O Most High;

Leader To declare your steadfast love in the morning,

All And your faithfulness by night (Ps. 92.1f.).

Leader O God make speed to save us.

All O Lord make haste to help us.

Leader Glory be to the Father and to the Son and to the Holy Spirit.

All As it was in the beginning, is now and ever shall be, world without end. Amen.

Psalm 95

Reader Isaiah 43.1–7 (The Pilgrimage back from Babylon)

Leader We give thanks to you, heavenly Father, for the blessings of this pilgrimage

All We give thanks.

Leader for the enjoyment we have had together

All We give thanks.

Leader for the fellowship we have experienced

All We give thanks.

Leader for the greater sense of our unity in Christ that we have developed

All We give thanks.

Nunc dimittis

Guard us waking, O Lord,
and guard us sleeping,
that awake we may watch with Christ,
and asleep we may rest in peace. Amen.

Little more needs to be said, but one suggestion may be acceptable: on the Sunday following arrival home, should not the pilgrims attend their local church, give a brief account of their experience and ask their fellow members in the congregation to join with them in an act of thanksgiving?

References

Books listed in the Bibliography are referred to by section and number

1. Christian Pilgrimage in the Later Middle Ages

1. Boccacio (H 3), Day 6, Tale 10
2. Gutsch (M 12), 193
3. Benton (F 4), 197
4. Chrysostom (J 10), 99
5. Caesarius (J 9), viii, 85
6. von Harff (K(a) 26), 262
7. Fabri (K(a) 20), II.40
8. von Harff, op. cit., 268
9. Caesarius, op. cit., viii, 69
10. Augustine (J 2), 36
11. Delehaye (M 3), 205
12. For one such text see PL.71. 1185–6
13. Geary (L 3)
14. Caesarius, op. cit., x.67
15. Wilson (M 6), 22
16. Jerome (J 31), 109
17. Paulinus (J 40); ACW.40, 81
18. Prudentius (J 47); ACW.43.259
19. Wilson, op. cit., 18
20. Ibid., 16f.
21. Martoni (K(a)), 37
22. Dickinson (C 16), 42
23. Tafur (K(a) 50), 27
24. Erasmus (B 3), 2
25. Chrysostom (J 15), 5
26. Bede (J 7), iv, 21
27. Northcote & Brownlow (H 23), 20
28. Gregory (A 6), I.278
29. Gregory (J 24), 13.45
30. Chrysostom (J 12), 8.2
31. Gregory of Tours (J 23), II.4
32. von Harff (K(a) 26), 28
33. cf. Moore (C 35)
34. Petrarch (J 42), XIX (XVI)
35. Dante (J 19), xli
36. Chrysostom (J 11), V.1
37. Jerome (J 31), 58.3
38. Eusebius (J 21), iv.26.14
39.* This was a primary motive of many Scandinavian pilgrims who, from the eleventh century on, went in large numbers to the Holy Land. Rome did not initially exercise an attraction but in due course the authority of the holy city induced many to visit it to venerate the relics and seek indulgences (Riant (C42))
40. Leo (J 37), 139.1
41. Jerome (J 32)
42. Fabri (K(a) 20), I.2
43. Origen (J 39), 6.40
44. Abbot Daniel (K(a) 2), 1
45. Shakespeare, *Henry IV*, Pt 1, Act 1, Sc. 1
46. Fabri (K(a) 20), I.4
47. von Harff, op. cit., 2
48. Fabri, op. cit., I.4
49. Telfer (C 47)
50. Eusebius (J 22), 3.25
51. Cyril (J 16), iv.10
52. Cyril, op. cit., x.19
53. Egeria (J 20), 5.8; 7.2f.
54. Chrysostom (J 13)
55. Fabri, op. cit., I.278
56. Paetow (F 18), 13
57. Leclercq (C 32), 23
58. Hughes (C 23)
59. Vogel (C 49)
60. Brewyn (E 1)
61. *Dictionnaire* (H 11), cols 1713–28

62. Purcell (F 190), 36
63. Labande (D 20), E 247
64. Constable (F 6), 248–52
65. Berlière (C 6)
66. Brundage (D 6)
67. Paetow (F 18), 83ff.
68. Merton (C 34), 102ff.
69. Labande (D 20), F 15
70. Purchas (K(b) 3), VII.450
71. Pernoud (E 11), 5
72. Hopkins (H 16), 20f.
73. Cuntz (H 8)
74. Wilkinson (K(b) 5), 153–63
75. Magoun (C 33)
76. Barker (C 3), 112–5
77. Parks (C 38), 83ff.
78. Barker, op. cit., 119–23
79. Bernard (K(a) 5), 43–9
80. Golubovich (E 7)
81. Parks, op. cit., 529
82. Ibid., 526
83. Wilkinson, op. cit., 162
84. Ibid., 85
85. Wright (K(b) 7), 31–50
86. Magoun, op. cit., 278f.
87. Furnivall (E 6), 4
88. Ibid., 10
89. Capgrave (K(a) 11), 63
90. Furnivall, op. cit., 31
91. Duff (E 4), xiii, n.1
92. Davies (C 15), 6
93. Hulbert (C 24)
94. Parks, op. cit., 179–84
95. Nebenzahl (H 21), 19
96. Ibid., 30
97. Ibid., figs 9, 10
98. Ibid., (H 21) pls 17, 18
99. de Sandoli (K(b) 4), 306
100. Ibid., 391
101. Davies, op. cit., xviii
102. Nebenzahl, op. cit., pl. 41
103. Frescobaldi (K(a) 22), 35
104. Fabri (K(a) 20), I.290
105. de Castro (D 7), 451–70
106. Bernouilli (D 3), 79–86
107. de Castro, art. cit., 470–8
108. Pernoud (E 11)
109. Pernoud, ibid., 6, n.1
110. de Castro, art. cit., 452f.; Bernouilli, art. cit., 81f.; Pernoud, op. cit., 164f.
111. de Castro, ibid., 170–96
112. Ibid., 483
113. Aquinas (J 5), 1a. 1, 10
114. Dante (J 18), X.7

115. Gregory (J 25), III.X; PL 75.513C
116. Owst (F 17), 57–61
117. Origen (J 38), I; SC 71.234
118. Origen (J 38), IX; SC 71.334
119. Gregory of Nyssa (J 27), I.5
120. Ibid., I.2
121. Ibid., I.15
122. Ibid., II.49
123. Ibid., II.37
124. Ibid., II.125
125. Ibid., II.269
126. Fetellus (E 5), 14
127. Gregory of Nyssa (J 26), 17
128. Purcell (C 40), 37–40
129. Pernoud, op. cit.
130. Wey (K(a) 57)
131. See the analysis of one guide book by Pernoud, op. cit., 6–19
132. Parks, op. cit., 294
133. von Harff (K(a) 26), xviii; for the *Information* see Duff, op. cit.
134. *Guide-Book* (E 8), 1
135. Nichols (E 10), 120–52
136. Fife (F 10), 169
137. Davies (C 15), 37
138. Hulbert (C 24), 415
139. *Compostela Guide* (E 3)
140. de Lannoy (K(a) 33)
141. Howard (C 22), 17
142. Niccolò (K(a) 41), 11
143. Abbot Daniel (K(a) 2), 2
144. Theoderich (K(a) 52), 1
145. Burchard (K(a) 8), 4
146. Willibald (K(a) 58), 1
147. Wright (K(b) 7), 129
148. von Harff, op. cit., 2
149. Torkington (K(a) 54); Guylforde (K(a) 25)
150. Niccolò, op. cit., 4
151.* Giacomo (K(a) 23). There is a list of those obtainable at Acre in a manuscript dated c. 1280 by its editors, but they acknowledge that this is uncertain and it could be post-1300 (Michelant & Reynaud (K(b) 1), 235f.)
152. Frescobaldi (K(a) 22), 186–201
153. Ludolph (K(a) 35), 12
154. Anonymous (K(a) 4), 457–9
155. Wey, op. cit., 1ff.
156. Ibid., 5
157. Frescobaldi, op. cit., 149–56
158. Fabri, op. cit., II.216
159. Quoted in (K(a) 13), 10
160. Kempe (K(a) 30), 77f.

161. Langland (J 35), Passus V
162. Davies (C 14), 77
163. Fabri (F(a) 20), I.54f.
164. Vogel (C 49), 150
165. Henderson (D 15), 207f.
166. Brundage (D 6), 303–6
167. Vogel, loc. cit.
168. Warren (D 24), 170
169. See below, p. o
170.* An example of such a letter is printed in PL 87.755
171. Fabri (K(a) 20), I.47
172. Giacomo (K(a) 23), 171
173. John of Canterbury (K(a) 28)
174. Wey (K(a) 57), 153f.
175. Casola (K(a) 13), 25
176. Guylforde (K(a) 25), 85
177. Wright (K(b) 7), 36
178. Niccolò (K(a) 41), 4
179. Casola, op. cit., 55
180. Ibid., 102f.
181. Fabri, op. cit., I.148ff.
182. Furnivall (E 6), 39
183. Joranson (F.14), 3–34
184. Frescobaldi, op. cit., 57
185. Labande (D 20), E 248
186. Brightman (D 4), 1034
187. Frescobaldi, op. cit., 35
188. Wright, op. cit., 185
189. Cutts (F 8), 179n.
190. von Harff (K(a) 26), 134
191. Oursel (C 37), 47
192. Psalms 6, 32, 38, 51, 102, 130, 143
193. de Sanseverino (K(a) 48), 37
194. Oursel, op. cit., 92ff.
195. Ibid., 45, 47
196. Sigal (C 44), 54
197. Labande, op. cit., C 109f.
198. Fabri, op. cit., I.323
199. Ibid., I.70
200. von Harff, op. cit., 258
201. Svobada (M 5), 14
202. Compostela Guide (E 3), 361
203. Vogel (C 49), 150
204. Compostela Guide (E 3), 369
205. Torkington (K(a) 54), 3
206. von Harff, op. cit., 41 n.1
207. Casola, op. cit., 117
208. Torkington, op. cit., 14f.
209. Fabri, op. cit., I.140–6
210. Casola, op. cit., 189
211. Fabri, op. cit., I.141–5
212. Ibid., I.78
213. Ibid., I.180

214. Ibid., I.203–9
215. Guylforde, op. cit., 15
216. de Sanseverino, op. cit., 87
217. Wright (K(b) 7), 175
218. Egeria (J 20), 37.5; Piacenza Pilgrim (K(a) 44), 20; Wilkinson (K(b) 6), 83
219. Adomnan (K(a) 1), 8; Wilkinson, op. cit., 97
220. Adomnan, ibid., 8; Wilkinson, ibid., 97
221. Adomnan, ibid., 7.2; Wilkinson, loc. cit.
222. Piacenza Pilgrim, op. cit., 20; Wilkinson, op. cit., 83
223. Adomnan, op. cit., 21.4; Wilkinson, op. cit., 108
224. Fabri (K(a) 20), I.299
225. Piacenza Pilgrim, op. cit., 4; Wilkinson, op. cit., 79
226. Fabri, op. cit., II.13
227. Wright, op. cit., 57
228. Labande (D 20), D n.51
229. Frescobaldi (K(a) 22), 78
230. Piacenza Pilgrim, op. cit., 31; Wilkinson, op. cit., 85
231. Frescobaldi, op. cit., 127
232. Ibid., 124
233. Finucane (C 17), 96f.
234. Adomnan, op. cit., 6.2; Wilkinson, op. cit., 97
235. Sigal (C 44), 82
236. Piacenza Pilgrim, op. cit., 18; Wilkinson, op. cit., 83
237. Delanielle (D 12), 530
238. Compostela Guide (E 3), 367
239. Paulinus (J 40), 20; ACW 40, 159
240. Labande, op. cit., D 285f.
241. Piacenza Pilgrim, op. cit., 37; Wilkinson, op. cit., 87
242. Fabri, op. cit., I.54
243.* This incident comes almost at the end of the account; the pilgrim then went on to Alexandria before returning to Jerusalem, but it is clear that by the time he had reached Sinai he regarded his pilgrimage as virtually complete
244. Davies (N 4), 18f.
245. Piacenza Pilgrim, op. cit., 7; Wilkinson, op. cit., 81
246. Egeria, op. cit., 37.2
247. Burchard (K(a) 8), 73
248. von Harff (K(a) 26), 211
249. Fabri, op. cit., I.567

250. Ibid., I.564
251. von Harff, op. cit., 231
252. Ibid., 224
253. Ibid., 142
254. Casola (K(a) 13), 247
255. Fabri, op. cit., II.13
256. Ibid., I.93
257. Piacenza Pilgrim, op. cit., 18; Wilkinson, op. cit., 83
258. Adomnan, op. cit., 23.8; Wilkinson, ibid., 101
259. Piacenza Pilgrim, op. cit., 22; Wilkinson, ibid., 84
260. Fabri, op. cit., I.349
261. Grabar (L 4)
262. Piacenza Pilgrim, op. cit., 20; Wilkinson, op. cit., 83
263. Niccolò (K(a) 41), XXII.4
264. Phocas (K(a) 43), 32
265. Jerome (J 31), 108.9f.
266. Burchard (K(a) 8), 73
267. Fabri, op. cit., I.283f.
268. Burchard, op. cit., 64
269. Fabri, op. cit., I.47
270. Jerome, op. cit., 108.11f.
271. Fabri, op. cit., I.387
272. Ibid., I.291
273. Ibid., I.4/3
274. Ibid., II.60
275. Ibid., I.388
276. Niccolò, op. cit., 15
277. Wey (K(a) 57), 156
278. Fabri, op. cit., I.633
279. Ibid., I.548
280. Ibid., I.557
281. Ludolph (K(a) 35), 96
282. Frescobaldi, op. cit., 78
283. Fabri, op. cit., I.78
284. Ibid., I.347, 373, 364, 379, 291f.
285. von Harff, op. cit., 18f.
286. Capgrave (K(a) 11), 75
287. Abbot Daniel (K(a) 2), 1
288. Frescobaldi, op. cit., 136
289. Theoderich (K(a) 52), 35
290. Frescobaldi, op. cit., 189
291. John of Würzburg (K(a) 29), 14
292. Ibid., 37
293. Theoderich, op. cit., 14
294. Ibid., 17
295. Frescobaldi, op. cit., 125
296. Fabri, op. cit., I.472
297. Davies (D 10), 35f.
298. Purchas (K(b) 3), IX.490f.
299. Piacenza Pilgrim, op. cit., 37; Wilkinson, op. cit., 87
300. Frescobaldi, op. cit., 63, 113
301. Guylforde, op. cit., 21, 25
302. Fabri, op. cit., I.346
303. e.g. ibid., II.214
304. (D 7), 451; (D 3), 81; (E 11), 64
305. (D 7), 454
306. (D 7), 455; (D 3), 83; (E 11), 66
307. Theoderich, op. cit., 20
308. Ludolph, op. cit., 107
309. *City of Jerusalem* (K(a) 15), 9
310. Guylforde, op. cit., 27f.
311. *Compostela Guide*, op. cit., 313
312. John of Würzburg, op. cit., 38
313. (D 7), 483
314. Ibid., 459
315. Casola, op. cit., 247
316. John of Würzburg, op. cit., 13
317. Theodosius in Wilkinson, op. cit., 61
318. Piacenza Pilgrim, op. cit., 4; Wilkinson, op. cit., 79
319. Ibid., 17; Wilkinson, op. cit., 83
320. Fabri, op. cit., I.299
321. Ibid., II.114
322. Abbot Daniel, op. cit., 81f.
323. Fabri, op. cit., I.622
324. Borenius (C 9)
325. Labande, op. cit., B 343
326. Dante (J 19), xli.35–52
327. Clarke (C 13)
328. von Harff, op. cit., 275
329. *Compostela Guide*, op. cit., 380
330. Borenius (C 8), 20
331. Ward-Perkins (H 30) 254–64
332. Fletcher (C 18), 63
333. Fabri (K(a) 20), II.398
334. Wright (K(b) 7), 292
335. Guylforde (K(a) 25), 65
336. Ibid., 68
337. Davies (C 15), xvii
338. Ibid., loc. cit.
339. Labande (D 20), E 241
340. Dugdale (H 12), 144

2. Criticisms of Pilgrimage and the Protestant Condemnation

1. Gregory of Nyssa (J 26), PG.46. 1009C
2. Jerome (J 31), 47.2
3. Ibid., 58.3

4. Gregory, op. cit., 1012C
5. Ibid., 1013C
6. Jerome, loc. cit.
7. Ibid.
8. Gregory, op. cit., 1012C
9. à Kempis (D 19), IV.1.8
10. Labande (D 20), D 284f.; E 244
11. La-Tour Landry (J 36), 51
12. Davies (C 14), 26
13. Mansi (H 20), col. 103
14. Quoted by Constable (F 6), 142
15. Bromyard (J 8), art. 1.6
16. Honorius (J 28), II.23
17. Jerome (J 30), 4
18. Jerome (J 31), 109.1
19. Morris (L 5), 55–60
20. PL.156.621
21. Ibid., 624–5
22. von Harff (K(a) 26), 292
23. Geary (L 3), 28f.
24. Finucane (C 17), 196
25. à Kempis, op. cit., IV.1.8
26. Quoted by Owst (G 17), 141
27. Quoted, ibid., 137ff.
28. Zacher (C 52), 53
29. Augustine (J 3), 18
30. à Kempis, loc. cit.
31. Casola (K(a) 13), 10
32. Zacher, op. cit., 132, 154
33. Leclercq (C 32)
34. Delanielle (D 12)
35. Quoted by Constable, op. cit., 129
36. Vogel (C 49), 138
37. Dan Michel (J 17), 104
38. Owst, op. cit., 104
39. Texts in Young (H 31), I.451–83, 688–94
40. Gardiner (C 19), 12
41. Robertson (H 27), 301
42. Casola, op. cit., 36–9
43. von Harff, op. cit., 140
44. See above, pp. 9, 80f.
45. Wey (K(a) 57), 138–46
46. Workman (F 24), 18
47. Wyclif (G 22), 156
48. Spinka (F 21), 68, 134
49. Todd (G.21), 12, 126
50. Crompton (F 7), 130–224
51. (G 7), 364f.
52. Aston (F 1), 159–67
53. Pecock (G 19), I.194
54. Haines (G 10), 143–54
55. Pecock, op. cit., 191
56. *Lanterne* (G.15), 85ff.

57. Aston, op. cit., 55
58. Dynmok (G 6), 192
59. Green (A 12), 88
60. Pecock, op. cit., 136–75
61. Ibid., 182
62. Ibid., 190
63. Ibid., 215
64. Ibid., 235f.
65. Ibid., 179
66. Aston, op. cit., 147 n.45
67. Foxe (G 8), 268
68. *Advocates of Reform* (G 1), 337f.
69. Erasmus (B 5), 101f.
70. *The Usefulness of the Colloquies* (1526) in (B 6), 627
71. Ibid., 625
72. *A Pilgrimage for Religion's Sake*; ibid., 288
73. *Opus* . . . (B 4), 163, 228f.
74. *The Shipwreck* (1523); (B 6), 142
75. Ibid., 141
76. See above, p. 78
77. (B 6), 6
78. Ibid., 627
79. Ibid., 289
80. Fife (F 10), 168f., 172
81. Cap. 8. Sermo 3 (G 18), 23, 335f.
82. Ibid., 13, 326ff.
83. Heath (C 21), 29
84. Severus (J 48), *Dialogues* III.10
85. Gregory of Tours (J 23), V.22
86. *Lectures on Genesis* 22 (G 18), 14, 130
87. Ps. 110.4 (G 18), 13, 327
88. (G 18), 51, 81f.
89. (G 18), 53. 154
90. (G 18), 53. 268 n.1
91. (G 18), 31. 198
92. (G 18), 44. 171
93. (G 18), 44. 180
94. (G 18), 53. 327
95. (G 18), 53. 326
96. Gen. 24 14; 51, 233
97. Isa. 40.2; 17, 5
98. Gen. 8.21; 2, 123
99. Cap. 6 Sermon 1 on John, 23, 15
100. First Sermon at Weimar, 51, 110
101. Cap. 3 Sermon 32 on John, 22, 370
102. Cap. 6 Sermon 17 on John, 23, 138
103. Gen. 32.34; 6, 129
104. Table Talk No. 3588; 54
105. Erasmus (B 6), 288
106. Scarisbrick (F 20), 163
107. *Ordinances* (G 2), 80
108. Calvin (G 2), 120

109. Ibid., 239
110. Ibid., 188
111. Ibid., 190
112. Higman (G 13), 49–52
113. Ibid., 53–8
114. Ibid., 62
115. Ibid., 94
116. Erasmus (B 6), 305
117. Ibid., 306f., 310
118. Ibid., 285
119. Scarisbrick, op. cit., 55
120. Ibid., 18
121. Cooke (G 4), 39
122. Ibid., 198
123. Ibid., 40
124. Ibid., 66
125. Ibid., 188f.
126. Ibid., 207
127. Ibid., 144
128. Ibid., 169
129. Ibid., 165ff.
130. Ibid., 113
131. Ibid., 200f.
132. Stow (G 20), 1012
133. Ibid., 1014
134. Cranmer (G 5), 490
135. Lloyd (G 17), xxviii
136. From the Bishop's Book: Lloyd, op. cit., 136. For The King's Book see (G 14), 88
137. (G 14), 136f.
138. Ibid., 89
139. Frere & Kennedy (G 9), 38
140. 14. Ibid., 57
141. Gairdner (F 12), 371
142. Cardwell (G 3), 39
143. 34. Frere & Kennedy, op. cit., 107
144. 16. Ibid., 285
145. 20. Ibid., 169
146. Frere (G 10), 381
147. Frere & Kennedy, op. cit., 6
148. Ibid., 236
149. 15. Ibid., 264
150. 9. Ibid., 269

151. Huizinga (F 13), 159
152. Latimer (G 16), 55
153. 10. Frere & Kennedy, op. cit., 39
154. 15. Ibid., 57
155. 18. Ibid., 58f.
156. 20. Ibid., 179
157. Cranmer (G 5), 63
158. Ibid., 147
159. Frere, op. cit., 21
160. Cardwell, op. cit., 234
161. Latimer, op. cit., 474
162. See above, p. 102
163. Campbell & Read (B 2), 193
164. Ibid., 61
165. Ibid., 156f.
166. Ibid., 159
167. Ibid., 62
168. Ibid., 15–19
169. Ibid., 163
170. Ibid., 20
171. Ibid., 164
172. Ibid., 28
173. Ibid., 164
174. Ibid., 6off.
175. Ibid., 22
176. Ibid., 149f.
177. Ibid., 159
178. Ibid., 28ff.
179. Ibid., 31f.
180. Ibid., 16
181. Ibid., 160
182. Ibid., 168
183. Ibid., 170; 158
184. Ibid., 78
185. Ibid., 72
186. Gardiner (G 11), 169
187. Ibid., 484f.
188. Ibid., 256
189. Ibid., 273–6
190. Muller (F 16), 174–82
191. Waterworth (B 7), 235
192. Ibid., 234
193. Donovan (B 1), 318-24

3. The Death and Resurrection of Protestant Pilgrimages

1. Moryson (K(a) 39), I.275
2. Lithgow (K(a) 34), 18
3. Bates (C 4), 54
4. Ibid., 302
5. Owen (K(a) 42), 18
6. Munday (K(a) 40), 45f.

7. Ibid., 32
8. Ibid., 76
9. Ibid., 64
10. Sanderson (K(a) 46), 92–5
11. Lithgow, op. cit., 16f.
12. Owen, op. cit., 23, 30

13. Moryson, op. cit., I.169
14. Lithgow, op. cit., 22
15. Mortoft (K(a) 38), 70
16. Ibid., 95
17. Ibid., 104
18. Ibid., 82
19. Ibid., 88
20. Pepys (H 25), 291
21. Owen, op. cit., 29
22. Ibid., 33
23. Ibid., 15
24. Ibid., 48
25. Mortoft, op. cit., 171
26. Lithgow, op. cit., 31
27. Moryson, op. cit., I.213f.
28. Ibid., I.216
29. Lithgow, op. cit., 224
30. Mortoft, op. cit., 89f.
31. Ibid., 61f.
32. Ibid., 118
33. Moryson, op. cit., I.xix
34. Bates, op. cit., 207
35. Casola (K(a) 13), 112
36. *Two Journeys* (K(a) 55), 52f.
37. Ibid., 103
38. Volney (K(a) 56), 308f.
39. Moryson, op. cit., II.46f.
40. Ibid., II.20
41. Lithgow, op. cit., 210
42. Ibid., 219
43. *Two Journeys*, op. cit., 64
44. Ibid., 86
45. See above, p. 26
46. *Two Journeys*, 59
47. Sanderson, op. cit., 19, 108f., 122f.
48. Lithgow, op. cit., 221
49. Ibid., 251
50. Ibid., 217
51. Ibid., 204
52. Ibid., 207f.
53. Moryson, op. cit., II.1
54. Ibid., I.452
55. Lithgow, op. cit., 236
56. Moryson, op. cit., III, 371
57. Ibid., II.41
58. Lithgow, op. cit., 221
59. Sandys (K(a) 47), 163
60. *Two Journeys*, op. cit., 93
61. Sandys, op. cit., 167
62. Ibid., 174
63. Purchas (K(b) 3), VIII. 278, 300
64. *Two Journeys*, op. cit., 59
65. Purchas, op. cit., VIII.19
66. Ibid., 54

67. Moryson, op. cit., I.447
68. Sanderson, op. cit., 5f.
69. Ibid., 105
70. *Two Journeys*, op. cit., 69
71. Terry (K(a) 51), 61
72. *Two Journeys*, op. cit., 86
73. Wright, (K(b) 7), 445f.
74. Coryate (K(a) 16), 52
75. Ibid., 4
76. Sanderson, op. cit., 111
77. Ibid., 19
78. Ibid., 104
79. Wright, op. cit., 433
80. Ibid., 430f.
81. Ibid., 390
82. Richards (C 43), 45
83. Thurston (F 23), 83
84. Ibid., 99
85. Ibid., 108
86. Ignatius (A 7), 72
87. Ignatius (D 17), 106
88. Ibid., 72
89. Possot & Philippe (K(a) 45), 12
90. Thurston (F 23), 82
91. Ibid., 92f.
92. Ibid., 98
93. Noted under 18.2.1645
94. Parks (C 38), 358f.
95. Chateaubriand reproduced the account by Delehayes (K(a) 14), 225–31
96. de Thévenot (K(a) 53)
97. Ibid., I.II.XLVI. 201
98. Ibid., I.II.XXIX. 191
99. Ibid., I.II.XLII. 195f.
100. *Two Journeys* (K(a) 55), 100
101. Chateaubriand, op. cit., 1
102. Ibid., 235
103. Laborde (K(a) 31), 318n.
104. Lamartine (K(a) 31), 158
105. Ibid., 7
106. Ibid., 133
107. Ibid., 218
108. Burton (K(a) 10), e.g. II.36f.
109. Ibid., II.21
110. Ibid., II.38f.
111. Ibid., II.680
112. Turner (C 48), 175f.
113. Cutts (F 8), 182n.
114. Lithgow (K(a) 34), 24
115. Gross (C 20), 129–49
116. Boussel (L 1), 77
117. Pascal (C 39), 239, 241f. For a map see Arseniev (C 1), 414
118. See above, p. 14

119. Graham (K(a) 24), 248–56
120. Purchas (K(b) 3), VIII.298
121. Ibid., 28
122. Lithgow, op. cit., 182
123. Purchas, op. cit., X.446
124. de Thévenot, op. cit., I.II.XLI. 193
125. Burckhardt (K(a) 9), 552
126. Curzon (K(a) 17), 231
127. Ben-Arieh (I 2), 99
128. Stanley (K(a) 49), 356
129. Noakes (H 22), 155, 221f.
130. Pascal, art. cit., 240
131. Graham, op. cit., 99f.
132. Ibid., 101
133. Ibid., 216–25
134. Ibid., 44
135. Ibid., 68
136. Ibid., 181
137. Ibid., 190f., 214
138. Ibid., 128
139. Ibid., 261
140. See above, p. 74
141. Pascal, art. cit., 246
142. Browne (K(a) 7)
143. Ibid., x
144. Ibid., 361
145. Jowett (A 9), 14
146. Ben-Arieh (I 2), 15
147. Kinglake (H 19), 21
148. Ibid., 219
149. Stanley (K(a) 49), 359
150. Walker (C 50), 122–32
151. Quoted, ibid., 223
152. Ibid., 185
153. Ibid., 73
154. Dixon (K(a) 18), II.299–307
155. Martineau (K(a) 36), 411
156. Ibid., 434
157. Ibid., 412
158. de Forest (K(a) 21), 80
159. Walker, op. cit., 30
160. Martineau, op. cit., 304, 408
161. Ibid., 425
162. Curzon (K(a) 17), 192ff.
163. See above, pp. 9f.
164. Dixon, op. cit., vf.
165. E. Robinson (I 6), 227
166. Ben-Arieh, op. cit., 58
167. P.E.F. (I 5), 13f.
168. Ibid., 3
169. Ibid., 37f.
170. Ibid., 164f., 97
171.* Morrison (I 4). Morrison was Hon. Treasurer of the P.E.F.
172. George Williams consulted it at

every site (I 7) II.5, and it was constantly in the hands of Dean Stanley (Prothero & Bradley (A 13), I.450
173.* Bacon (I 1), 19. This volume reprints all the archaeological reports from *The Illustrated London News* between 1842 and 1976. In his preface the editor remarks how much of the work initially was aimed at demonstrating 'the truth of the Bible'
174. Ibid., 26f.
175. Ibid., 45
176. Stanley (N 15), 31
177. Ben-Arieh, op. cit., 175
178. Wright (K(b) 7)
179. MacAlister (I 3), 25
180. Ben-Arieh (I 2), 191
181. Swinglehurst (H 29), 88
182. Cook's Excursionist (H 5); Series 22.7; 20.7.1872, 2
183. Ibid., 18.12; 5.9.1868, 3
184. 19.2; 15.5.1869, 6f.
185. Pudney (H 26), 188
186. (H 5); 32.7; 1.8.1882
187. Ibid., 22.2; 4.5.1872, 2
188. 22.8; 5.8.1872, 2
189. Pudney, op. cit., 188
190. Rowe (H 28), 208–15
191. Swinglehurst, op. cit., 106
192. Burton (K(a) 10), II.19
193. *Excursionist* 22.1; 20.4.1872, 5
194. Ibid., 22.2; 4.5.1872, 2
195. Ibid., loc. cit.
196. Ibid., 23.1; 21.4.1873, 2
197. Ibid., 22.1; 20.4.1872, 6
198. Ibid., 22.7; 20.7.1872, 4
199. Ibid., e.g. 20.1; 7.5.1870, 4
200. Ibid., 23.4; 14.6.1873, 2
201. *The Diary of Miss Riggs of Hampstead*, 1869, manuscript in Thomas Cook's Archives
202. *A Cook's Tour* (H 6), 66
203. See above, p. 33
204. Heath (C 21), 167
205. Jerome (K(a) 27), 159f.
206. Kilvert (A 8), III.333
207. Thompson (F 22), 98–102
208. Ibid., 191f.
209. Chadwick (Γ 5), I.140
210. Goulburn (H 15), xif.
211. Howson (H 17), 65
212. Browne (A 2), 355

213. Ibid., 387
214. Lloyd (F 15), I.31
215. Benson (H 20), 52
216. Ibid., 134
217. Temple (A 15), I.541
218. *A Day* (H 9), 4
219. *Final Report* (H 14), 1
220. Quoted by Chadwick, op. cit., II.383
221. Jusserand (C 28)
222. Cartwright (C 11)
223.* Belloc (C 5). A new edition was issued in 1910, and it was reprinted 3 times up to and including 1921
224. Quiller-Couch (C 41)
225. Ibid., vf.
226. Garbett (A 4), 149
227. Ibid., 150, 216, 272f.
228. Lloyd, op. cit., II.238
229. Bennett (D 1 & 2)
230. Bennett (F 3), 4, 6f.
231. Bennet (F 2), 467f.
232. Ibid., (F 3), 45
233. Ibid., (F 2), 111f.
234. Ibid., 89
235. Ibid., (F 3), 52
236. Ibid., 48–52
237. Bennett (D 1), 2

238. Ibid., (F 3), 62
239. *Handbook* (D 14), 51
240. Lang (A 10), 296f.; Alymer & Cant (H 1), 551
241. Lloyd, op. cit., II.246
242. Ibid., 247
243. Quoted by Stephenson (C 45), 144
244. Ibid., 131
245. Purcell (C 40), 40–8
246. Ibid., 51–3
247. Ibid., 31–4
248. Ibid., 107–11
249. Kellet (C 30)
250. From the forewords to (D 13 & 14)
251. Wavell (A 1), 230
252. Gore (A 5) 491–3
253. Temple (A 14), 396f.
254. Ibid., 322
255. Lang (A 10), 323
256. Garbett (A 4), 491
257. Ibid., 230 n.1
258. Ibid., 493
259. Ibid., 494
260. Fisher (A 3), 277
261. Woods (A 17), 35
262. (D 5)
263. (E 2)

4. The Meaning of Pilgrimage Today

1. Morinos (C 36), 253
2. Sumption (C 46), *passim*
3. Wilson (M 6), 6f.
4. Delehaye (M 4), *passim*
5. Tertullian (J 49), 2.4
6. Tertullian (J 50), 22
7. Augustine (J 1), XXII.10
8. Dickens (F 9), 17–20
9. Delehaye (M 3), 243
10. Cunningham (M 2), 24
11. Nunn (H 24), 37
12. Jerome (J 31), 39.6
13. Gregory (J 24), XI.13
14. See above, p. 106.
15. (J 45), 17f.
16. See above, pp. 109, 114
17. *Calvin's Commentaries* (N 2), 140
18. Haenchen (N 9), 562
19. Waugh (C 51), 21
20. Kirkegaard (N 11), 83
21. Proclus (J 46), I.9

22. Quick (N 13), 102
23. Jerome (J 31), 58.3
24. Davies (N 6), 46
25. Kamal (C 29), 44
26. See above, p. 99
27. Quick, op. cit., 2–6
28. Chrysostom (J 14), 82.4
29. Aquinas (J 6), 3.c.119
30. Rahner (N 15), 709f.
31. Morinos (C 36), 65
32. Amal (K(a) 3), 1
33. Birks (C 7)
34. Stanley (N 18), 31f.
35. V.1, 5f., 8–12
36. See above, pp. 13ff
37. Campenhausen (C 10), 231–51
38. Ladner (C 31), 233–59
39. See above, p. 127
40. Tinsley (N 19)

44. *Dictionary of Christian Spirituality* (H 10), 208f.
45. *Mishnah*, loc. cit.
46. Cullmann & Leenhardt (D 8), 40
47. See above, pp. 28ff., 71f., 125
48. Bonhoeffer (N 1), 80
49. Stanley (N 18), 36
50. Jungmann (D 18), 180
51. Cunningham (M 2), 20
52. Ibid., 75
53. John of Damascus (J 33), 4.15
54. Rahner (N 14), 100
55. *Common Catechism* (N 3), 632
56. Paulinus (J 41), ACW 40, 91
57. Stanley, op. cit., 104, 93
58. Cunningham, op. cit., 162, 173
59. Chrysostom (J 13)
60. Graham (K(a) 24), 85
61. Philo (J 43), I.70
62. Malcolm X (A 11), 269
63. Chateaubriand (K(a) 14), 269
64.* Those familiar with anthropo-

logical studies will have noted that I have not made use of the Turners' concept of liminality (C 47). I have not done so because I accept the validity of the criticism by Morinos (C 36), 255–61
65. Brown (M 1), cap. 5
66. See above, p. 165
67. Quoted by Clark (C 12), 5
68. Davies (D 11), 97–108
69. Coser (H 7), 172
70. Hurlcy (N 10), 104f.
71. Jerome (J 32)
72. Egeria (J 20), 5.8
73. Prothero & Bradley (A 13), I.456
74. Jerome (J 29), iii.22
75. Stanley (K(a) 49), xii
76. Cyril (J 16), iv.10
77. Jerome (J 31), 78.1
78. Josephus (J 34), 4.8.7; 17.9.3
79. Lewis (N 12), 94
80. Gardiner (C 19), 11

5. Devotions for Today's Pilgrims

1. See above, pp. 44ff., 49
2. Warren (D 24), 166–70
3. Opening verses from *Sarum Missal*
4. Confession, absolution and peace adapted from *ASB*
5. Psalm 25 is the first of three prescribed for use at Sarum
6. The proposed readings are for use if there is no celebration of the eucharist, i.e. the service is complete in itself, whereas in the Middle Ages it invariably culminated with the mass
7. Versicle, response and collects from Sarum
8. The blank is to be filled in with the name of the destination
9. This and the following prayers are adapted from Sarum
10. The dismissal is the author's composition drawing on the collect from the 'mass for travellers' (D 24), 173
11. Warren (D 24), 170–3
12. See above, p. 49
13. Allenby (A 1), 236
14. Eliade (H 31), 104
15. Frei (N 8), 163

16. Ibid., 16f.
17. Ibid., 56
18. Ramsey (N 16), 113
19. Witvliet (N 21), 26
20. Williams (A 16), 368
21. Quoted by Underhill ((D 21), 122
22. See above, p. 26
23. Pernoud (E 11), 42
24. Fabri (K(a) 20), I.291
25. Revised edn 1979
26. Brownrigg (D 5)
27. Huddlestone (D 16), xvii.
28. Witvliet (N 21), 9
29. See above, p. 131
30. Underhill (D 22), 271
31. Underhill (D 23), 46
32. Hudlestone, op. cit., 178
33. Egeria (J 20), 13.1
34. Possot & Philippe (K(a) 45), 173
35. Augustine in Ps. cxlviii
36. Pernoud (E 11), 41–67
37. See above, pp. 210f.
38. Theodore (J 15); trans. C.P. Roth, St Vladimir's Seminary, New York 1981, 27
39. de Castro (D 7), 455
40. Egeria (J 20), 31
41. Kermode (H 18), 24
42. Brownrigg (D 5), 115

43. Davies (N 7), 138–41
44. Fabri (K(a) 20), I.280
45. Giacomo (K(a) 23), 170
46. Davies, op. cit., 160f.
47. Brightman (D 4), 446
48. Brownrigg, op. cit., 105
49. Waterland (N 20), 261

50. Davies (N 4), 131ff.
51. Augustine (J 4), 57.7
52. Schmemann (N 17), 14
53. Ibid., 77
54. Davies, op. cit., 128f.
55. Davies (N 6), 175
56. Davies (N 4), 125f.

Bibliography

For ease of reference this bibliography has been divided into sections, but of course some books could have been included under more than one heading. Unless otherwise stated, the place of publication is London.

A. *Autobiography and Biography*

1. Allenby: A. Wavell, *Allenby. A Study in Greatness*, Harrap 1940
2. Browne: G. W. Kitchin, *Edward Harold Browne, D.D.*, Murray 1895
3. Fisher: W. Purcell, *Fisher of Lambeth. A Portrait from Life*, Hodder & Stoughton 1969
4. Garbett: Charles Smyth, *Cyril Foster Garbett. Archbishop of York*, Hodder & Stoughton 1959
5. Gore: G. L. Prestige, *The Life of Charles Gore*, Heinemann 1935
6. Gregory: F. H. Dudden, *Gregory the Great. His Place in History and Thought*, 2 vols, Longmans, Green 1915
7. Ignatius: *The Autobiography of St Ignatius* ed. J. F. X. O'Conor, Benziger Bros., New York 1980
8. Kilvert: *Kilvert's Diary* ed. W. Plommer, 3 vols, Cape 1971
9. Kinglake: B. M. Jowett, *Alexander W. Kinglake*, Twayne, Boston 1981
10. Lang: J. G. Lockhart, *Cosmo Gordon Lang*, Hodder & Stoughton 1949
11. Malcolm X: *The Autobiography of Malcolm X*, Hutchinson 1966
12. Pecock: V. -H. H. Green, *Bishop Reginald Pecock*, CUP 1943
13. Stanley: R. E. Prothero & G. G. Bradley, *The Life and Correspondence of Arthur Penrhyn Stanley D.D., Late Dean of Westminster*, 2 vols, Murray 1894
14. W. Temple: F. A. Iremonger, *William Temple*, OUP 1948
15. W. F. Temple: *Memoirs of Archbishop Temple by Several Friends*, ed. E. G. Sandford, 2 vols, Macmillan 1906
16. H. A. Williams: *'Some Day I'll Find you'*, Mitchell Beazley 1982
17. Robin Woods: *Robin Woods. An Autobiography*, SCM Press 1986

B. *Catholic Criticism and Defence*

1. J. Donovan, *Catechism of the Council of Trent*, Duffy, Dublin, n.d.

2. W. E. Campbell & A. W. Reed, *The English Works of Sir Thomas More*, II, Eyre & ,Spottiswoode 1931

3. Erasmus, *Pilgrimages to St Mary of Walsingham and St Thomas of Canterbury*, trans. J. G. Nichols, Bowyer Nichols 1849

4. – *Opus epistolarum Des. Erasmi Roterodami*, ed. P. S. Allen, H. M. Allen & H. W. Garrod, IX, Oxford

5. – *The Praise of Folly (1511)*, trans. J. Wilson (1668), ed. P. S. Allen, Clarendon, Oxford 1913

6. – *The Colloquies of Erasmus*, trans. C. R. Thompson, University of Chicago Press 1965

7. J. Waterworth, *The Canons and Decrees of the Sacred and Oecumenical Council of Trent*, Dolman 1848

C. *Critical Studies*

1. N. Arseniev, 'Russian Piety', *Lumen Vitae*, 1.3, 1946

2. G. Bardy, 'Pèlerinage à Rome vers la fin du ivè siècle', *Revue Béne'dictine*, 67, 1949, 224–35

3. E. R. Barker, *Rome of the Pilgrims and Martyrs*, Methuen 1913

4. E. S. Bates, *Touring in 1600*, Franklin, New York 1911

5. H. Belloc, *The Old Road*, Constable 1904

6. V. Berlière, 'Les pèlerinages judiciaires au moyen âge', *Revue Béne'dictine*, 7, 1890, 520–6

7. J. S. Birks, 'The Mecca Pilgrimage of the West African Nomads', *Journal of Modern African Studies*, 15.1, 1977, 47–58

8. T. Borenius, 'The Iconography of St Thomas of Canterbury', *Archaeologia*, LXXIX, 29–54

9. – *Mediaeval Pilgrims' Badges*, Ye Sette of Odd Volumes 90, 1930

10. H. von Campenhausen, *Tradition and Life in the Church*, Collins 1968

11. J. Cartwright, *The Pilgrims' Way from Winchester to Canterbury*, Virtue 1893

12. J. Clark, *Visiting the Holy Land Today*, Church Missionary Society, n.d.

13. M. L. Clarke, 'English Visitors to Rome in the Middle Ages', *History Today*, 28, 1978, 43–9

14. H. & M. -H. Davies, *Holy Days and Holidays. The Medieval Pilgrimage to Compostela*, Bucknell University, Lewisburg 1982

15. H. W. Davies, *Bernhard von Breydenbach and his Journey to the Holy Land, 1483–4. A Bibliography*, Leighton 1911

16. J. C. Dickinson, *The Shrine of our Lady of Walsingham*, CUP 1956

17. R. C. Finucane, *Miracles and Pilgrims*, Dent 1977

18. R. A. Fletcher, *St James's Catapult*, Clarendon, Oxford 1984

19. F. C. Gardiner, *The Pilgrimage of Desire. A Study of Theme and Genre in Medieval Literature*, Brill, Leiden 1971

20. D. R. Gross, 'Ritual and Conformity: A Religious Pilgrimage to Northeastern Brazil', *Ethnology*, X, 1971, 129–48

21. S. Heath, *Pilgrim Life in the Middle Ages*, Unwin 1911

22. D. R. Howard, *Writers and Pilgrims*, University of California Press,

Berkeley 1980

23. K. Hughes, 'The Changing Theory and Practice of Irish Pilgrimages', *Journal of Ecclesiastical History*, XI, 1960, 143–5

24. J. R. Hulbert, 'Some Medieval Advertisements of Rome', *Modern Philology*, 20, 1922/3, 403–24

25. E. D. Hunt, *Holy Land Pilgrimage in the Later Roman Empire*, AD 312–460, Clarendon, Oxford 1982

26. E. R. James, *Notes on the Pilgrims' Way in West Sussex*, Stanford 1871

27. G. Hartwell Jones, 'Celtic Britain and the Pilgrim Movement', *Y Cymmrodor*, 23, 1912

28. J. J. Jusserand, *English Wayfaring Life in the Middle Ages*, Unwin 1889

29. A. Kamal, *The Sacred Journey*, Allen & Unwin 1964

30. J. Kellet, *The Iona Pilgrimage*, Iona Community 1986

31. G. B. Ladner, '*Homo Viator*. Medieval Ideas on Alienation and Order', *Speculum*, 42, 1967, 233–59

32. S. Leclercq, 'Monachisme et pérégrinations du ixè au xiiè siècle', *Studia Monastica*, III, 1961, 35–52

33. F. P. Magoun, 'The Rome of Two Northern Pilgrims: Archbishop Sigeric of Canterbury and Abbot Nikolas of Munkarthvera', *Harvard Theological Review*, 33, 1940, 267–89

34. T. Merton, 'From Pilgrimage to Crusade', *Mystics and Zen Masters*, Dalton Books 1967, 91–112

35. W. J. More, *The Saxon Pilgrims to Rome and the Schola Saxonum*, Doctoral Thesis, Fribourg 1937

36. E. A. Morinos, *Pilgrimage in Hindu Tradition. A Case Study of West Bengal*, OUP, Delhi 1984

37. R. Oursel, *Les pèlerins du moyen âge*, Fayard, Paris 1963

38. G. B. Parks, *The English Traveler in Italy*, I, Stanford University Press 1954

39. P. Pascal, 'Pilgrimage in the Orthodox Church', *Lumen Vitae*, 13.2, 1958, 328–46

40. W. Purcell, *Pilgrims' England*, Longman 1981

41. A. T. Quiller-Couch, *The Pilgrims' Way. A Little Scrip of Good Counsel for Travellers*, Seeley 1906

42. P. Riant, *Expéditions et pèlerinages des Scandinaves en Terre Sainte au temps des croisades*, Laine et Harvard, Paris 1865

43. J. Richards, *The Great Folly, Superstition and Idolatry of Pilgrimage in Ireland, especially of that of St Patrick's Purgatory*, Dublin 1729

44. P. Sigal, *Les marcheurs de Dieu*, Armand Colin, Paris 1974

45. C. Stephenson, *Walsingham Way*, Darton, Longman & Todd 1970

46. J. Sumption, *Pilgrimage. An Image of Medieval Religion*, Faber & Faber 1975

47. W. Telfer, 'Constantine's Holy Land Plan', *Studia Patristica*, I.1, 1957, 696–700

48. V. & E. Turner, *Image and Pilgrimage in Christian Culture. Anthropological Perspectives*, Blackwell, Oxford 1978

49. C. Vogel, 'Le pèlerinage pénitentiel', *Revue des Sciences Religieuses*,

38.2, 1964, 113–53
50. F. D. Walker, *Irreverent Pilgrims*, University of Washington Press, Seattle 1974
51. E. Waugh, *The Holy Places*, Queen Anne Press 1952
52. C. K. Zacher, *Curiosity and Pilgrimage. The Literature of Discovery in Fourteenth Century England*, John Hopkins University, Baltimore & London 1976

D. *Devotional and Liturgical Material*

1. F. S. M. Bennett, *Handbook for Pilgrims*, Phillipson & Golder, Chester 1925
2. – *The Pilgrim's Way*, Phillipson & Golder, Chester 1925
3. A. Bernouilli, '*Ein Reisebüchlein für Jerusalemspilger*', *Zeitschrift für Kirchengeschichte*, 28, 1970, 79–86
4. F. E. Brightman, *The English Rite*, II, Rivingtons 1921
5. R. Brownrigg, *Come and See*, Darton, Longman & Todd 1968
6. J. A. Brundage, '*"Cruce Signari"*. The Rite of Taking the Cross in England', *Traditio*, XII, 1926, 289–310
7. M. de Castro, 'Dos itinerarios de Terra Sante de los siglos xiv y xv', *Hispania Sacra*, 10, 1957, 451–70
8. O. Cullman & F. J. Leenhardt, *Essays on the Lord's Supper*, Lutterworth Press 1958
9. G. L. Cuming & D. Baker (ed.), *Popular Belief and Practice*, Studies in Church History 8, CUP 1972
10. J. G. Davies, *Holy Week. A Short History*, Lutterworth Press 1963
11. – *New Perspectives on Worship Today*, SCM Press 1978
12. E. Delanielle, 'Le pèlerinage intérieur au xvè siècle', *La piété populaire au moyen âge*, Erasmo, Turin, 1975, 556–61
13. *Handbook of the Birmingham Canterbury Pilgrimage*, 21 June 1986
14. *Handbook of the Portsmouth Diocesan Pilgrimage to Canterbury*, 30 May 1984
15. W. G. Henderson, *Manuale et processionale ad usum insignis ecclesiae Eboracensis*, Surtees Society 63, 1875
16. R. Hudleston (ed.), *The Spiritual Letters of Dom John Chapman O.S.B.*, Sheed & Ward, 2nd edn 1938
17. Ignatius Loyola, *Spiritual Exercises*, trans. A. Mottola, Doubleday, New York 1964
18. J. A. Jungmann, *The Early Liturgy*, Darton, Longman & Todd 1960
19. Thomas à Kempis, *On the Imitation of Christ*
20. E.-R. Labande, *Spiritualité et vie littéraire de l'occident, Xè – XIVè siècles*, Variorum Reprints, 1974, (six articles marked A to F)
21. E. Underhill, *Mysticism*, Methuen, 14th edn 1942
22. – *Letters*, ed. C. Williams, Longmans, Green 1943
23. – *Practical Mysticism*, Dent, reprint 1931
24. F. E. Warren, *The Sarum Missal in English*, II, Moring, 1911

E. *Guide Books*

1. W. Brewyn, *A XVth Century Guide-Book to the Principal Churches of Rome. Compiled c. 1470 by William Brewyn*, trans. C. E. Woodruff, Marshall 1933
2. R. Brownrigg, *Come, See the Place. A Pilgrim Guide to the Holy Land*, Hodder & Stoughton 1985
3. *Compostela Guide* – Latin text by W. M. Whitehill, Santiago, 1944; French text by J. Vieillard, Protat, Macon, 2nd edn 1950
4. E. G. Duff (ed.), *Information for Pilgrims unto the Holy Land*, (1498), Lawrence and Bulle 1893
5. Fetellus, *Guide Book*, Palestine Pilgrims' Text Society, V, 1896
6. F. J. Furnivall (ed.), *The Stacyons of Rome*, Early English Text Society, OS 25, 1867
7. G. Golubovich, 'Peregrinationes Terrae Sanctae', *Archivum Franciscanum Historicum*, XI, 1918, 559–63
8. *Guide-Book to Palestine, c. 1350*, Palestine Pilgrims' Text Society, VI, 1894
9. Inter-Church Travel Ltd, *A Pilgrim's Handbook for the Holy Land*, 1959; revd. edn 1979
10. F. M. Nichols, *Mirabilia Urbis Romae. The Marvels of Rome or A Picture of the Golden City*, Ellis and Elvery 1894
11. R. Pernoud, *Un guide du pèlerin de Terre Sainte au XVè siècle*, Cahiers d'histoire et de bibliographie, I, Petit Mantan, Mantes, 1940

F. *History*

1. M. Aston, *Lollards and Reform*, Hambledon 1984
2. F. S. M. Bennett, *Chester Cathedral*, Phillipson & Golder, Chester 1925
3. – *The Nature of a Cathedral*, Phillipson & Golder, Chester 1925
4. J. F. Benton, *Self and Society in Medieval France. The Memoirs of Abbot Guibert de Nogent*, Harper & Row, New York, 1970
5. O. Chadwick, *The Victorian Church*, I, A. & C. Black 1966; II, A. & C. Black 1970; both vols reissued SCM Press 1987
6. G. Constable, *Religious Life and Thought (11th–12th Centuries)*, Variorum Reprints 1979
7. J. Crompton, *Lollard Doctrine with Special Reference to the Controversy over Image Worship and Pilgrimage*, B.Litt. Thesis, Oxford 1949
8. E. L. Cutts, *Scenes and Characters of the Middle Ages*, Virtue 1872
9. A. G. Dickens, *The English Reformation*, Arnold 1967
10. R. H. Fife, *The Revolt of Martin Luther*, Columbia University Press, New York 1957
11. J. Gairdner, *Lollardy and the Reformation in England*, II, Macmillan 1908
12. M. R. Gutsch, 'A Twelfth Century Preacher – Fulk of Neuilly', Paetow (ed.), F.18 below, 183–206
13. J. Huizinga, *The Waning of the Middle Ages*, Arnold 1924

14. E. Joranson, 'The Great German Pilgrimage of 1064–1065', Paetow (ed.) F.18 below, 3–43
15. R. Lloyd, *The Church of England in the Twentieth Century*, I, Longmans 1946; II, Longmans 1950: revised and expanded as *The Church of England 1900–1965*, SCM Press 1966
16. J. A. Muller, *Stephen Gardiner and the Tudor Reaction*, Macmillan, New York 1926
17. G. R. Owst, *Literature and Pulpit in Medieval England*, Blackwell, Oxford 1933
18. L. J. Paetow (ed.), *The Crusades and Other Historical Essays*, Crofts, New York 1928
19. M. Purcell, *Papal Crusading Policy*, Brill, Leiden 1975
20. J. J. Scarisbrick, *The Reformation and the English People*, Blackwell, Oxford 1964
21. M. Spinka, *John Huss. A Biography*, Princeton University Press 1968
22. A. H. Thompson, *The Cathedral Churches of England*, SPCK 1925
23. H. Thurston, *The Holy Year of Jubilee*, Newman, Westminster, Maryland 1949
24. H. B. Workman, *John Wyclif*, II Clarendon, Oxford, 1926

G. *Lollard and Reformation Documents*

1. *Advocates of Reform* ed. M. Spinka, LCC XV, SCM Press and Westminster Press 1953
2. *Calvin: Theological Treatises* ed. J. K. S. Reid, LCC XXII, SCM Press and Westminster Press 1954
3. E. Cardwell, *Documentary Annals of the Reformed Church of England*, I, Oxford 1839
4. G. H. Cooke (ed.), *Letters to Cromwell and Others on the Suppression of the Monasteries*, Baker 1965
5. Cranmer, *Miscellaneous Writings and Letters* ed. J. E. Cox, Parker Society 18, Cambridge 1846
6. Rogeri Dynmok, *Liber contra XII errores et hereses Lollardorum* ed. H. S. Cronin, Wyclif Society, Kegan Paul, Trench & Trubner [1922]
7. *Fasciculi zizanorium* ed. W. W. Shirley, Rolls Series 5, Longman, Brown & Green 1858
8. John Foxe, *Acts and Monuments* ed. S. R. Cattley, Seeley & Burnside, III, 1837
9. W. H. Frere & W. M. Kennedy, *Visitation Articles and Injunctions of the Period of the Reformation, II, 1536–58*, Alcuin Club 15, 1910
10. W. H. Frere, *Visitation Articles and Injunctions of the Period of the Reformation, III, 1559–1575*, Alcuin Club 16, 1910
11. Stephen Gardiner, *Letters* ed. J. A. Muller, CUP 1933
12. R. M. Haines, '"Wilde wittes and wilfulness": John Swetstock's attack on those "poyswun mongers", the Lollards', Cuming & Baker D 9 above, 143–54
13. F. M. Higman, *Jean Calvin. Three French Treatises*, Athlone 1970

14. *The King's Book or A Necessary Doctrine and Erudition for Any Christian Man, 1543* ed. E. A. Lacey, SPCK 1932
15. *The Lanterne of Light* ed. L. M. Swinburn, Early English Text Society, OS 151, 1917
16. Hugh Latimer, *Sermons*, I, Parker Society 22, 1844
17. C. Lloyd (ed.), *Formularies of the Faith Put Forth by Authority during the Reign of Henry VIII*, Clarendon, Oxford 1825
18. Martin Luther, *Works*: published in 54 volumes by Concordia, St Louis, and Fortress, Philadelphia, from 1958 on
19. R. Pecock, *The Repressor of Over Much Blaming of the Clergy (1449)* ed. C. Babington, Longmans, Green 1860
20. J. Stow, *The Chronicles of England from Brut unto the present year*, Newberie 1580
21. J. H. Todd (ed.), *An Apology for Lollard Doctrine*, Camden Society 20, 1844
22. John Wyclif, *Tractatus de Mandatis Divinis* ed. J. Loserth & F. D. Mathew, Wyclif Society 1922

H. *Miscellaneous*

1. G. E. Aylmer & R. Cant (ed.), *A History of York Minster*, Oxford 1977
2. E. W. Benson, *The Cathedral. Its Necessary Place in the Life and Work of the Church*, Murray 1878
3. Boccacio, *Decameron*
4. W. Caxton, *Dialogues in French and English (1486)* ed. H. Bradley, Early English Text Society, ES 79, 1900
5. *A Cook's Tour to the Holy Land in 1874. The Letters of William Henry Leighton*, James 1947
6. *Cook's Excursionist and Advertiser*, first issued in 1851
7. R. L. Coser, 'Some Social Functions of Laughter. A Study of Humour in a Hospital Setting', *Human Relations*, 12, 1959, 171–82
8. O. Cuntz, *Itineraria Romana*, Leipzig, 1929
9. *A Day at Lichfield*, Lomax, Lichfield, and Masters, London 1856
10. *A Dictionary of Christian Spirituality* ed. Gordon S. Wakefield, SCM Press 1983
11. *Dictionaire de spiritualité*, 7 Beauchesne, Paris 1971
12. W. Dugdale, *Monasticon Anglicanum* IV, March 1848
13. M. Eliade, *The Myth of Eternal Return*, Princeton University Press 1971
14. *Final Report of the Commission on Cathedrals*, 1885
15. E. M. Goulburn, *The Principles of the Cathedral System*, Rivingtons 1870
16. C. Hopkins, *The Discovery of Dura Europos*, Yale University Press, New Haven & London 1979
17. J. S. Howson (ed.), *Essays on Cathedrals*, 1872
18. F. Kermode, *The Genesis of Secrecy. On the Interpretation of Narrative*, Harvard University Press, Cambridge, Mass. 1979
19. A. W. Kinglake, *Eothen*, 4th edn, Ollivier 1845

20. J. D. Mansi, *Sacrorum Conciliorum Nova et Amplissima Collectio*, 14, reprint 1960
21. K. Nebenzahl, *Maps of the Bible Lands*, Times Books 1986
22. V. Noakes, *Edward Lear. The Life of a Wanderer*, Collins Fontana 1979
23. J. S. Northcote & W. R. Brownlow, *Roma Sotterranea*, Longmans, Green, Reader & Dyer 1869
24. H. V. P. Nunn, *Christian Inscriptions*, Savile, Eton 1951
25. Samuel Pepys, *Diary and Correspondence*, IV, Bohn, 6th edn 1858
26. J. Pudney, *The Thomas Cook Story*, Non-fiction Book Club 1954
27. D. W. Robertson, *A Preface to Chaucer*, Princeton University Press 1963
28. W. F. Rowe, *The Business of Travel. A Fifty Years' Record*, Cook 1891
29. E. Swinglehurst, *Cook's Tours. The Story of Popular Travel*, Blanford, Poole 1982
30. J. B. Ward-Perkins, *Medieval Catalogue of the London Museum*, 1940
31. K. Young, *Drama of the Medieval Church*, Oxford 1933/1962

I. *Palestine Research*

1. E. Bacon (ed.), *The Great Archaeologists*, Secker & Warburg 1976
2. Ben-Arieh, *The Rediscovery of the Holy Land in the Nineteenth Century*, Magnes, Jerusalem, 2nd edn 1983
3. R. A. S. MacAlister, *A Century of Excavation in Palestine*, Religious Tract Society 1925
4. W. Morrison, *The Recovery of Jerusalem. A Narrative of Exploration and Discovery in the City and the Holy Land*, Bentley 1871
5. Palestine Exploration Fund, *Our Work in Palestine*, Bentley 1871
6. E. Robinson, *Biblical Researches in Palestine*, Murray, 1st edn 1841; 3rd edn 1867
7. G. Williams, *The Holy City*, 2 vols, Parkes 1849

J. *Patristic and Mediaeval sources (apart from Pilgrims' Narratives)*

1. Augustine, *De Civitate Dei*
2. – *De Opere Monachorum*
3. – *Ennaratio in Psalmos XXXVIII*
4. – *Sermones*
5. Aquinas, *Contra Gentes*
6. – *Summa Theologica*
7. Bede, *Historia Ecclesiastica*
8. John Bromyard, *Summa Praedicanti Feriae*, Dominicus Nicolinus, Venice, I, 1586
9. Caesarius of Heisterbach, *The Dialogue on Miracles*, 2 vols, Routledge 1929
10. John Chrysostom, *De Sancto Babyla contra Julianum et Gentiles*
11. – *Homiliae de Statuis*
12. – *Homiliae in Epistolam ad Ephesios*
13. – *Homiliae in Epistolam ad Philemonem*

14. – *Homiliae in Matthaeum*
15. – *Panegyricus in S. Ignatium*
16. Cyril of Jerusalem, *Catecheses*
17. Dan Michel, *Dan Michel's Ayenbite of Inwyte* ed. R. Morris, Early English Text Society, OS 23, 1866
18. Dante, *Epistolae*
19. – *La Vita Nuova*
20. Egeria, *Itinerarium*
21. Eusebius, *Historia Ecclesiastica*
22. – *De Vita Constantini*
23. Gregory of Tours, *Historia Francorum*
24. Gregory the Great, *Epistolae*
25. – *Moralia*
26. Gregory of Nyssa, *Epistolae*
27. – *De Vita Mosis*
28. Honorius of Autun, *Elucidarium*
29. Jerome, *Apologia contra Rufinum*
30. – *Contra Vigilantium*
31. – *Epistolae*
32. – *Praefatio in Libro Paralipomenon*
33. John of Damascus, *De Fide orthodoxa*
34. Josephus, *The Antiquities of the Jews*
35. W. Langland, *Piers Plowman*
36. La-Tour Landry, *The Book of the Knight of La-Tour Landry* ed. T. Wright, Early English Text Society, OS 33, new edn 1906
37. Leo the Great, *Epistolae*
38. Origen, *Homiliae in Exodum*
39. – *Homiliae in Joannem*
40. – *Homiliae in Numeros*
41. Paulinus, *Carmina*
42. Petrarch, *Sonnets*
43. Philo, *De Specialibus Legis*
44. *The Pilgrims' Sea-Voyage and Sickness*, Early English Text Society, OS 25, 1867
45. *S.Polycarpi Passio*
46. Proclus, *Orationes*
47. Prudentius, *Carmina*
48. Sulpicius Severus, *Dialogi*, III
49. Tertullian, *Ad Uxorem*
50. – *De Pudicitia*
51. Theodore the Studite, *On the Holy Icons*

K. *Pilgrims' Narratives*

(a) *Designated by the name of the pilgrim*

1. Adomnan, *On the Holy Places*, Wilkinson K(b) 6 below
2. Abbot Daniel, *The Pilgrimage of the Russian Abbot Daniel in the Holy*

Land 1106–1107 AD, PPTS, IV, 1895

3. Amal: *The Pilgrimage of Amal*, trans. H. T. Norris, Atis & Phillips, Warminster
4. Anonymous: H. Omont, '*Journal d'un pèlerin français en Terre Sainte (1383)*, *Revue de l'Orient Latin*, III, 1895, 457–9
5. Bernard of Ascoli, *Descriptio Terrae Sanctae*, Sandoli K(b) 3 below
6. Bordeaux Pilgrim, *Itinerarium Burdigalense*, Wilkinson K(b) 6 below
7. W. G. Browne, *Travels in Africa, Egypt, and Syria, for the Years 1792 to 1798*, Cadell 1799
8. Burchard of Mount Sion, *The Holy Places*, PPTS, XII, 1896
9. J. L. Burckhardt, *Travels in Syria and the Holy Land*, Murray 1822
10. I. Burton, *The Inner Life of Syria, Palestine, and the Holy Land*, King, 2 vols, 2nd edn 1876
11. J. Capgrave, *Ye Solace of Pilgrims (c. 1450)* ed. C. A. Mills, OUP 1911
12. Gabriele Capodilista, *Itinerario in Terra Santa (1458)*, Vydenast, Perugia 1475
13. Pietro Casola, *Canon Pietro Casola's Pilgrimage to Jerusalem in the Year 1494* ed. M. M. Newett, Manchester University Press 1907
14. F. -R. de Chateaubriand, *Itinéraire de Paris à Jérusalem*, Furne et Jouvet, Paris 1827
15. *The City of Jerusalem, 1220 AD*, PPTS, VI, 1896
16. T. Coryate, *Traveller for the English Writers: Greeting*, Iaggard & Featherstone 1616
17. R. Curzon, *Visits to Monasteries in the Levant (1849)*, Century 1983
18. H. Dixon, *The Holy Land*, 2 vols, Chapman & Hall 1865
19. Egeria: J 20 above
20. Fabri: *The Wanderings of Felix Fabri*, PPTS, VII–X; AMS reprint, 2 vols, New York 1971
21. J. W. de Forest, *Oriental Acquaintances or Letters from Syria*, Dix & Edwards, New York 1856
22. Frescobaldi, Gucci & Sigoli, *Visits to the Holy Places of Egypt, Sinai, Palestine and Syria in 1384* trans. T. Bellorini & E. Hoade. Preface and Notes by B. Bagatti, *Studium Biblicum Franciscanum* 6, Franciscan Press, Jerusalem 1948
23. Giacomo de Verona, *Peregrinationes et Indulgentie Terre Sancte*; R. Röhricht, 'Le pèlerinage du moine augustin Jacques de Verone', *Revue de l'Orient Latin*, III, 1895, 155–302
24. Stephen Graham, *With the Russian Pilgrims to Jerusalem*, Macmillan 1913
25. Sir Richard Guylforde, *Pylgrymage to the Holy Land, AD 1506* ed. H. Ellis, Camden Society, Series 1, 151, 1851
26. A. von Harff: M. Letts, *The Pilgrimage of Arnold von Harff*, Hakluyt Society 1946
27. Jerome K. Jerome, *Diary of a Pilgrimage [1891]*, Dent, reprint 1955
28. John of Canterbury, *Epistolae Cantuarienses*
29. John of Würzburg, *Description of the Holy Land, AD 1169–1170*, PPTS, V, 1890

30. Margery Kempe, *The Book of Margery Kempe*, OUP 1954
31. L. de Laborde, *Journey through Arabia Petraea to Mount Sion and the Excavated City of Petra (Paris 1830)*, Murray 1836
32. A. de Lamartine, *A Pilgrimage to the Holy Land (Paris 1835)*, Facsimiles and Reprints, Delmar, New York 1928
33. Sir Gilbert de Lannoy, 'A Survey of Egypt and Syria undertaken in the year 1422', Text and trans J. Webb, *Archaeologia*, XXII, 1827, 281–444
34. William Lithgow, *The Totall Discourse of the Rare Adventures and Paineful Peregrinations (1632)*, MacLehose, Glasgow 1906
35. Ludolph von Suchem, *Description of the Holy Land, and of the Way Thither*, PPTS, XII, 1895
36. H. Martineau, *Eastern Life, Present and Past*, Lea & Blanchard, Philadelphia 1848
37. Nicolas di Martoni: L. Legrand, 'Relations du pèlerinage à Jérusalem de Nicolas di Martoni, notaire Italien (1394–95)', *Revue de l'Orient Latin*, III, 1895, 566–669
38. Francis Mortoft: *His Book, being his Travels through France and Italy, 1658–1659* ed. M. Letts, Hakluyut Society, 2nd Series, LVII, 1925
39. Fynes Moryson, *An Itinerary (1617)*, 3 vols, MacLehose, Glasgow 1907
40. A Munday, *The English Roman Life (1582)* ed. P. J. Ayres, Clarendon, Oxford 1980
41. Niccolò of Poggibonsi, *A Voyage beyond the Seas (1346–50)*, trans T. Bellorini & E. Hoade, *Studium Biblicum Franciscanum* 2, Franciscan Press, Jerusalem 1945
42. L. Owen, *The Running Register: Recording a True Relation of the State of the English Colleges, Seminaries and Cloisters in all Forraine Parts (Milbourne 1624)*, Facsimile Da Capo, New York, & Theatrum Orbis Terrarum, Amsterdam 1968
43. Phocas the Cretan, *The Pilgrimage of Joannes Phocas in the Holy Land, 1185*, PPTS, V, 1896
44. Piacenza Pilgrim, *Travels*, Wilkinson K(b) 6 below
45. Possot and Philippe: *Le voyage de la terre sainte composé par Maître Denis Possot et achevé par Messire Charles Philippe (1532)* ed. C. Schefer, Slatkin Reprints, Geneva 1971
46. J. Sanderson: *The Travels of John Sanderson in the Levant 1584–1602* ed. W. Foster, Hakluyt Society, LXVII, 1931
47. G. Sandys, *A Relation of a Journey Begun An: Dom. 1610*, 3rd edn, Allet 1632
48. R. de Sanseverino, *Viaggio in Terra Sante (1408)*, Manuffi, Bologna 1888
49. A. P. Stanley, *Sinai and Palestine*, Murray 1910
50. Pero Tafur, *Travels and Adventures 1435–1439*, trans M. Letts, Routledge 1926
51. E. Terry, *A Voyage to East-India (1655)*, Wilkie, Carter & Easton 1777
52. Theoderich: *Theoderich's Description of the Holy Places, c. 1172 AD*, PPTS, V, 1891
53. de Thévenot: *The Travels of Monsieur de Thévenot to the Levant*, Faitborne, Adamson, Skegnes & Newborough 1687

54. R. Torkington, *Ye Oldest Diarie of Englysshe Travell* ed. W. J. Loftie, Field & Tuer 1884
55. *Two Journeys to Jerusalem*, Nath. Crouch 1695
56. M. C. -F. Volney, *Travels through Syria and Egypt in the Years 1783, 1784 and 1785*, 2nd edn, Robinson 1788
57. William Wey, *The Itineraries of William Wey*, Roxburghe Club, Nichols 1857
58. Willibald: *The Hodoeporicon of St Willibald*, PPTS, III, 1895

(b) *Designated by the name(s) of the editor(s)*

1. H. Michelant & G. Reynaud, *Itinéraires à Jerusalem*, Fick, Geneva 1882
2. Palestine Pilgrims' Text Society, 12 vols, 1897: individual volumes and parts within each volume have different years
3. S. Purchas, *Hakluytus Posthumus or Purchas His Pilgrimes*, 10 vols, MacLehose, Glasgow 1905
4. S. de Sandoli, *Itinera Hierosolymitana Crucesignatorum*, II, Franciscan Press, Jerusalem 1980
5. J. Wilkinson, *Egeria's Travels*, SPCK 1971
6. – *Jerusalem Pilgrims before the Crusades*, Aris & Phillips, Warminster 1977
7. T. Wright, *Early Travels in Palestine*, Bohn 1848

L. *Relics*

1. P. Boussel, *Des reliques et de leur bon usage*, Ballard, Paris 1971
2. J. Calvin, *Traité des reliques 1523*; Higman G 13 above
3. P. J. Geary, *Furta Sacra. The Theft of Relics in the Central Middle Ages*, Princeton University Press 1978
4. A. Grabar, *Les ampoules de la Terre Sainte. Monza, Bobbio*, Paris 1958
5. C. Morris, 'A Criticism of Popular Religion: Guibert of Nogent on *The Relics of the Saints*', in Cuming & Baker, D 9 above

M. *Saints*

1. P. Brown, *The Cult of the Saints*, SCM Press 1981
2. L. Cunningham, *The Meaning of Saints*, Harper & Row, San Francisco 1980
3. H. Delehaye, *Sanctus. Essai sur le culte des saints dans l'antiquité*, Bollandistes, Brussels 1927
4. – *Les origines du culte des martyrs*, Bollandistes, Brussels, 2nd edn 1933
5. R. A. Svobada, *The Illustrations of the Life of St Omer*, University of Minnesota, Ph.D. Thesis 1983
6. S. Wilson (ed.), *Saints and their Cults*, CUP 1983

N. Theology

1. D. Bonhoeffer, *Ethics*, SCM Press 1955
2. *Calvin's Commentaries. The Acts of the Apostles*, trans. W. J. G. MacDonald & J. W. Fraser, Oliver & Boyd, Edinburgh 1965
3. *The Common Catechism*, Search Press, London & Seabury Press, New York 1975
4. J. G. Davies, *The Spirit, the Church and the Sacraments*, Faith Press 1954
5. – *The Secular Use of Church Buildings*, SCM Press 1968
6. – *Every Day God. Encountering the Holy in World and Worship*, SCM Press 1973
7. – *Liturgical Dance. An Historical, Theological and Practical Handbook*, SCM Press 1984
8. H. W. Frei, *The Eclipse of Biblical Narrative. A Study in Eighteenth and Nineteenth Century Hermeneutics*, Yale University Press, New Haven & London 1974
9. E. Haenchen, *The Acts of the Apostles. A Commentary*, Blackwell, Oxford 1971
10. N. Hurley, *The Real Revolution*, Orbis Books, Maryknoll 1978
11. S. Kirkegaard, *Journals* ed. A. Dru, OUP 1938
12. C. S. Lewis, *Reflections on the Psalms*, Bles 1958
13. O. C. Quick, *The Christian Sacraments*, Nisbet, reprint 1941
14. K. Rahner, *Theological Investigations*, III, Darton, Longman & Todd 1967
15. – ed., *Encyclopedia of Theology*, Burns & Oates 1975
16. I. T. Ramsey, *Religious Language*, SCM Press 1957
17. A. Schmemann, *For the Life of the World*, National Student Christian Federation, New York, 1963
18. A. P. Stanley, *Sermons Preached Before His Royal Highness the Prince of Wales, During His Tour in the East in the Spring of 1862*, Murray 1863
19. E. J. Tinsley, *The Imitation of God in Christ*, SCM Press 1960
20. D. Waterland, *The Doctrine of the Eucharist*, Clarendon, Oxford 1868
21. T. Witvliet, *The Way of the Black Messiah*, SCM Press 1987

Index

Aaron, 43
Abellas, 58
Abgar, 109
Abraham, 13, 45, 50, 75, 90, 188f., 207, 209
Absolution, 15, 17, 38, 51, 215
Adam, 85, 97
Adomnan, 56f.
Adriatic, 47
Agincourt, 222
Aidan, St, 159
Albert, Prince, 145
Albert Victor, Prince, 149
Aleppo, 121, 127f.
Alexandria, 41, 47, 55, 137, 202
Alexandrovitch, Grand Duke, 138
Allenby, General, 161, 222
Allerton, R., 87
Alms, 57f., 66, 81, 90f.
Alphabets, 40f.
Alps, 33, 47, 117
Altar, 37, 44, 51f., 69, 72, 79, 106, 117f., 120, 169, 226, 238
Ambrose, St, 174, 230
Ambrosia, 32
America, 145
Amiens, 75, 102
Amsterdam, 165
Anchorite, 14
Ancona, 78
Angeby, 51
Angers, 36
Anne, Empress, 136
Anne, Queen, 129
Anne, St, 6
Annunciation, 1, 75
Antakya, 195
Anthony, St, 51, 101
Antioch, 6, 195
Antiphon(s), 11, 27, 70, 73, 232
Apostle(s), 4, 7, 43, 82, 97, 101, 131, 195, 210

Arabia, 9
Arabs, 48
Aravatus, 7
Archaeology, 145f.
Arculf, 56f.
Armenian Christians, 123, 137, 140, 234
Arundel, T., 92
Asaph, St, 91, 104
Ascension, 10, 61, 67, 122, 141, 191, 230, 238
Ascetic(ism), 5, 14, 16f., 86, 149, 170
Asia Minor, 48
Assisi, 90, 228
Assyria, 145
Athanasius, St, 228
Athens, 197
Augustine of Canterbury, St, 159
Augustine of Hippo, St, 4, 85, 169ff., 174, 229, 232, 235
Austria, 165
Autun, 101
Avalon, 101
Avignon, 20

Babylas, St, 3
Babylon, 209
Bamberg, 22
Bangor, 107
Baptism, 6, 11, 31, 56, 90, 99, 124, 151, 190, 204, 206f., 216, 219, 226, 234–8
Bari, 47, 137
Barlow, Bishop, 104
Basil, St, 171
Basilissa, 32
Bassett, Sir W., 104
Bathsheba, 224
Bavaria, 33
Beads, 117ff., 124
Bede, St, 7, 62
Bedford, F., 14

Belgium, 41, 164
Bell(s), 61, 77, 79, 93, 162
Bell, G. K. A., 158
Belloc, H., 155
Bellulca, 129
Belzoni, G. B., 140
Benares, 1
Bencham, Bishop, 106
Benediction, 2, 53, 84, 129
Bennett, F. S. M., 156ff., 167
Benson, E. W., 154
Bentwick, N., 164
Bernard of Ascoli, 20
Bernard of Clairvaux, 16, 85
Bertrand de la Brocquière, 77
Bethany, 64, 161
Bethesda, 81
Bethlehem, 10, 20f., 26f., 32, 45, 55ff., 60,
    62ff., 66, 72, 103, 122, 128, 163, 178,
    185f., 207, 229f.
Bethphage, 67
Beyrouth, 148
Bible, 9, 11, 28ff., 71, 90f., 111, 128, 134,
    142, 144, 146, 148f., 162, 206–14, 221–
    8, 232, 235, 238
Bidding the Bedes, 49, 220
Biddulph, W., 126, 137
Bilney, T., 102, 109
Birmingham, 159f., 227
Bishop, E., 164
Blesilla, 172
Blessing(s), 2, 5f., 44f., 52, 61f., 73, 79, 97,
    138f., 172
Bletchingley, 166
Boccacio, 1, 3
Bohemia, 89
Bologna, 4
Bom Jesus da Lapa, 136
Bonhoeffer, D., 192
Boniface VIII, 8, 16, 22, 39
Bordeaux Pilgrim, 19f.
Boulogne, 59, 75
Boxley, 104
Brazil, 136
Brewyn, W., 15, 22
Breydenbach, B. von, 23, 25, 35, 40f.
Brigitte, St, 89
Brisbane, 227
Bristol, 103, 156, 165
Brittany, 6
Bromholm, 32
Bromyard, J., 82
Browne, E. H., 153
Browne, W. G., 140
Brownrigg, R., 164ff., 226, 232, 234

Buddhists, 1
Bulgaria, 48
Bulkeley, Bishop, 107
Bunel, J., 121f., 124, 126, 132
Bunyan, J., 108
Burchard of Mount Sion, 23, 36, 38, 60,
    63f.
Burckhardt, J. L., 137
Burgos, 88
Burton, I., 134f., 149
Burton-upon-Trent, 104
Bury St Edmunds, 103
Butt of Lewis, 159
Buxton, 104

Caen, 59
Caesarea, 10, 23, 48, 232
Caesarius of Heisterbach, 3f.
Cairo, 26, 41, 48, 50, 55, 137
Calais, 33
Calixtus II, 36
Calvary, 8, 70f., 134, 185
Calvin, 84, 100f., 109, 175
Cambrai, 23
Cambridge, 102
Cana, 56, 73f., 191, 232
Canaan, 148
Candles, 52, 68, 70, 74, 95, 106, 110, 120,
    122, 140
Canterbury, 7, 20, 46f., 75, 77ff., 93, 97,
    103, 152, 155, 157ff., 161, 191, 202, 228
Canticles, 55, 57, 66, 221, 230
Capernaum, 192
Capgrave, J., 22f., 67
Capodilista, G., 23
Cartwright, J., 155
Cashel, 153
Casola, P., 5, 54, 61, 72
Catacombs, 7
Cathedral(s), 152–60
Catherine, Empress, 136
Catherine, St, 6, 22, 49, 61, 69, 89, 91
Cavalier Santo Brasca, 42, 86
Caxton, W., 41
Cevennes, 203
Chadwick, O., 153
Châlons, 82
Chamber, G., 104
Chambéry, 52
Champarnoy, C. P. de, 229
Chaplin, C., 205f.
Chapman, J., 227
Chateaubriand, 133, 203
Chaucer, 32, 46, 82
Chester, 156, 167

Chichester, 97, 158
Choir Festival, 154
Christmas, 147, 160, 185, 228
Church, 112, 184, 203, 215, 228
Churchill, W., 201
Cipolla, 1ff.
Clare, St, 66
Claremont, 17
Clement VII, 129f.
Cockles, *see* Shells
Colet, J., 102, 108
Collect(s), 26ff., 70, 220
Cologne, 7, 42, 136
Colosseum, 199
Columbia, St, 159
Colyn, W., 92
Commissioning, 215–21
Compostela, 2, 4, 6ff., 22, 31f., 47, 49, 51,
    55, 58, 65f., 72, 75, 77, 79, 89, 96f., 99,
    115, 132, 178, 201
Confession, 15, 82, 84
Conques, 58
Constantine, 10, 21, 232
Constantinople, 7, 11, 17f., 48, 178
Contact-relics, 5, 61f., 134, 174
Cook, T., 147–152, 166
Cook's Excursionist, 147f.
Coptic Christians, 135, 137
Corbigny, 58
Cordoba, 6
Corinth, 197, 199
Corpus Christi, 47, 52, 121
Corunna, 47
Coryate, T., 127, 137
Counter Reformation, 113, 132
Coventry, 106
Cranmer, T., 106f., 173
Cromwell, T., 102–105
Cross(es), 7, 14, 16f., 23, 28, 32, 39, 45f.,
    51f., 56, 60, 62ff., 70f., 74, 81, 86, 94,
    124, 134, 138, 140, 162, 178, 185, 191,
    207, 215f., 219, 225, 231, 233
Crowland, 159
Crucifixion, 11, 52, 81, 86, 101, 117
Crusade(s), 13, 16ff., 33, 38, 48, 164,
    168
Cunningham, L., 194, 199
Curiositas, 85f.
Curzon, R., 137, 142
Cuthbert, St, 159
Cyril of Jerusalem, St, 11, 68, 206, 227

Damascus, 41, 137
Damasus, 7, 60
Dance, 232

Dangers, 46–49, 138
Daniel, Abbot, 10, 38, 74, 139
Dante, 8, 29f., 75
Darwin, C., 142
David, 43, 221
Demetrius, 195
Desert, *see* Wilderness
Devereux, J., 91
Devotion(s), 8, 10, 17, 19ff., 26–9, 50,
    55–77, 89, 91, 96, 101, 105, 111, 120,
    122ff., 126f., 135, 138, 141, 157, 161,
    170f., 173, 182, 184, 203, 214–240
Diaries, 19
Dickens, C., 223
Dioceses, 152–60
Diognetus, 187
Discipleship, 13, 31, 86, 100, 188
Discipline, 14, 188
Disraeli, B., 146
Dixon, W. H., 141f.
Donegal, 129
Dover, 33, 103, 118
Drama, 87, 139, 214, 232f.
Dulia, 5, 90, 110, 173, 201
Dura-Europos, 19
Durham, 30, 159
Dynmok, R., 91, 111

Easter, 13, 66, 71f., 87, 126, 137f., 162, 223
Eckhart, 225
Ecumenism, 164
Edmund, St, 103
Edward the Confessor, St, 75
Edward VI, 101, 112
Edward VII, 145, 186, 188, 192
Edwards, L., 165
Egeria, 11, 56, 60, 68, 73, 147, 206, 229,
    232
Egypt, 21, 29, 37. 148, 180, 190, 208f., 237
Elijah, 122, 136
Elisha, 151
Elizabeth, Empress, 136
Elizabeth, Queen, 117
Elizabeth, St, 66, 230
Elkanah, 176
Ely, 153
Emmaus, 13, 87f., 126, 201, 208
England, 3, 33, 41, 130
Ephesus, 195f., 199
Erasmus, 6, 93–6, 99f., 105, 108, 111, 157
Esther, 209
Etheldreda, St, 153
Eucharist, *see* Mass
Eugenius III, 16
Eugenius IV, 16

Eulogius, 7
Eusebius, 10, 23, 109
Eustathia, 12
Eutropius, St, 37
Evelyn, J., 118, 131
Example(s), 65, 92f., 101, 189, 193
Ex-votos, _see_ Votive Offerings
Exegesis, 28ff., 71, 87
Exeter, 154
Exodus, 25, 29–32, 43, 177, 188, 190f., 208ff., 235, 238f.

Fabri, F., 3, 9f., 13, 26, 39, 41f., 48, 51f., 54, 56, 59–65, 68f., 73, 132, 134, 226, 233
Fafnir, 21
Fatima, 135f.
Felix, St, 4, 58
Fetellus, 31
Fetters, 7, 58
Filocalus, F., 7
Finucane, R. C., 84
Fisher, G., 162f., 166
Fisk, P., 144
Fison, J., 164
Fitzralph of Armagh, 85
Flasks, 62, 75, 77
Forgiveness, 9f., 15, 99, 183
Fortunatus, V., 230
Foy, St, 58
France, 17, 26, 33, 145
Francis, St, 69, 206, 228
Frankfurt, 128
Franzini, G., 36
Frederick of Heilo, 81
Frescobaldi, 26, 29, 48, 57, 68f.
Frith, F., 146
Fulk de Neuilly, 2

Gadara, 59
Galerius, 199
Galicia, 206
Galilee, 152, 204
Gallio, 197
Ganges, 182, 204
Garbett, G. F., 156, 162
Gardiner, F. C., 211
Gardiner, S., 112f.
Gargano, 8
Gatharen, D., 104
Gaul, 7
Gaza, 64
Genantius, 172
Genoa, 6
George, St, 60, 157

George V, 149
Germany, 26, 129, 145, 160, 164f.
Gesture(s), 56, 64, 110, 231, 233f.
Gethsemane, 11, 60, 64, 72f., 128, 161f., 231
Giacomo de Verona, 23f., 39, 46, 233
Gifford, Sir J., 102
Gloucester, 106
Golgotha, _see_ Holy Sepulchre
Goliath, 43, 57
Good Friday, 132, 134
Gore, C., 161
Gospel(s), 9, 26, 46, 71, 94
Gotha, 145
Gouda, W. de, 27
Graham, S., 138, 202
Gravesend, 108
Greece, 199
Greek Orthodox Christians, 137f., 140
Gregory I, 7, 26, 29, 173
Gregory IX, 17
Gregory XIII, 129, 131
Gregory of Nyssa, St, 30ff.
Gregory of Tours, 97
Grove, G., 147
Growth, Spiritual, 184
Groves, Sir C., 145
Gucci, G., 41, 57, 67, 69
Guibert de Nogent, 3, 83
Guide Books, 15, 19, 21, 26, 31, 33–8, 51, 157, 222, 225f.
Gunther of Bamberg, 48
Guthlac, St, 159
Guylforde, Sir R., 39, 47, 69, 71, 78, 95

Hadley, J., 102
Hadrian, 9
Hajj, 203
Hamadan, 209
Haraeus, F., 25
Haran, 189
Harff, A. von, 3f., 7, 10, 34, 39, 41, 49, 51, 60f., 66f., 75, 84, 89
Hawkes, F. O. T., 162
Hayles, 103f.
Healing (Health), 6, 59f., 85, 92, 126, 159
Heath, S., 151
Hebrides, 159
Helena, St, 70
Henry II, 77, 191
Henry IV, 10
Henry V, 38
Henry VI, 48
Henry VII, 6

Henry VIII, 102ff.
Henson, H., 159
Herod, 229
Hilton, W., 85
History, 9, 13, 28–31, 87, 122, 124, 142, 145, 148, 190f., 206, 222ff.
Hindus, 1, 182, 204
Hippo, 33
Holland, 165
Holy, *passim*
Holy Land, *see* Palestine
Holy Sepulchre, 10f., 18, 22, 26f., 32f., 46, 55ff., 65f., 68ff., 72, 74, 91, 94, 121–5, 127, 131f., 134, 137, 140–52, 161f., 185, 207, 228, 237
Holy Week, 11, 118, 161f., 237
Honorius of Autun, 83, 85
Honorius III, 90
Hooper, Bishop, 106f.
Hope, 28, 31, 188, 195
Howard, A., 149
Howson, J. S., 153
Huizinga, J., 107
Hunt, Holman, 146
Humour, 205f.
Hungary, 48
Hurley, N., 205
Huss, J., 89
Huysmans, J. K., 135
Hyde, 103
Hymn(s), 11, 26f., 53f., 56, 66, 70, 98, 158, 210, 225f., 229f.
Hyperdulia, 110f.

Identity, 202–6
Ignatius of Antioch, St, 6, 228
Ignatius Loyola, 130ff., 227
Image(s), 83, 85, 89–93, 98, 101, 105, 108, 110–15, 171, 173, 184
Imitation, 2, 13, 31, 84, 93, 189–202, 208, 237
Incubation, 59
India, 84, 127
Indulgences, 13–16, 19, 21ff., 39, 41, 58, 64f., 67, 89, 96–9, 112, 119, 124, 127, 130f., 167f., 175, 180, 182
Ingworth, Bishop, 103
Inter-Church Travel, 161, 163, 165f., 204, 226, 231
Intercession, 5, 13, 49, 74, 98, 100, 107, 139, 172, 220, 229
Interiorization, *see* Internalization
Internalization, 32, 86f., 90f., 93, 96, 100, 123, 167f., 175, 180ff., 193

Iona, 159
Ipswich, 109f.
Iran, 209
Ireland, 6, 14f.
Italy, 117, 120, 141, 160, 199
Itineraries, 19ff., 26, 72f., 133, 166
Izmir, 228

Jackson, J., 119
Jacob, 14, 56, 68, 123
Jaffa, 33f., 47, 55, 137, 148
James, E. R., 155
James, St, 6, 8, 22, 36f., 49, 66, 94f., 97, 201, 227
Japan, 1
Jeddah, 149
Jericho, 65, 72, 75, 137, 148, 151, 232
Jerome, J. K., 151f.
Jerome, St, 5, 9, 23, 62, 64, 80f., 83, 89, 122, 172, 178, 206f., 232
Jerusalem, 1, 9ff., 13, 18–23, 25f., 29, 33, 38, 39, 41f., 44f., 49, 55, 57, 62, 64, 66–9, 71, 75, 80f., 86, 91, 94f., 99, 109, 121–4, 126f., 131, 137–52, 161–5, 176f., 178, 185f., 188, 202, 204, 207f., 210, 215, 232f.
Jews, 1, 204
Job, 8, 26, 226, 229
John XV, 20
John, St, 6, 199, 227, 232
John of Canterbury, 47
John Chrysostom, St, 3, 6ff., 13, 171, 174, 181, 201
John the Baptist, St, 51, 54, 56, 75, 230
John of Damascus, 194
John of Jerusalem, 206
John of Würzburg, 67, 72f.
Jonah, 78
Joppa, *see* Jaffa
Jordan, 26, 56f., 61, 66, 78, 124, 133f., 137, 139, 142, 151, 191, 232f.
Joseph of Arimathea, 139
Joshua, 222
Journey, 13f., 17, 46–55, 138, 176ff., 181ff., 189, 208f., 211, 213f., 235
Jowett, W., 144
Joy, 6, 14, 62, 64f., 69, 126, 131, 142, 205, 209f., 238
Jubilee(s), 8, 16, 129ff., 135
Judaea, 9, 208
Judas, 11, 90, 195
Julian of Norwich, 159
Jusserand, J. J., 155
Justification, 96, 99, 183f.

Juvenal of Jerusalem, 9

Ka'bah, 179
Kaiser Wilhelm, 149, 161
Kamal, A., 179, 183
Kempe, M., 42
Kierkegaard, S., 176
Kiev, 136
Kilvert, Parson, 152, 155
Kinglake, A., 140
Kingston, 162
Kishon, Brook, 129
Kiss, 8f., 51f., 55f., 63, 65, 67, 77, 107, 110, 114, 119f., 124, 127, 131, 139

La-Tour Landry, 81
Laborde, L. de, 133
Lake Ladoga, 136
Lamartine, A. de, 133
Lambeth, 32
Lang, C. G., 158, 161
Lannoy, Sir G. de, 37
Laodicea, 199
Laon, 3, 7
La Rochelle, 59
Latimer, H., 103, 107f.
Latria, 5, 90, 110f., 173
Lawrence, St, 103, 173
Layton, R., 103
Lazarus, 101, 230
Lear, E., 137, 146
Leighton, W. H., 151
Leo the Great, 9, 89
Leonard, St, 58
Lewis, C. S., 181, 210
Lichfield, 106, 154
Light(s), 21, 58, 104
Limoges, 58
Lincoln Memorial, 201
Lindisfarne, 159
Litanies, 50, 54, 57, 70, 74, 98
Lithgow, W., 115, 118, 120–4, 135, 137
Llandyfodwg, 44
Lloyd, R., 154, 156
Lollard(s), 83, 89ff.
London, 87, 91, 102, 104, 129, 132, 140, 155
London, J., 104
Loreto, 78, 135
Lot's wife, 61
Lough Dergh, 129
Louis XIII, 132
Lourdes, 135f.

Lübeck, 36
Luchino del Campo, 62
Ludolph von Suchem, 41, 66, 71
Luke, St, 8
Luther, 36, 67, 82, 96–100, 105f., 108, 130f., 180, 183, 191
Lyons, 36

Maastricht, 84
MacLeod, G., 159
Madden, T., 231
Maiden Bradley, 103
Maidstone, 104
Mainz, 23
Malchus, 103
Malcolm X, 203
Malplaquet, 222
Manchester, 161
Manresa, 130
Maps, 19
Mark, St, 230
Marseilles, 47, 101
Martin, St, 8, 97, 173, 228, 237
Martineau, H., 141ff.
Martyr(s), 3ff., 7f., 9, 51, 75, 83, 96, 169f., 174f., 180, 204
Mary Magdalene, St, 27, 70, 72
Mary, Queen, 112
Mary, The Virgin, 1, 3, 8, 20f., 52, 54, 60, 62, 64, 66, 68, 71, 73, 75, 78, 81, 84, 90, 92f., 95, 97f., 110, 118, 120, 135, 170f., 201, 230
Mass, 44, 51, 58, 62, 69, 71f., 99, 123, 134, 190, 193, 214, 219, 234–8
—, Dry, 53f.
Matthias, St, 67, 195
Maundeville, Sir J., 38, 49, 55, 88
Maundrell, H., 127
Maundy Thursday, 162, 231
Mauretania, 183
Maurice of Sully, 82
Measures, 61
Mecca, 1f., 179, 183, 203
Meditation(s), 26, 30, 51, 64f., 70, 84, 87, 101, 131, 134, 155, 176, 184, 190, 192, 207, 214, 226ff., 230, 234
Medjugorje, 135
Meinwerc, St, 4
Melito, 9, 143
Melle, 76f.
Melville, H., 141
Merit-theology, 98ff., 123f.
Mersina, 138

Michael's Mount, St, *see* Mont-Saint–Michel
Michel, D., 87
Milan, 36, 52
Miletus, 195, 198
Milos, 78
Milton, J., 125
Mini-pilgrimage, 55–77, 157, 159, 165, 185
Miracle(s), 3f., 51, 62, 91, 102, 105, 107, 109ff., 171, 175, 178, 193
Mirfield, 224
Mission, 32, 144, 161, 204
Modone, 48
Mole, J., 115
Monks, 4f., 14, 43f., 48, 51, 132f., 136, 162
Monstrances, 84
Monte Sant'Angelo, 8
Mont-Saint-Michel, 3, 16, 48, 75, 81
Monza, 62
Mordecai, 209
More, Sir T., 108–11, 114, 174
Mortimer, R. C., 163
Mortoft, F., 118ff.
Moryson, F., 115, 118, 120–4, 127
Moses, 11, 29ff., 54f., 57, 235
Motive(s), 2–7, 20, 67, 74, 90, 120, 128, 135, 138
Mount Gerizim, 128
Mount Gilboa, 57
Mount Hermon, 129
Mountjoy, 55
Mount of Olives, 10, 26, 32, 55, 64, 72, 74, 128, 134, 161, 232
Mount Sion, 27, 33, 49, 52, 68f., 74, 77, 128, 132, 138, 164, 225
Mount Tabor, 180, 227f.
Movement-prayers, 64, 233
Mulberton, 39
Munday, A., 117f.
Murray, J., 140
Muslims, 1, 203
Musée du Désert, 203

Naaman, 151
Naples, 115, 222
Napoleon, 133
Nathan, 224
Nazareth, 1, 26, 32, 34, 138, 162, 192, 224, 228
Nazirite, 59
Neapolis, 212
Newcastle, 180
Nicaragua, 135

Niccolò of Poggibonsi, 38, 39, 47, 65
Nicholas, St, 137f.
Nicholson, H., 158
Nicolas di Martoni, 6
Nikolaevitch, Grand Duke, 137
Nikolas of Munkathvera, 21
Nineveh, 145
Nola, 5, 58
Norway, 6
Norwich, 153
Novena, 75
Nuns, 5, 44, 170, 206

Oberammergau, 151
Ogygius, 6
Olaf, St, 159
Omnipresence, 80, 90, 111, 175–8
Origen, 10, 30, 143
Orthodox Christians, 74, 122, 130, 135–40, 162, 173, 233
Owen, L., 117ff., 121
Oxford, 161

Padwick, C., 164
Palestine, 3, 6, 8ff., 13, 17, 21ff., 25, 31, 33ff., 37f., 51f., 53, 65, 67, 75, 79, 89f., 98, 118, 120f., 123, 128ff., 131ff., 135, 137f., 140–52, 160–7, 176, 186, 191, 193, 199, 201, 204, 207, 209, 214, 223, 225, 227, 235, 237ff.
Palestine Exploration Fund, 144f.
Palestine Pilgrims' Text Society, 147
Palms, 75, 232
Palm Sunday, 161
Palmers, 75, 87, 123, 138, 163
Paris, 23, 36, 82, 84, 132, 140
Paris, Matthew, 22
Parker, M., 106, 108
Pascal, P., 139
Passover, 190f., 208, 211, 237f.
Patten, A. H., 159
Paul, St, 4, 7, 25, 31, 75, 89, 93f., 109, 119, 133, 171, 178, 180, 184, 186, 189–97, 199, 201, 207ff., 214, 223, 228, 232, 235
Paula, 62, 64, 172, 232
Paulinus, St, 5, 10, 58, 197
Payton, A., 161, 164ff.
Peace, 52, 157, 205, 210, 233, 235
Pecock, R., 91
Peel, Sir R., 153
Penance, 13, 15f., 135, 182
Penitence, 14–17, 91, 124, 211, 227
Pentecost, 132, 208

Pepys, S., 119
Perry of Lincoln, 155
Petchersk, 136
Peter, St, 4, 7, 10, 13, 67, 72, 75, 93, 103, 118f., 180, 195, 201, 227, 232, 237f.
Peterborough, 156
Petrarch, 8
Philemon, 201
Philippi, 185, 195, 207, 232, 236
Philo, 202
Philomelium, 174
Phocas the Cretan, 62
Piacenza Pilgrim, 20, 56–9, 62, 69, 73f.
Pilgrimage, criticism of, 80–108
—, diocesan, 153–60
—, exilic, 13ff.
—, judicial, 13, 16f., 50, 168
—, literature, 19–37
—, penitential, 2, 13–16, 50f., 58, 64, 211
—, preparation for, 42–6
—, universality of, 1f.
Pisgah, 54
Pius II, 48f.
Pius XII, 135
Planck, S., 34
Plymouth, 47
Pole, R., 157
Poloner, J., 23
Polycarp, St, 174, 228
Portsea, 162
Portsmouth, 113, 159
Portugal, 135
Possot, D., 131, 229
Postures, 56, 64, 234
Praise, 10, 80, 106, 126, 210, 229
Prayer(s), 7, 11, 26f., 44f., 50, 56f., 64f., 73f., 81f., 85, 110, 123f., 128, 134, 184, 190, 192, 203, 220f., 225, 228f., 231
Prayer Card, 32
Price, E., 104
Probatic Pool, 20
Procession(s), 26, 52, 70, 72, 79, 226, 231f.
Processional(s), 26, 29f., 70, 72, 122, 132, 151, 192, 225, 231
Proclus, 178
Prudentius, St, 5, 7
Psalms, 26, 44, 50, 66, 99, 123, 210f., 221, 232
Purchas, S., 126f., 137

Quency, 5
Quiller-Couch, A. T., 155

Rachel, 21
Rahner, K., 182, 195
Ramah, 21
Rameshwaran, 2
Ramlah, 150
Reading, 104
Red Sea, 13, 31, 190, 235
Re-enactment, *see* Drama
Reformation, 1, 3, 79, 84ff., 89, 93, 95, 100f., 115, 124, 128, 132, 147, 152f., 159f., 166, 168, 170, 173, 175, 180, 201
Relic(s), 1–4, 7, 17, 32, 39, 51, 56, 58, 60f., 78f., 83f., 89f., 93, 100–3, 105, 109, 111, 114f., 117f., 126, 130, 136, 138, 141, 168f., 171, 173ff., 193, 199, 201
Reliquaries, 3, 84, 103, 109
Reschen Pass, 33
Responses, 26f., 70, 231
Resurrection, 8, 10, 27, 32, 63, 65, 68, 71, 81, 87, 138, 191, 197, 207, 232, 238
Retreats, 186, 188, 202
Reuwich of Utrecht, E., 23
Rhodes, 23f., 35
Rice, J. ap, 103
Ridley, N., 107, 113
Riggs of Hampstead, Miss, 150
Riparius, 83
Roberto de Sanseverino, 50, 55
Robert of Flanders, 17
Roberts, D., 137, 146
Robinson, E., 142, 145
Rocamadour, 58
Rochester, 104
Roger of Wansford, 6
Role-playing, 13, 232
Roman Catholics, 122f., 128, 130–5, 148, 173f., 182, 194
Romania, 18
Rome, 4, 7f., 10, 15ff., 19ff., 33, 35f., 39, 47, 49, 51f., 55, 66f., 75, 86f., 93–6, 98f., 112, 115, 117–20, 129, 131, 135, 137, 165, 172, 176, 180, 199, 201, 203, 207, 215, 232, 237, 239
Rood, 32, 104
Roos, Lord, 117
Rosaries, 50, 61, 117, 134, 140
Runcie, R., 159f.
Russian Christians, 137
Rye, 39
Rypon, R., 30

Sacrament(s), 234–8
Sadolet, 100
Saewulf, 21, 47

Saint(s), 2–5, 9, 13, 51, 75, 83ff., 90–93,
  95ff., 100f., 105, 107f., 110–114, 136,
  168f., 171f., 174f., 193–201, 203ff.,
  237
Saint-Gilles, 51
Saint-Hilaire, Melle, 76f.
Saint-Jouin-de-Marnes, 11f., 97
Salisbury, 106, 156, 164
Salonika, 199
Samuels, Mrs, 150
Sanctification, 92, 183f.
Sanctify, 2, 5, 57, 61, 126, 129, 141, 194
Sanderson, J., 118, 122, 127f.
San Domingo de la Calzada, 4
San Domingo de Silos, 88
Sant Cugat del Valles, 50
Sandys, E., 124
Sandys, G., 124ff.
Santiago, *see* Compostela
Sanuti, M., 23
Sapientza, 78
Sarnath, 1
Sarov, 136
Satalia, Gulf of, 48
Sceva, 175
Schmemann, A., 235
Scrip, *see* Wallet
Scripture, Senses of: historical (literal)
  28ff., 71f., 87, 125, 192, 222f.; spiritual
  (mystical): allegorical ((typological)
  28ff.; anagogical (eschatological), 28ff.,
  71f., 125, 225; tropological (moral))
  28ff., 72, 125
Sedulius, C., 229
Seelzen, M., 145
Sermon(s), 8, 51f., 84, 146, 152, 192, 199
Sernin, St, 3
Sessia, B. da, 36
Severus, S., 97
Seville, 26
Shackles, *see* Fetters
Shakespeare, 10
Shalom, *see* Peace
Shaxton, N., 106f.
Shells, 2, 74ff., 79, 133f.
Shiloh, 76
Shintoism, 1
Shrewsbury, 103
Shrine(s), 5ff., 13, 20, 51, 62, 83, 90, 92f.,
  101, 105f., 111, 115, 129, 152, 168f.,
  193, 201
Siegfried of Mainz, 13, 48
Siena, 21
Sigeric, 19, 21
Sigoli, 39

Simeon Stylites, St, 169
Simmonds, B., 165
Sin(s), 2, 6, 10f., 13, 15f., 21, 38, 57, 65, 70,
  75, 82, 86, 89f., 94, 99, 107, 119, 123,
  146, 172, 182f., 207, 210f., 225, 235,
  237
Sinai, Mount, 6, 11, 22ff., 26, 41, 48, 50,
  55, 59, 61, 89, 137
Smithfield, 104
Smyrna, 174, 228
Solomon, 1
Solovki, 136
Songs, 50, 65f.
Soubirous, B., 135
Southampton, 160
South Creake, 91
Southwark, 156, 100, 166
Spain, 26, 130, 132, 160
Spiritual Exercise(s), 26, 70, 73, 87, 105,
  123, 183–9, 199, 202, 211, 214, 231
Spirituality, 30, 169
Staff(s), 26, 43ff., 52, 79, 87, 215
Stanley, A. P., 137, 141, 145f., 186, 192,
  199, 206
Stations, 19ff., 26f., 30, 69, 185
Stations of the Cross, 87, 131, 184f., 231
Statues, 5, 7, 83, 91f., 173
Stephen, St, 9, 177
Storms, 6, 78
Suez, 133
Sweden, 165
Swithin, St, 103
Syria, 19, 48

Tafur, P., 6
Taizé, 160
Tantur, 163
Tarsus, 138
Tattoo, 46, 127, 132, 139, 188
Tel Aviv, 55
Temple, W., 161
Temple, W. F., 154
Tenri-Kyo, 1
Tertullian, 169
Thanksgiving, 6, 10, 79, 126, 138, 210,
  229, 240
Theft, 4, 49, 78
Theoderich, 38, 67f.
Theodore of Studios, St, 231
Theodosius, 73
Thévenot, de, 132f., 137
Thomas, St, 84
Thomas Aquinas, St, 28f., 85, 181
Thomas à Becket, St, 7, 77, 97, 102f., 170,
  191, 228
Thomas à Kempis, 81, 84f., 189

Thompson, H., 152f.
Thorpe, W., 92f.
Thurston, H., 129f.
Timberlake, H., 121f., 124, 132
Tinsley, E. J., 189f.
Tobias, 45
Tobit, 45
Tobler, T., 146
Tokens, 32f., 35, 75–78, 120, 124, 133, 136, 156f., 214f., 219
Tomb(s), 2, 7ff., 13, 51, 65, 68, 77, 124, 127, 131, 133, 140, 175, 203f., 207
Tomkins, O., 165
Tongres, 7
Torkington, R., 39, 51f.
Toulouse, 3, 7
Tour, J. de la, 36
Tours, 8, 228, 237
Toxeter, 164
Transfiguration, 180, 227, 238
Travel Accounts, 37–42
Trent, Council of, 113f., 174
Trindle, 61
Turkey, 199, 214
Twain, Mark, 141
Tyndale, W., 108, 111
Tyrol, 33

Ulm, 9
Underhill, E., 227, 229
Unity, 10, 157, 202–6, 221, 234f., 239
Ur, 13, 207, 209
Urban II, 16ff.
Uriah, 224

Valaam, 136
Vaughan, E., 113
Veneration, 1, 83, 90ff., 101, 107, 112f., 118, 168, 170, 194
Venice, 20, 26, 33f., 36, 39, 47f., 52f., 61, 78f., 118, 121, 131
Venus, 9
Vernicle, 8, 22, 109
Veronica, St, 8
Versicle(s), 26f., 70, 231
Vesconti, P., 23
Via Crucis, see Way of the Cross
Via Egnatia, 212
Victoria, Queen, 145
Vienne, 51
Vigilantius, 83
Virgin, see Mary
Vocabularies, 34f., 41
Vogüé, E. M. de, 138
Volney, M. C.-F., 121

Votive Offerings, 52f., 95, 104, 106, 136, 138f.
Vow(s), 6, 13, 78, 99, 124, 136, 170

Wakefield, 87
Wallet, 26, 43ff., 52, 79, 87, 215
Walsingham, 6f., 75, 90, 92, 102, 108–10, 135, 138f.
Warren, C., 145
Waterland, D., 234
Waterloo, 222
Waugh, E., 176
Way of the Cross, 2, 161
Way, The, 2, 188f.
Wellington, 222
Werburgh, St, 156
Westminster Abbey, 75, 158
Wey, W., 23, 33, 39, 41, 65f., 89
Whitchurch Canonicorum, 60
Whitsunday, see Pentecost
Wilderness, 11, 31, 188f., 235
Wilhelm, Rabbi, 164
Wilkie, D., 146
William of Malmesbury, 20
William de Mandeville, 79
Williams, H. A., 224f.
Willibald, St, 38
Wilson, C., 145, 147
Wilson, S., 169
Winchester, 103, 106, 155f., 159, 162, 166
Winnock, 97
Wite, St, 60
Witness(es), 5, 9, 204
Wittenberg, 98, 149
Woods, R., 163
Woods, T., 155
Worcester, 43, 45, 156, 161
Works, (Good), 82, 99, 128, 175, 179f., 183f.
Worship, 9, 13, 80, 105, 107, 110, 112, 117, 120, 123, 126, 178, 181, 205, 227
Wright, T., 146
Wriothesley, T., 103
Wyclif, J., 89, 102
Wynkyn de Worde, 33f., 49

Yambo, 149
York, 156, 158, 162
Yugoslavia, 135, 160

Zion, see Jerusalem
Zola, E., 135
Zurich, 96
Zwingli, 96